# Outdoor Shelter Plans: Overheads, Sheds & Gazebos

*Created and Designed by the Editorial Staff of Ortho Books*

**Project Editor**
Gretchen Jacobson

**Writer**
Roger S. Grizzle

**Illustrators**
Angela Hildebrand
Ron Hildebrand

**Photo Editor**
JoAnn Masaoka Van Atta

**Principal Photographer**
Scott Atkinson

## Ortho Books

**Publisher**
Richard E. Pile, Jr.

**Editorial Director**
Christine Jordan

**Production Director**
Ernie S. Tasaki

**Managing Editors**
Robert J. Beckstrom
Michael D. Smith
Sally W. Smith

**System Manager**
Linda M. Bouchard

**Editorial Assistants**
Joni Christiansen
Sally J. French

**Marketing Specialist**
Daniel Stage

**Sales Manager**
Thomas J. Leahy

**Distribution Specialist**
Barbara F. Steadham

**Technical Consultant**
J. A. Crozier, Jr., Ph.D.




Before purchasing materials discussed in this book, be sure to check with local building authorities to verify and review all construction steps.

Every effort has been made at the time of publication to guarantee the accuracy of the names and addresses of information sources and suppliers, and in the technical data and recommendations contained. However, readers should check for their own assurance and must be responsible for selection and use of suppliers, supplies, materials, and chemical products.


Address all inquiries to:
Ortho Books
Box 5047
San Ramon, CA 94583-0947





2 3 4 5 6 7 8 9
93 94 95 96 97 98 99

ISBN 0-89721-252-5
Library of Congress Catalog Card Number 92-71350

THE SOLARIS GROUP
6001 Bollinger Canyon Road
San Ramon, CA 94583

**Editorial Coordinator**
Cass Dempsey

**Copyeditor**
Elizabeth von Radics

**Proofreader**
Barbara Ferenstein

**Indexer**
Elinor Lindheimer

**Composition by**
Laurie A. Steele

**Production by**
Studio 165

**Separations by**
Color Tech Corp.

**Lithographed in the USA by**
Webcrafters, Inc.

**Photographers**
Names of photographers are followed by the page numbers on which their work appears. R = right, C = center, L = left, T = top, B = bottom. With the exception of the following, all photographs in this book are by Scott Atkinson.

Crandall & Crandall Photography: 4–5, 7, 8B, 17B, 48, 49TL, 49B
Derek Fell: 46T, 49TR, 85TL, 85TR
Barbara J. Ferguson: 46B
Horticultural Photography®: 17T
Saxon Holt Photography: 85BL
Sam's Gazebos, Torrance, Calif.: 84B

**Designers**
2 M Associates, Landscape Architects: front cover
Berrington-Mathias & Associates: 8B
Hugh Dargan & Associates: 48B
Michael Glassman, Environmental Creations, Inc.: 4-5, 9, 12B, 14TC, 85BR
Mary Gordon: 10-11
John Herbst, Jr. & Associates: 17B
Stanley Allan Johnson: 14TR, 15
Kikuchi & Associates: 3T, 14CT, 16T
Peter Koenig Designs: 3B, 82-83
David A. and Evelyne T. Lennette & Morimoto Architects: 6, 84T
Ron Lutsko, Landscape Architect: 8T
Carol B. Malcolm/Peter Agras: 44-45
Nature Care Landscape Industries: 16BR
Rogers' Gardens: 49TL
Sam's Gazebos: 84B
David Sedlack, Landscape Architect: 14TR
Scott Soderquist: Low Profile Yard Storage Plan, 62-65
Byron Tarnitzer: 49B
The Brickman Group: 85TL
The Steinberg Group in collaboration with Elden Beck Associates: 1, 14CB
Dennis Tromburg Associates Landscape Architects: 12TR, 14BC, 14BR, 16BL
Nick Williams & Associates: 7B
Zierden: 12TL, 14C, 14BL
Steven R. Zimmerman: 47


**Front Cover**
An ordinary backyard deck has been transformed into a dramatic and inviting outdoor room by this redwood roof. The oversized posts, beams, lattice, and trim impart a feeling of strength and protection, as well as shade. See pages 26 to 29 for detailed plans and complete instructions for building a similar patio roof.

**Title Page**
A dramatic setting adds to the allure of this functional patio cover. The structure defines the space around the seating area, and its paint scheme and simple lines complement the accompanying building and stonework. Seasonal vines provide needed shade over the canopy in the summer and, when bare during the colder months, allow sun and warmth through.

**Page 3**
**Top:** This closeup view reveals in detail the post-and-beam construction of the overhead shown on page 16 (top). The beams are through-bolted to built-up posts; slats are comprised of 2 by 4s laid on edge. The beam ends are chamfered for a decorative effect.
**Bottom:** This is the view looking upward from inside the gazebo shown on page 82. The main rafters are joined to a hub in the center. To prevent rafter crowding at the top of the ceiling, header blocking is used to provide connections for the eight intermediate rafters.

**Back Cover**
Each project features full-color drawings of the complete structure as well as details to guide you in building it.

# Outdoor Shelter Plans: Overheads, Sheds & Gazebos

W
E

# PLANNING YOUR OUTDOOR SHELTER

*This book contains 15 plans for a variety of patio roofs, sheds, and gazebos. Some are simple projects that can be completed in a weekend or two. Others are more ambitious undertakings that might occupy your free time for most of a summer; these include outdoor rooms—extensions of the indoor living space. The purposes of these shelters range from attractive storage for yard equipment to transforming a landscape with an expansive trellis or intimate gazebo.*

*Whether you choose to use a plan directly from this book or modify one to suit your particular needs, the following pages will help you get off to the right start on the construction of your overhead shelter.*

*Constructed of naturally weathered redwood and roofed with cedar shingles, this inviting gazebo looks right at home with its backdrop of conifers, rocks, and stream. Arch headers carry the rafters between the built-up posts, and low, open railings provide a sense of enclosure without blocking the view.*

# THE CONSTRUCTION PLAN

*Proper planning is the key to a successful building project. You'll have to decide on a design and choose a site, prepare a plan and obtain permits, establish a budget and draft a rough schedule. What follows is a nuts-and-bolts guide to this process.*

## Choosing a Design

There are two basic considerations when deciding on a design. The first is the practical one: Will the structure do what it is supposed to do? If it's a patio roof, will it provide shade where it's needed? If it's a storage shed, will it accommodate the items you want to store and provide easy access when you need them? Take time to define your needs in detail, and let these requirements dictate the basic layout of your design.

The second consideration is aesthetic. Even a perfectly functional design can be an eyesore in the wrong setting. An ideal design fits naturally into its surroundings, provides a feeling of comfort and shelter, and reflects the style and taste of its owners. All these considerations—along with basic elements of scale, proportion, and choice of materials—are significant. Yet ultimately, it may come down to a certain something, difficult to define yet impossible to ignore, that makes one design seem right. You need to trust your instincts from the start, and then work on developing your design into its final form.

## Choosing a Site

The selection of a building site deserves special attention. Where you place a structure will affect not only the usefulness of the structure itself, but also the character of the surrounding area.

The place to start is with your local building department. The building inspector can simplify the task of choosing a site by telling you what you can't do: Most municipalities have specific requirements for setbacks from property lines, maximum lot coverage, and maximum height of outbuildings.

In some cases, the choice of a site will be obvious—a new trellis might have to go over an existing patio, for instance, or a storage shed out by the garage—but even if you have already settled on a location, there are certain things you can do to get the most from an outdoor room.

Consider traffic patterns and how the structure will be used. If you'll be dining outdoors frequently, it's desirable to locate a barbecue area within easy access to and from the kitchen. If privacy is a consideration, take advantage of trees, fences, or an out-of-the-way location in the yard.

Pay attention to patterns of sunlight and wind. Study how the sun affects the site at different times of day and different times of year. This is particularly relevant for overhead structures, where you may want shade during the hottest part of the day, and sunlight in the morning and evening. (See "Adapting Overhead Structures" on page 42 for more on this subject.) Consider the effects of prevailing winds on your proposed site. A cool afternoon breeze may be welcome on a hot summer day, but strong, gusty winds in an unprotected area can make an outdoor room uninhabitable.

Finally, use your choice of site to establish the architectural character of the new structure. Using materials, colors, and detailing that match or complement existing fences, outbuildings, or the house itself will help the new structure blend naturally with the existing ones.

*This little garden shed borrows details from the wall behind it to fit in successfully with its surroundings, yet its high-pitched roof and arch door trim give it a character of its own. The ingenious use of 1 by 3 trim creates a grid similar to that of the wall blocking, and its gray stain finish matches the wall as well.*

## Plans and Permits

Once you've decided what to build and where to locate it, you will have to prepare plans and, in most cases, obtain permits for the work. This process can take weeks and sometimes months to complete, so it's wise to initiate it early in the year. You can then begin and complete construction when the weather is most favorable.

Check with the local building department to find out if you will need a permit for your proposed project. Some detached outdoor structures will not require permits, but most attached ones will. If a permit is required, you'll most likely have to prepare a site plan showing the location of the structure on the property, and enough detailed drawings to demonstrate that it will conform to building and safety codes. You'll also have to pay a fee, which will be based on the estimated value of the improvements.

You can use this book as a guide to prepare your own drawings, or you can have them done by a professional; but if you will be making any structural changes (increasing a beam span, for instance), you should enlist the help of an architect or engineer.

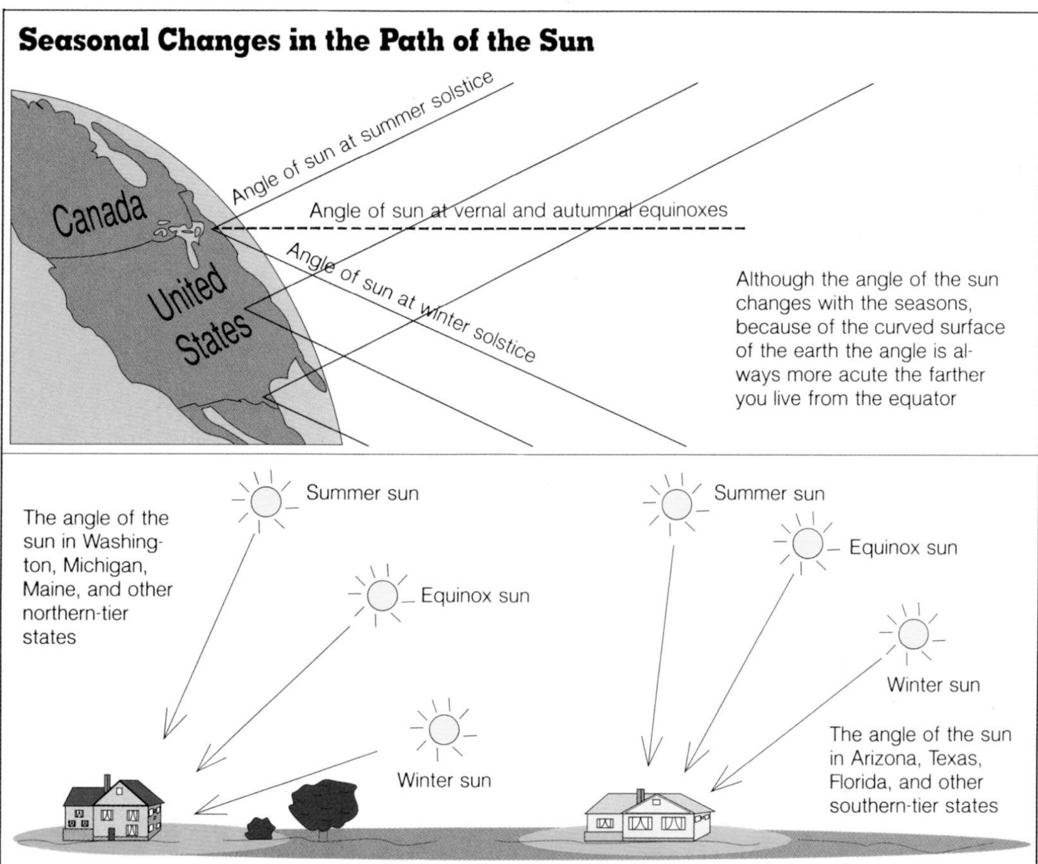


## Budget and Schedule

Before jumping into construction, find out how much the project will cost and how long it will take to finish. Try to set aside enough time and money to complete construction in a reasonable amount of time. A project that sits half-finished for months can become weathered and deteriorated on exposed areas before it's even completed.

Figuring the cost of materials is usually a straightforward proposition. Each project in this book is accompanied by a list of the materials needed to build it. You may have to modify the list if you will be making any changes in design or overall dimensions of the structure.

*An overhead doesn't have to provide much shade in order to give a strong sense of definition and enclosure. Though minimal in structure, this log cabin–style design serves as a dramatic element in the yard. Log members can be obtained from manufacturers of log cabin kits.*

Some details, such as lumber grades and wood species, have been omitted from the materials list purposely because the specifics will depend on your budget and what is readily available in your area.

In addition to the basic costs of materials, you will have to figure expenses for any related work that might be necessary, such as electrical wiring, new landscaping, or the construction of a deck or patio. Make your list of materials as detailed as possible, and submit it to potential suppliers for pricing.

Estimating labor accurately is not so easy, especially if you are short on experience. The secret is to break the work down into manageable tasks and look at each one individually. Compile a list of everything you will have to do, from site preparation to painting, in as much detail as you can. Imagine yourself going through each phase of construction, one step at a time, and make an educated guess as to how many hours each step will take. Add up the total, and allow some extra time for head scratching and the inevitable run to the lumberyard for that missing piece of hardware.

You can also get a rough time estimate by remembering this rule of thumb: On most construction projects, the cost of labor is approximately equal to the cost of materials. If you are a beginner, assume that you will be working for something like minimum wage (pay yourself a little more if you have some construction experience), and divide the cost of materials by your rate to figure the number of weekends you can expect to spend with your tool belt on.

*Top: Adaptation of the typical rectangular overhead structure is necessary when the area around the house doesn't lend itself to standard dimensions and design. This bi-level patio roof conforms to the L shape of the yard, and the elevation contrast gives it interest and depth. Bottom: In keeping with its formal environment, this overhead utilizes elegant neoclassic columns juxtaposed with the simple lines of the roof. Bolted brackets secure the cross-beams to the main beams. Solid slats in the roof provide heavy shade in one area, while open cross-beams allow the sun through in another.*

If the result indicates that you will be giving up more of your spare time than you're willing to sacrifice, consider hiring a professional to help. You may want to subcontract the concrete work, for example, and do the carpentry yourself.

Once you have a labor estimate, you can prepare a construction schedule. Making a schedule is helpful even on small projects because it provides clear-cut goals for each day's work, and helps you avoid getting bogged down in small details. Remember, the object is to get from the beginning to the end in the most direct way possible.

Don't be afraid to tackle a project just because it looks complicated, even if you don't know a knee brace from a hip rafter. If you're unsure how to approach some phase of construction, the final chapter in this book, beginning on page 104, provides information on materials, tools, and construction techniques that supplement the instructions in each plan. In addition, the do-it-yourself trend of recent years has spawned hundreds of books on building techniques, so that tricks of the trade that were jealously guarded secrets a few generations ago are now no farther away than the nearest library or bookstore.

With planning and persistence, a dedicated amateur can produce work that is very close, if not equal, to that of a professional. It may take you a little longer, but the satisfaction of seeing and enjoying the finished product, built with your own hands, makes it worth everything you went through to accomplish it.

*An overhead can function simply as a strong design element in a landscape and, as this one does, provide partial shade for a pond and garden. This canopy is shaped to follow the curvature of the patio curb and planter. The paint matches that of the gates and fencing, to create a unified color scheme. Where posts have contact with the ground, they should be pressure treated or constructed of a naturally durable species of wood to prevent rot.*

# SIX OVERHEAD PLANS

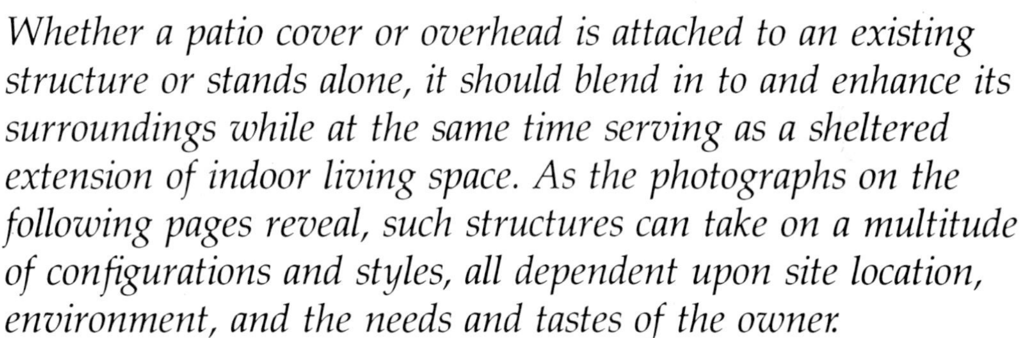

*Whether a patio cover or overhead is attached to an existing structure or stands alone, it should blend in to and enhance its surroundings while at the same time serving as a sheltered extension of indoor living space. As the photographs on the following pages reveal, such structures can take on a multitude of configurations and styles, all dependent upon site location, environment, and the needs and tastes of the owner.*

*Beginning on page 18 are complete and detailed plans for constructing six different types of overhead shelters. These original designs, which range from a basic and versatile shed awning to a lofty entry trellis on precast columns, are illustrated with renderings and construction details. Each plan contains step-by-step building instructions and a materials list of the items required.*

*The plans may be used exactly as they are or modified in materials or dimensions to better suit individual requirements. See "Adapting Overhead Structures" (page 42) for tips on how to adapt these or other overhead designs.*

*Direct sun is partially deflected from glass doors and windows, and a sweeping brick walkway is defined by this overhead. The widely spaced cross-beams are supported in joist hangers on a ledger attached to the house. The main beams are tied securely to the 4 by 4 posts with the 2 by 6s that are built up along them. Decoratively cut beam ends add an additional touch of style.*

*Top left: Brick rectangular posts solidly support the massive roof of this sturdy pavilion. The long spans between posts are achieved by utilizing glulam beams, which are available in longer lengths than sawn timbers.*
*Top right: The wood has been left unfinished on this overhead in order to weather and blend naturally into its leafy surroundings. Some type of bracing must be incorporated into a freestanding structure like this, such as burying the posts well into the ground, reinforcing the joints, or utilizing a knee-bracing technique like the one described on page 18.*
*Bottom: Weathered rough-sawn lumber gives a strong, rustic air to this attached patio cover. The sturdy posts are used elsewhere in the surrounding structures for a unified look. Louvered slats set at the appropriate angle allow sunlight into the patio area during the winter and block hot rays during months when the sun follows a higher path in the sky.*

*A rhythmic repetition of spacing between 2 by 2 slats yields attractive patterns of structure, sunlight, and shade to this pair of twin pavilions. The deck is adroitly incorporated into one of the overheads by utilizing its posts as structural members. The posts and roof-framing members are 6 by 6s; 4 by 4s serve as cross-beams.*

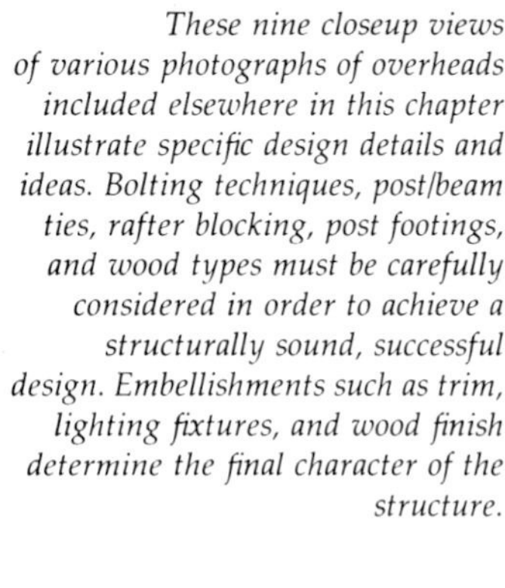

*These nine closeup views of various photographs of overheads included elsewhere in this chapter illustrate specific design details and ideas. Bolting techniques, post/beam ties, rafter blocking, post footings, and wood types must be carefully considered in order to achieve a structurally sound, successful design. Embellishments such as trim, lighting fixtures, and wood finish determine the final character of the structure.*

*Looking as though it grew up on its own from the floor of this abundant garden, this naturally weathered freestanding overhead provides an inviting oasis for potting tables and gardening work. Vines climbing along its posts and beams incorporate it fully into its lush surroundings.*

*Top: By following the shape of the adjoining house, this dramatic overhead shelters both a seating area and a poolside walkway. Lattice panels, built-up posts, and chamfered beam ends create a dignified style.*
*Bottom left: Constructed of unfinished redwood, this generous overhead converts a narrow side yard into shady and defined patio and spa areas, at the same time sheltering the windows of the house from direct sunlight.*
*Bottom right: A creative solution was required to tuck this overhead securely into its allotted space along the angled house. It is attached to a ledger on one portion of the building and is supported independently by posts and beams where it is too high to fit under the eaves.*

*Top: This simple, painted post-and-beam structure provides intersecting paths and doubles as a trellis for rows of roses that ramble into it from both sides.*
*Bottom: An entryway is formalized by this elaborate structure, which adds focus to the paths below. Multiple posts support both a lattice ceiling and the beam-frame roof; bands of trim add style and interest to the tops and bottoms of the posts. The white paint is not only decorative, but also protects the wood from the elements.*

# HED AWNING WITH KNEE-BRACED POSTS

*This awning roof may well be the most universal overhead structure there is. It can be used for porches, verandas, door canopies, and storage shelters. This particular plan is designed to be built onto the Basic Shed (page 50), but with minor modifications it can be made to suit a wide variety of other applications.*

## Preparation of the Main Structure

If you are attaching the awning to an existing structure, begin by stripping back the roofing to about 1 foot past the wall line. If the sheathing underneath is made of boards, remove enough of them to expose the wall below. If the existing roof has plywood sheathing, snap a chalk line across it, cut along the line with a circular saw, and remove the section that is over the wall.

Once the rafters have been exposed, remove any blocking between them with a reciprocating saw fitted with a nail-cutting blade. Then cut the rafter tails flush with the outside of the wall, using a handsaw or reciprocating saw.

If you are building the awning as part of a new structure, cut the rafters so their ends are flush with the outside of the wall where the awning attaches; don't put in any blocking until after the awning rafters have been installed.

## Posts and Beam

Lay out the locations of the posts as indicated on page 21. Dig the holes for the pier footings, fill them with concrete, and set the pier blocks as shown. The tops of the blocks should be at least 6 inches above grade.

Toenail the posts to the pier blocks and install 2 by 4 temporary bracing to hold them plumb. Use a level to mark the two end posts at the height of the wall of the main building; measure down from this mark 21½ inches and snap a chalk line across all the posts at this elevation. Cut off the posts at the chalk line. You will most likely have to cut from both sides.

Next, cut the main beam to length (20 feet). If you are unable to find one piece of wood long enough, use two pieces and locate the splice over the center of a post; then install a metal plate strap over the joint after the beams are in place.

To shape the ends of the beam, make a cardboard template and trace the shape onto both sides of the beam end. Make a series of straight cuts close to the curve and smooth the shape to its final profile with a rasp or block plane.

## Post Base and Post-and-Beam Detail

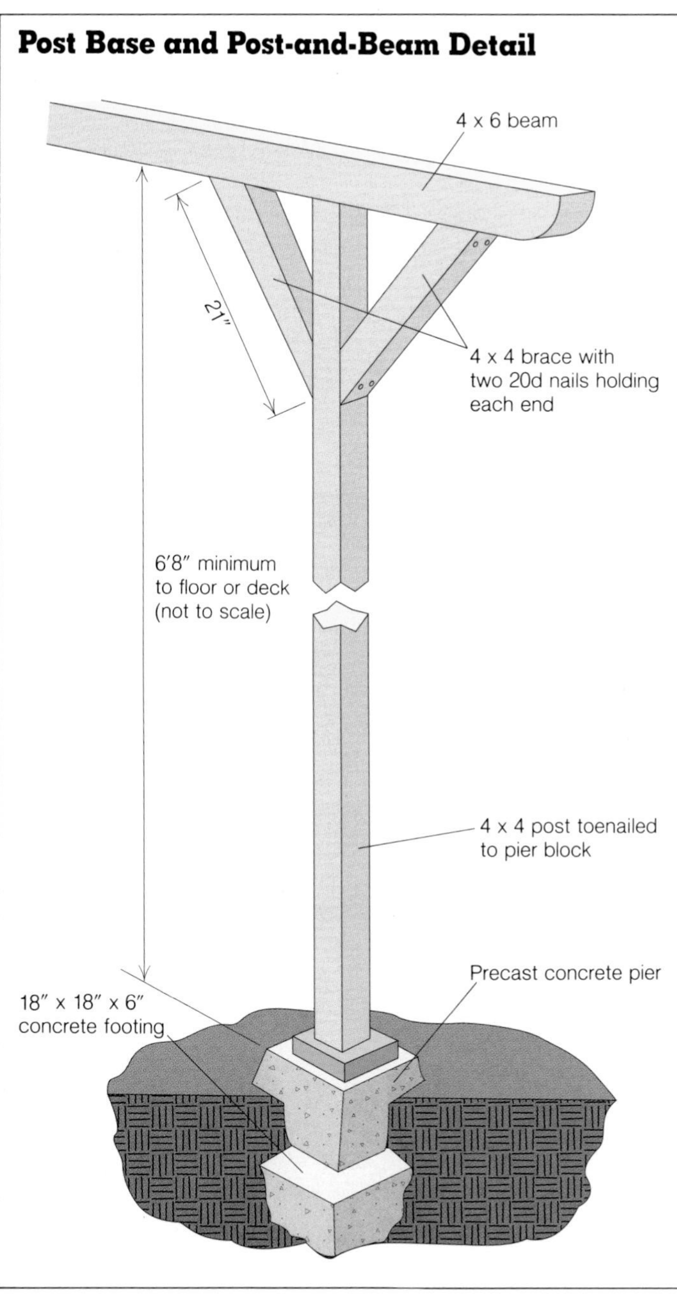


## Alternate Post Bases

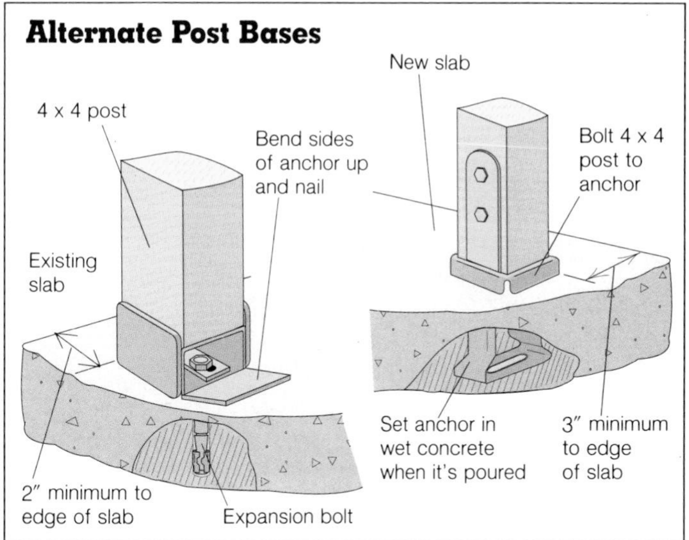


Before setting the beam on the posts, lay out the locations of the awning rafters on top of the beam. Use the rafter spacings on the existing building as a guide, making sure that the awning rafters will align with them.

Installing the beam usually takes two people. Lift it onto the tops of the posts, making sure that it overhangs both ends equally, and tack it temporarily with 8-penny (8d) nails. Also ensure that the layout marks on the beam align with the rafters on the building. Double-check all the posts for plumb, then toenail each post to the beam with four 16d nails (or use a metal post cap).

Install the 4 by 4 knee braces with two 20d nails in each end. If the beam is spliced, remember to install the plate strap on top of it.

## Rafters and Blocking

Cut the rafters as shown on page 21. Install the common rafters first, nailing them to the rafters on the main building with three 16d nails and to the beam with one 16d toenail on one side and two on the other. Then install the barge rafters. Check the joint where they abut the existing rafters and adjust the fit as necessary.

Measure and cut the first set of blocks that rests on the building wall. (These blocks will have to be ripped to width as well.) Nail them to the rafters and wall plate with 16d toenails.

Cut the next set of blocks from the same size stock you used for the rafters. Install them with the top edges flush with the tops of the rafters; nail them to both the rafters and the first set of blocks. Simply repeat the process for the blocks over the main beam.

## Roof Sheathing and Trim

To install the awning sheathing boards, start at the outside edge of the roof. Snap a chalk line across the awning rafters where the back edge of the first sheathing board will be—this will be your guide to getting a straight start. Nail the first board in place with three 8d nails into each rafter. Place the second board against the first. It may not fit very well because sheathing lumber is often bowed. If this is the case, just nail it down where it touches the first board, then start a nail over a rafter where you see a gap. Drive a screwdriver into the top edge of the rafter next to the board, pry it over until it fits snugly, and nail it down. Install the rest of the sheathing in the same manner.

Two useful tips for putting up roof sheathing are as follows. First, cut the boards a little long and let the excess extend past the barge rafters;

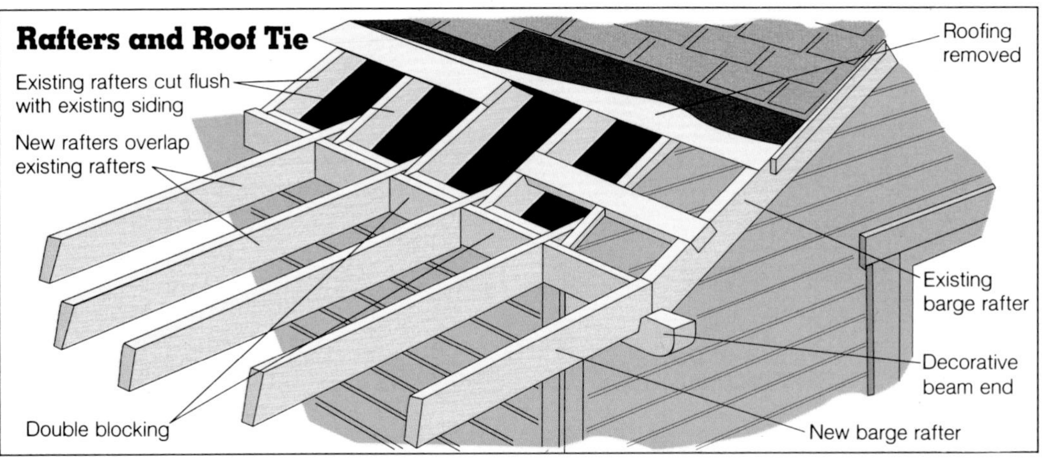


when the roof deck is completed, snap a line and cut off all the ends at once. Second, it is faster to use just enough nails to hold the sheathing boards firmly in place, and then fill in the rest after all the boards have been installed.

Once the awning roof deck is finished, install 1 by 2 trim around the edges. Miter the corners. Then patch the house roof wherever sheathing was removed.

## Alternate Detail With Wall Ledger

In some cases it may be easier to attach the awning to the wall of an existing structure with a ledger. However, there must be enough headroom under the outer beam if you choose to do so. In this case, the top of the ledger would have to be at least 9 feet above the deck or patio, and about a foot of clearance above that would be necessary to install flashing and roofing.

If fastening a ledger to a new building, bolt it to the studs or sheathing before you install the siding. Remember to shorten the ledger 1½ inches on each end so the barge rafters can be nailed to its ends. Nail a strip of 1 by 4 backing above the ledger, and install the Z-bar flashing over that. Fasten the rafters to the ledger with metal joist hangers. After the roofing has been installed, tuck the L flashing up under the Z bar and fasten it with 4d hot-dipped galvanized (HDG) box nails.

Attaching a ledger to an existing building is a bit more involved. In most cases, you will have to cut away a strip of siding about 4 inches wide above the ledger to install the flashing. If the siding is wood, you can do this with a circular saw, but first try to pull out any nails that may be in the way. If cutting stucco, use a masonry-cutting abrasive blade. It is imperative that you wear goggles to protect your eyes. Wear a dust mask as well, and tape a second one over the air intake of the saw motor to protect the saw.

Next, carefully pry away the siding at the top of the cutout just enough to slip the top flange of the Z-bar flashing behind it. Install the ledger and proceed as before.

On a brick or masonry wall, fasten the ledger with expansion bolts, and make a ½-inch-deep saw cut in the masonry 4 inches above it (use an abrasive blade). Fill the saw cut with caulk and press a piece of L flashing measuring 1 inch by 3 inches into the wet caulk.

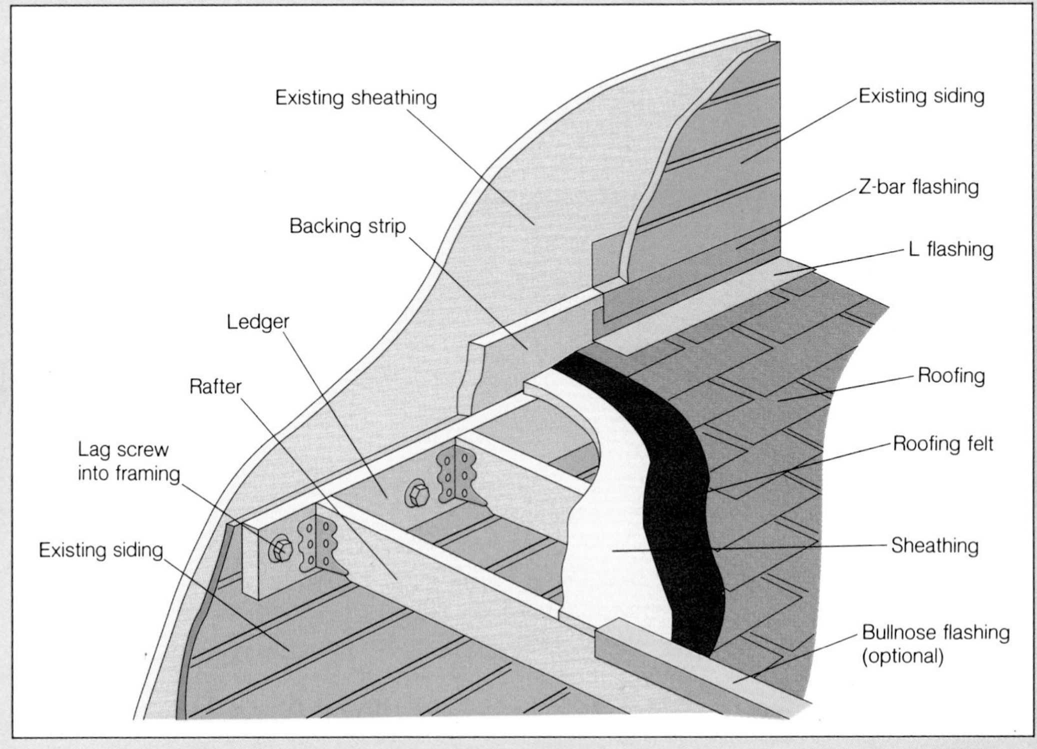

## Framing Plan

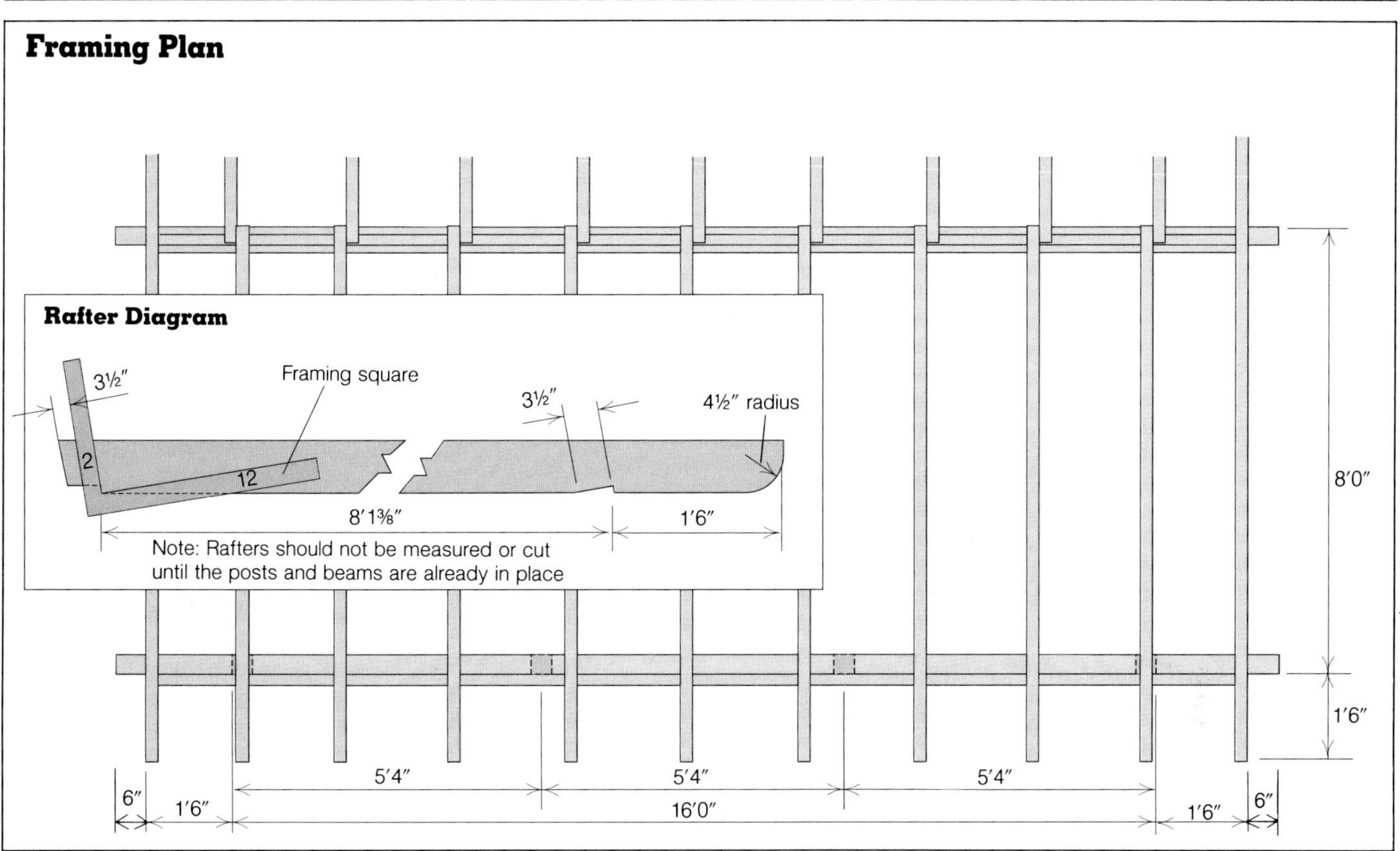


## Roofing

For a sloped roof like this one, roll roofing or built-up roofing (also known as hot mop) offers the best protection. You can install roll roofing yourself by following the manufacturer's instructions printed on the roll wrapper. A built-up roof must be installed by a professional. Extend the roofing up at least 1 foot onto the existing building, then shingle back down over it.

Wood or composition shingles can also be used where allowed by fire codes, but a double layer of 30-pound felt is required before the shingles are installed because of the low slope.

## Materials List

| Description | | Material/Size | Length | Quantity |
|---|---|---|---|---|
| Foundation | Pier blocks | — | — | 4 ea |
| | Concrete | — | — | 5 cu ft |
| Lumber | Posts/knee braces | 4×4 | 8′ (min) | 6 ea |
| | Beam | 4×6 | 14′<br>8′ | 1 ea<br>1 ea |
| | Rafters/blocking | 2×6 | 10′<br>RL | 11 ea<br>60 l.f. |
| | Sheathing | ½″ or ⅝″ plywd | 4′ × 8′ | 7 sh |
| | Trim | 1×2 | 10′ | 4 ea |
| | Misc. scrap lumber for temporary bracing as per text | | | |
| Hardware | Nails: framing | 16d sinker | — | 5 lb |
| | sheathing | 8d sinker | — | 5 lb |
| | knee braces | 20d HDG | — | ½ lb |
| | trim | 8d HDG | — | ½ lb |
| | Assorted metal fasteners as per text | | | |

See page 105 for materials list abbreviations.

# ATTACHED SHADE STRUCTURE

*This attached overhead structure uses built-up posts to support beams that have decoratively shaped ends. It employs a common system of trellis construction with an ascending order of cross-members in which each succeeding layer uses smaller and more closely spaced pieces.*

## Post Footings

Locate the centers of the posts. Here they are shown 8 feet center to center, but you may want to adjust their locations somewhat to frame a view or to align the spaces between posts with windows or door openings. Just be sure each post falls directly under one of the crossbeams above. If the posts are more than 10 feet apart, you may have to use a larger beam to span the distance.

Pour the footings and set the post bases in wet concrete. The bases don't necessarily have to be at the same elevation, but they should be in a straight line. Orient them so that later you can adjust the posts toward or away from the house if necessary to get everything lined up just right.

Most codes require that posts exposed to the weather be supported above the surface of a patio by at least 1 inch, so be sure to use post bases with a standoff plate.

## Ledger

Mount the ledger to the house. To do this, set its bottom edge at least 7 feet, 2 inches above the elevation of your highest post base. This will give you the minimum 6-foot 6-inch headroom under the outer beam. Locate and mark the wall studs. Cut the ledger to size, tack it in place, and drill for lag screws.

If the ledger will be protected by the eaves of the house, it can be fastened directly to the siding; but if it will be exposed to the weather you should space it off the wall at each lag screw with three or four washers to prevent water from getting trapped behind it.

## Posts and Main Beam

Temporarily set the two 4 by 4 end posts without cutting them to length. Level across from the bottom edge of the ledger and mark both posts at this height. This mark represents the top of the beam. Measure down from the mark the depth of the beam (about 7¼ inches for a 4 by 8), take the posts down, and cut them to length.

Reerect the posts, install the post-base bolts, and brace them in both directions with 2 by 4s.

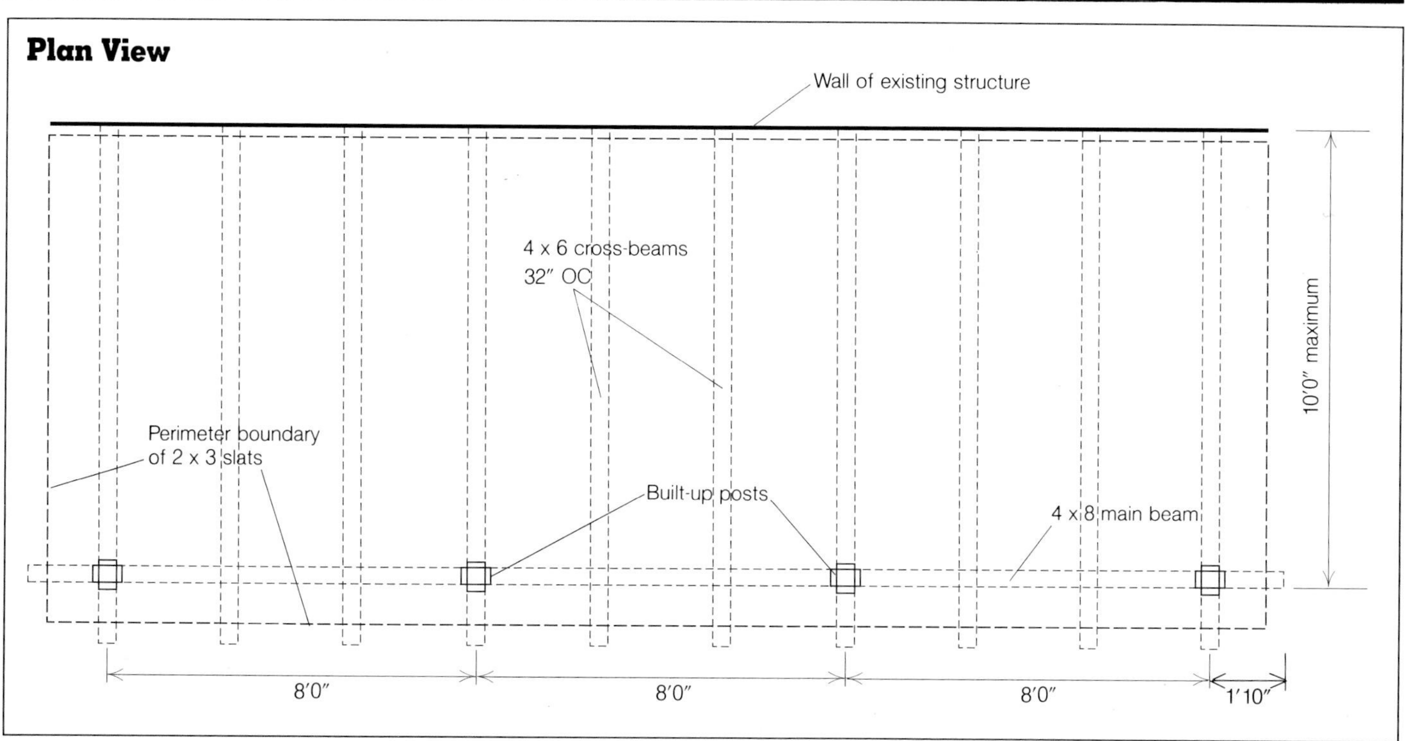


Pull a string across the tops of the posts and measure down to the remaining post bases to get the lengths of the other posts. Then cut and install the remaining posts.

Cut the main beams to length, locating splices over the centers of posts. With an assistant, lift the beams onto the posts and toenail them in place. Install metal plate straps on top of the beam over any joints.

## Cross-beams

Lay out the ledger for the cross-beams at 32 inches on center. Where cross-beams land over posts, you can maneuver your layout to one side or the other to get them to line up directly over the posts. Install the joist hangers.

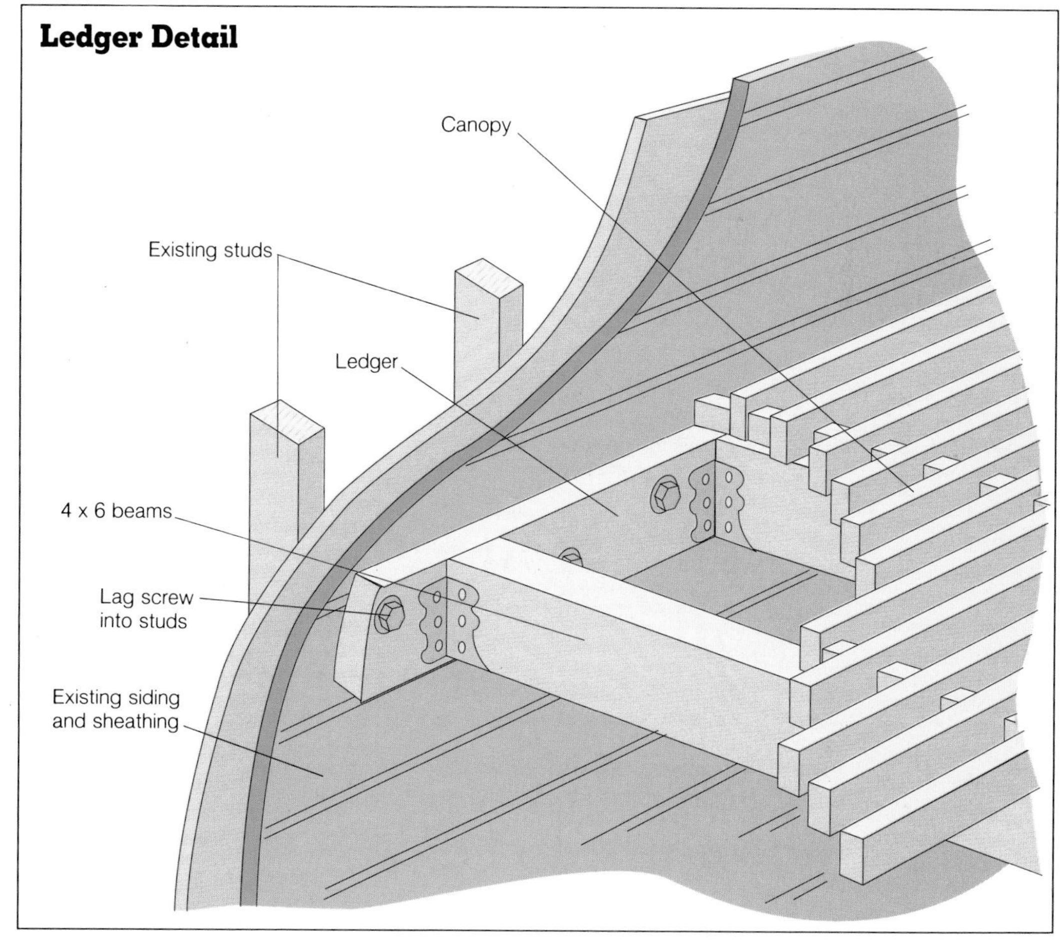

## Canopy Detail

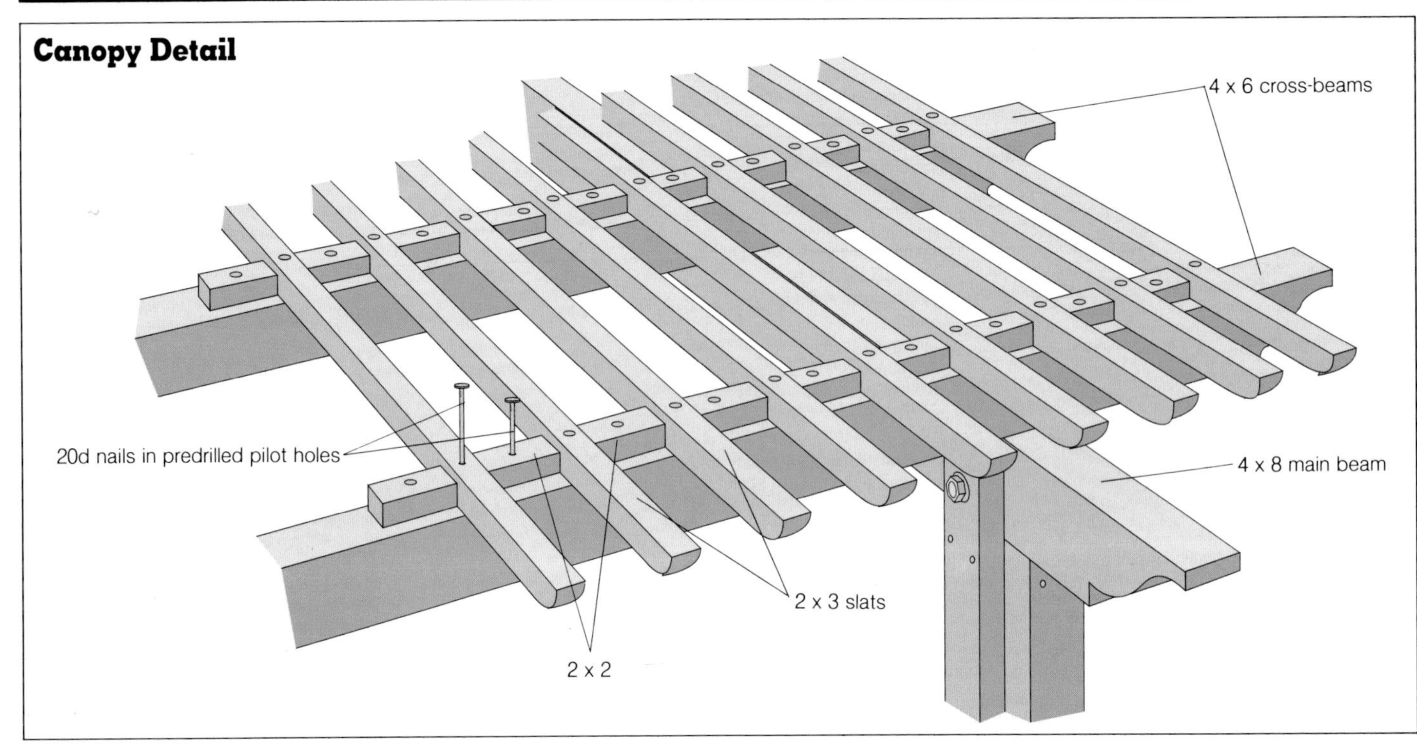


## Post and Base Detail

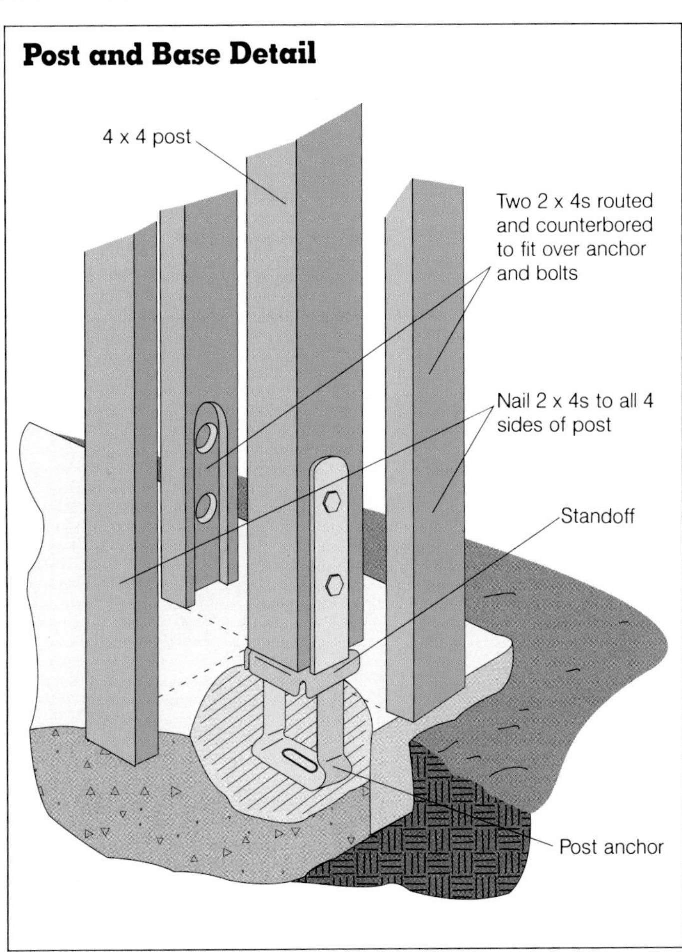


You may be able to have the shaped beam ends cut at the lumberyard when you buy your material, which is the preferable option, or you can cut them yourself. To do so, use a template to lay out and trace the shape on both sides, then make a series of saw cuts close to the traced line. Refine the shape with a block plane, chisel, and belt sander.

Cut the cross-beams (with ends preshaped) to length and install them with four 16d toenails into the main beam, using joist-hanger nails at the end of the ledger.

## Completing the Post Assembly

Once the cross-beams are in place, you can remove the temporary bracing you installed earlier and apply the 2 by 4 plant-on trim to the posts. You will have to relieve the backside of two of the 2 by 4s at each post to accommodate the post-base straps and bolts. Use a chisel or router to cut the shallow recess for the strap, and counterbore for bolt heads.

Nail the 2 by 4s to the posts with two 16d HDG nails every 24 inches. Extend the trim pieces on the front and back of the post to cover the main beam as shown, and install the ½-inch bolts.

## Lattice Covering

The 2 by 3 slats that cover this trellis are shown with the space between them equal to the depth of the slat. This arrangement will provide full shade during the hottest part of the day if the slats are oriented east-west. If you want more sun under the trellis, increase the spacing or decrease the depth of the slats.

Before you climb up on top of the structure to install slats, cut about 300 blocks 2½ inches long from 2 by 2 stock. These blocks are crucial because trellis coverings take a lot of punishment from the sun and rain, and without blocking, the lattice slats will warp and twist. If you have a power miter saw, simply clamp a stop to the fence to make the cutting go quickly. With a little imagination, you can do the job just as easily with a circular saw by improvising a cutoff jig that will allow you to make repeat cuts without having to measure every piece. While you're still on the ground, predrill every block for the 20d HDG nail that will hold it in place. If you don't predrill, the little blocks will definitely split when you nail them in.

Begin installing the lattice by toenailing the two end slats to the cross-beams. Pull a string line between the ends of these slats to align the remaining slats. Then start working your way from the outer edge toward the house. Lay blocks on the cross-beams between the first and second slats, then toenail the second slat on, pinching the blocks in snugly. Nail off the blocks and repeat the process. When you get to within a few feet of the house, measure back to the ledger. If your slats are not parallel to the building, cut some special-length blocks to make up the difference gradually over the remaining distance.

## Beam Ends

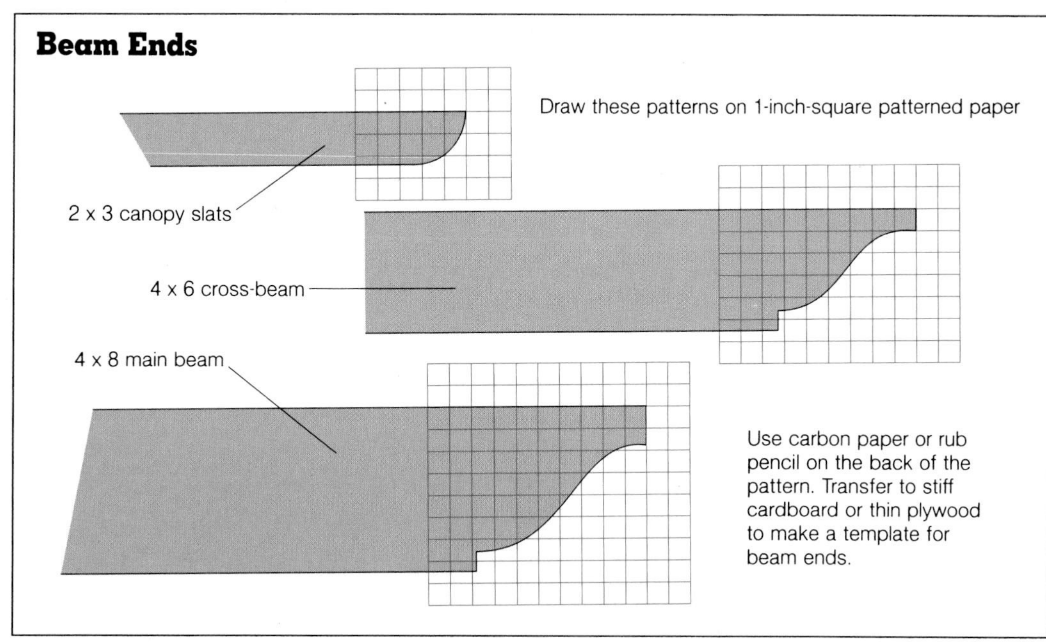


## Materials List

| Description | | Material/Size | Length | Quantity |
|---|---|---|---|---|
| Post footings | Concrete | — | — | .25 cu yd |
| Lumber | Ledger | 2×6 | 14′ | 2 ea |
| | Posts | 4×4 | 8′ | 4 ea |
| | Main beams | 4×8 | 18′<br>10′ | 1 ea<br>1 ea |
| | Cross-beams | 4×6 | 12′ | 10 ea |
| | Slats | 2×3 | RL | 1,060 l.f. |
| | Slat blocking | 2×2 | RL | 120 l.f. |
| | Post plant-on trim | 2×4 | 8′ | 16 ea |
| Hardware | Post bases | 4×4 elev post base | — | 4 ea |
| | Post-base bolts | ½″ MB (n) | 4½″ | 8 ea |
| | Ledger screws | ½″ lag screw (w) | 5″ | 18 ea |
| | Post/beam bolts | ½″ MB (n/w) | 7½″ | 4 ea |
| | Joist hangers | 4×6 hgr | — | 10 ea |
| | Nails: joist hanger<br>framing<br>block | 1½″ joist hgr<br>16d HDG<br>20d HDG | —<br>—<br>— | 2 lb<br>5 lb<br>5 lb |
| | Assorted metal fasteners as per text | | | |

See page 105 for materials list abbreviations.

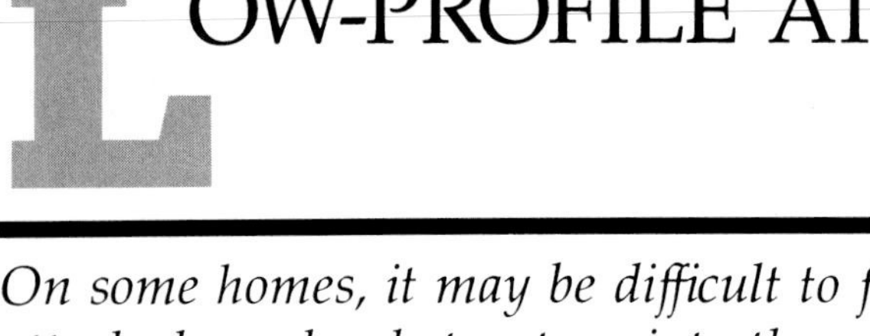

# LOW-PROFILE ATTACHED OVERHEAD

*On some homes, it may be difficult to fit an attached overhead structure into the narrow strip of space between the tops of windows and doors and the bottom of the roof overhang. At just 9¼ inches deep, this lattice-covered trellis can actually be tucked up under the eaves of almost any house.*

## Determine Clearance

To make sure the trellis will fit under your eaves, you'll have to check two things. First, you will need at least a foot of unobstructed wall space above any door or window opening to attach the ledger. Second, you must make sure the trellis joists will clear the bottom edge of the overhang. Mark the wall an inch or two above a door or window opening (this represents the bottom of the ledger), and then make a second mark 7¼ inches above the first to mark the top. Level out from this top mark to the outer edge of the overhang. If you are still below the rafters, you are ready to proceed. If the rafter tails or fascia board are in the way, you may still be able to go ahead if you can cut away some of the rafter tails or fascia to get the trellis joists underneath, without disturbing the roof sheathing or the roofing itself. Avoid the temptation to attach the ledger to the rafter tails or fascia board. These are usually not designed to carry any loads other than the overhang itself.

If it appears you don't have the necessary clearance, consider building your trellis as a completely detached structure, independent of the house altogether. If you decide on this option, consult an engineer or local building official for advice on how to brace it against winds and earthquakes.

## Layout and Post Footings

Lay out the frame of the trellis on the ground with batter boards and string lines. In the example, this is a rectangle 8 feet by 22 feet; if you decide to change the dimensions to fit a particular area, try to work in 2-foot increments. Square the rectangle by adjusting the strings until the diagonal measurements are equal.

The illustration on page 27 shows one type of footing for supporting posts on a concrete slab with metal post bases, but there are other options. For example, if you will be building the trellis over a wood deck, you can use precast concrete pier blocks and fasten the

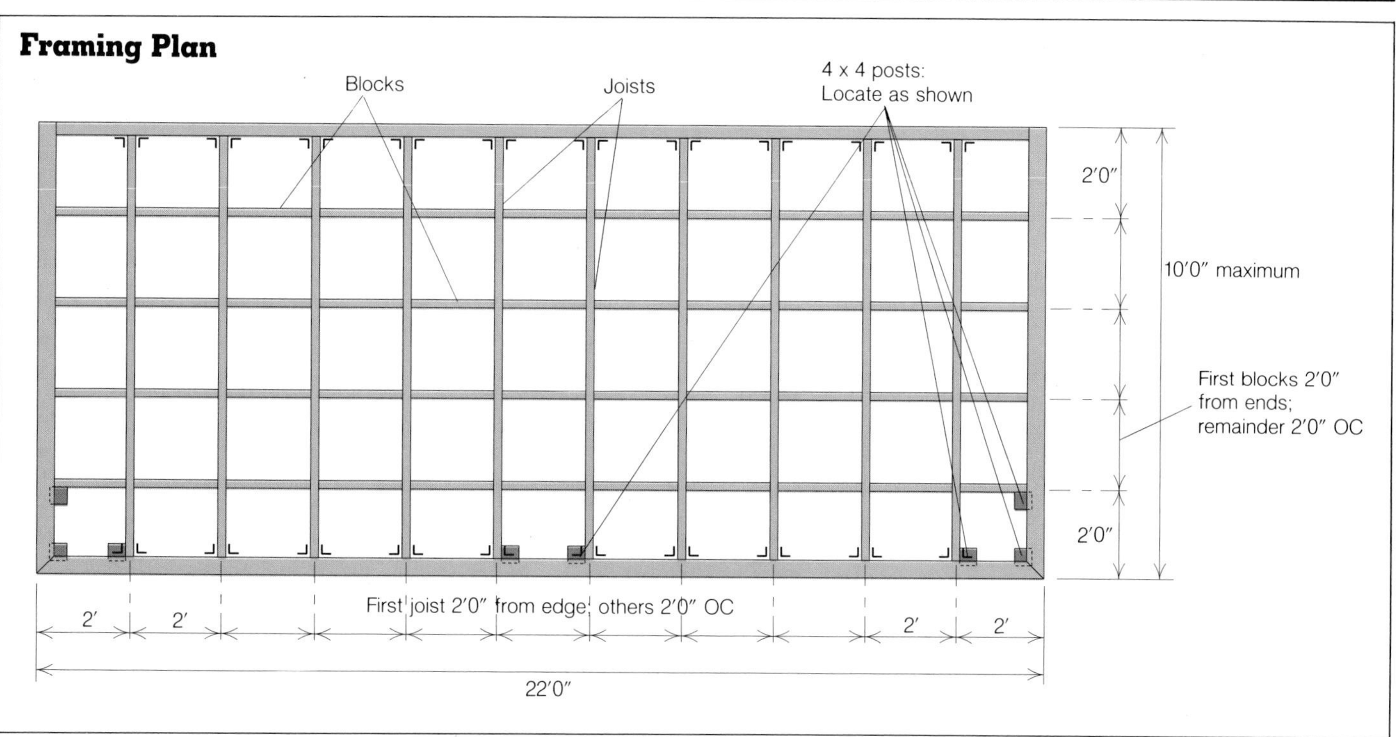


deck-perimeter beams directly to the posts. Most building codes will also allow posts for a light patio cover like this one to be supported on an existing slab so long as it is at least 4 inches thick. The primary task is to locate the posts accurately—2½ inches inside the string lines and 13¾ inches apart—so they will fit into the canopy framing later.

If you use metal post bases, it is best to select a type with side plates under 6 inches. Installing the lattice railing panels between the posts will be a lot easier without long straps and bolt heads in the way.

## Ledger

Locate the bottom edge of the ledger so that it will be at least 1 or 2 inches above doors and windows, and snap a chalk line on the wall at that height. Locate the ends of the ledger by plumbing up from the layout strings and measuring back 3½ inches at each end. This allows the 4 by 8 beams to cover the ends. Cut the 2 by 8 ledger to length and bolt it to the wall. If it won't be protected from the weather by the roof overhang, space it off the wall ½ inch or so with washers or plywood scraps at the bolts so water can't get trapped between the ledger and siding, where it can cause rot and structural damage.

## Posts and Beams

The next step is to establish the height of the two corner posts. To do this, set one corner post in place temporarily, level across from the top of the ledger (use a level taped to the edge of a long, straight 2 by 4), and mark the post. Cut it to length, and notch it on two

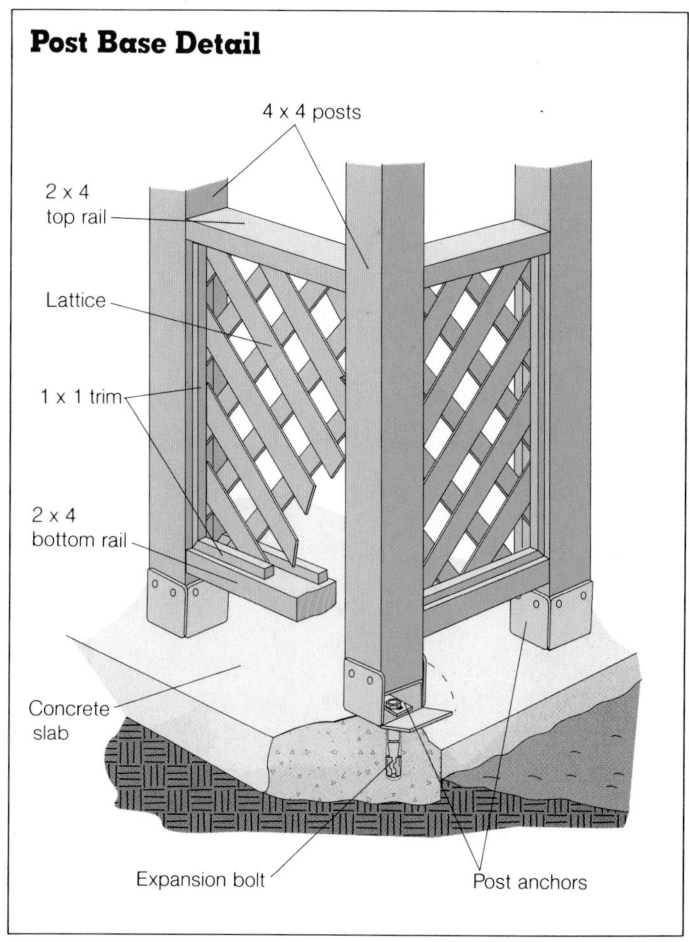

**Framing Detail**

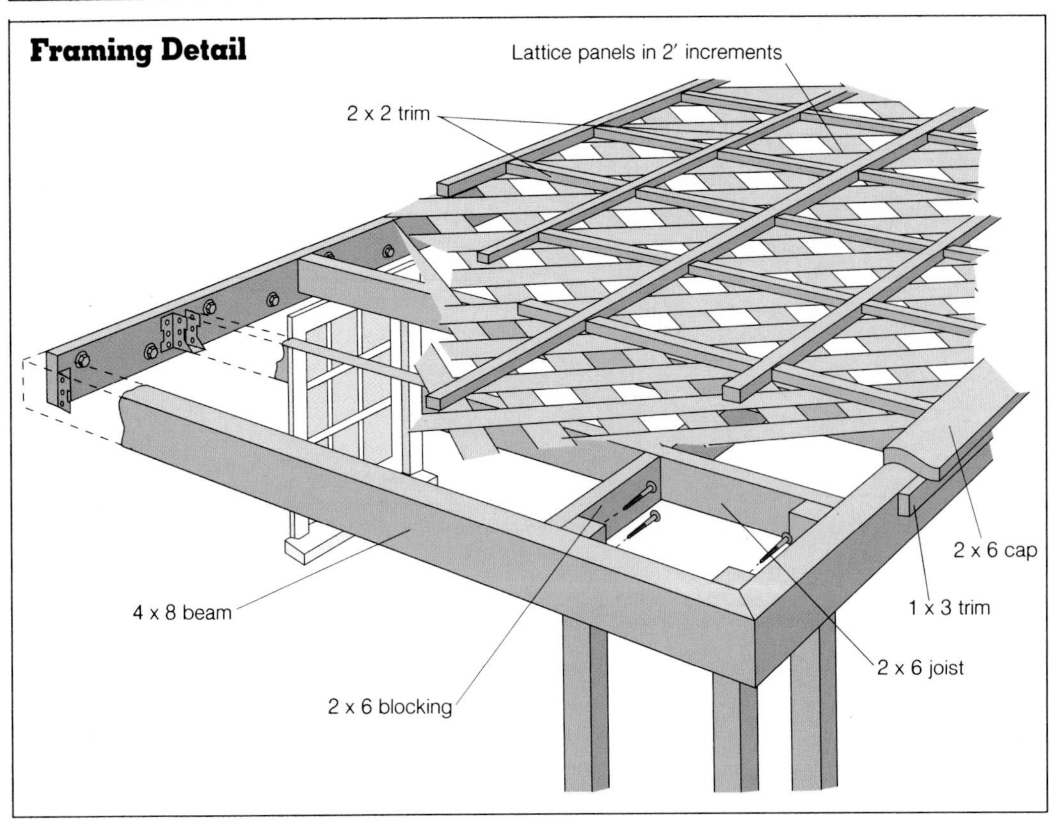


**Post-and-Beam Detail**

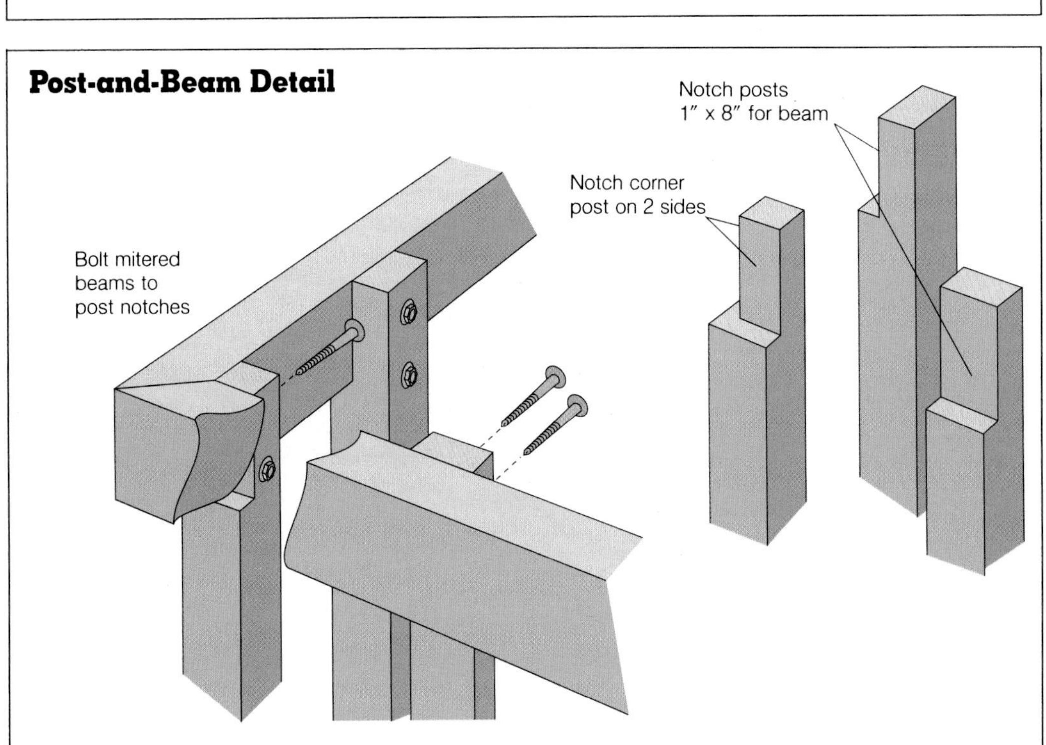


faces for the 4 by 8 beams as shown at lower left. The safest way to cut these notches is to make a series of parallel saw cuts, about ¼ inch apart and 1 inch deep, across the grain; then knock out the waste with a hammer and smooth the surface with a sharp chisel. Cut the other corner post in the same way.

Brace both corners plumb and measure for the 4 by 8 perimeter beams. Cut and install these as shown, mitering the corners. Where the end beams meet the ledger, install an L-shaped metal framing clip to tie them together. Measure and cut the rest of the posts (these will have to be notched on only one face). Temporarily brace the whole assembly plumb and square, and bolt the posts to the beams.

## Joists and Blocking

Lay out and mount the 2 by 6 joist hangers to the ledger and the outer beam, 24 inches on center, and install the joists. Snap chalk lines across the tops of the joists on 24-inch centers for the 2 by 6 blocks, and nail the blocks in place.

## Lattice Panels

Now you're ready to install the lattice panels, but, first, stain or paint them. Use a spray gun—rented if need be. If you try to use a brush or roller, you will regret it—painting all those little edges is extremely time-consuming, and preventing drips and runs is almost impossible.

## Lattice Detail

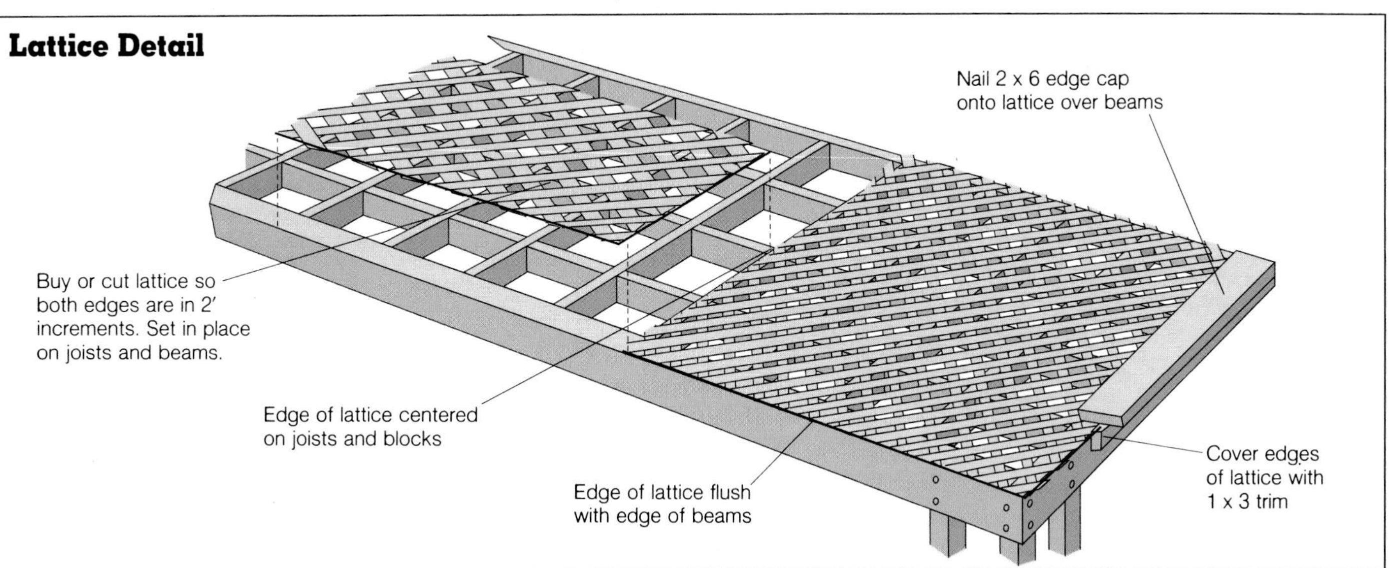


One alternative to painted wood lattice is prefinished vinyl lattice panels. These can be cut and nailed like wood, they don't need painting, and they hold up well in weather.

Install the lattice panels with 4d HDG box nails. Stagger end joints in adjacent courses. If you have to cut some of the panels, watch out for the little staples that hold the slats together.

## Trim and Railing Panels

Install the 2 by 6 trim on top of the beams first, setting the inside edge flush with the inside of the beams; then put in the 2 by 2s over the joists and blocks. The 1 by 3 trim under the overhanging 2 by 6 covers the edges of the lattice panels and completes the canopy.

To make the small railing panels between the posts, first fit the 2 by 4 top and bottom rails in place and install the 1 by 1 stops on one side. Fit a section of lattice loosely in the opening and secure it with the second set of stops.

## Materials List

| Description | | Material/Size | Length | Quantity |
|---|---|---|---|---|
| Lumber | Ledger | 2×8 fir or pine* | 12′ | 2 ea |
| | Posts | 4×4 fir or pine | 8′ min | 8 ea |
| | Perimeter beams | 4×8 fir or pine | 12′ | 4 ea |
| | Joists and blocking | 2×6 fir or pine | 10′<br>RL | 10 ea<br>66 l.f. |
| | Lattice panels | 4×8 wood or vinyl lattice | — | 8 sh |
| | Trim | 2×6 rwd or cedar**<br>2×2 rwd or cedar<br>1×3 rwd or cedar<br>2×4 rwd or cedar<br>1×1 rwd or cedar | 12′<br>RL<br>12′<br>16′<br>RL | 4 ea<br>190 l.f.<br>4 ea<br>1 ea<br>80 l.f. |
| Hardware | Post bases | 4×4 light post base | — | 8 ea |
| | Ledger screws, post/beam screws | ½″ lag screw (w) | 5″ | 32 ea |
| | Joist hangers | light 2×6 hgr | — | 16 ea |
| | Angle clips | light angle clip | — | 6 ea |
| | Nails: joist hanger<br>2×6 blocks and top trim<br>light trim<br>lattice panel | 1½″ hgr<br>16d HDG<br>8d HDG<br>4d HDG | —<br>—<br>—<br>— | 2 lb<br>5 lb<br>1 lb<br>2 lb |

*or other suitable structural lumber
**or other naturally durable species
See page 105 for materials list abbreviations.

# FREESTANDING OVERHEAD ON POLES

*The dominant feature of this overhead canopy is its wide, low-pitched roof—a generous shelter for outdoor dining and social gatherings. There is enough room underneath for a large picnic table, with a barbecue and food-preparation counter nestled into the area between the poles at one end.*

## Structure

The basic structure of this canopy is simple, consisting of six poles, three beams, and nine pairs of rafters. The poles are buried 4 feet into the ground for lateral stability against wind and earthquake loads.

The heavy-timber style of construction requires several bolted connections and uses some readily available metal framing connectors. It also requires a bit of heavy lifting. Make sure you have plenty of help when the time comes to set the poles and raise those 22-foot beams.

Beams this long may not be readily available in your area. Although the plans for this project call for 6 by 12s, you can substitute 5⅛-inch-wide by 12-inch glulam beams if they are easier to find. Be sure to use beam saddles made to fit glulam sizes if you do.

## Preparing Footings

Use string lines to locate the centers of the postholes as shown on page 31, and mark each one with a small stake. The holes can be dug by hand with a posthole digger or, if you have adequate access to the site, by a truck-mounted power auger. Hiring one of these machines is expensive, but can save a lot of time and hard work. Check the telephone directory under "Drilling Companies" for contractors who are qualified to do this kind of work.

Once the holes have been dug to the correct diameter and depth, place about 6 inches of gravel in the bottom of each one to provide drainage for the bases of the poles.

## Poles

The poles for this structure must be pressure-treated to protect them from termites and decay. Some chemical treatments leave the wood with a greenish tint, which may be objectionable if it is not going to be painted later. However, if you don't care for the color, lumber treated this way can be stained like untreated wood.

## Pole Layout

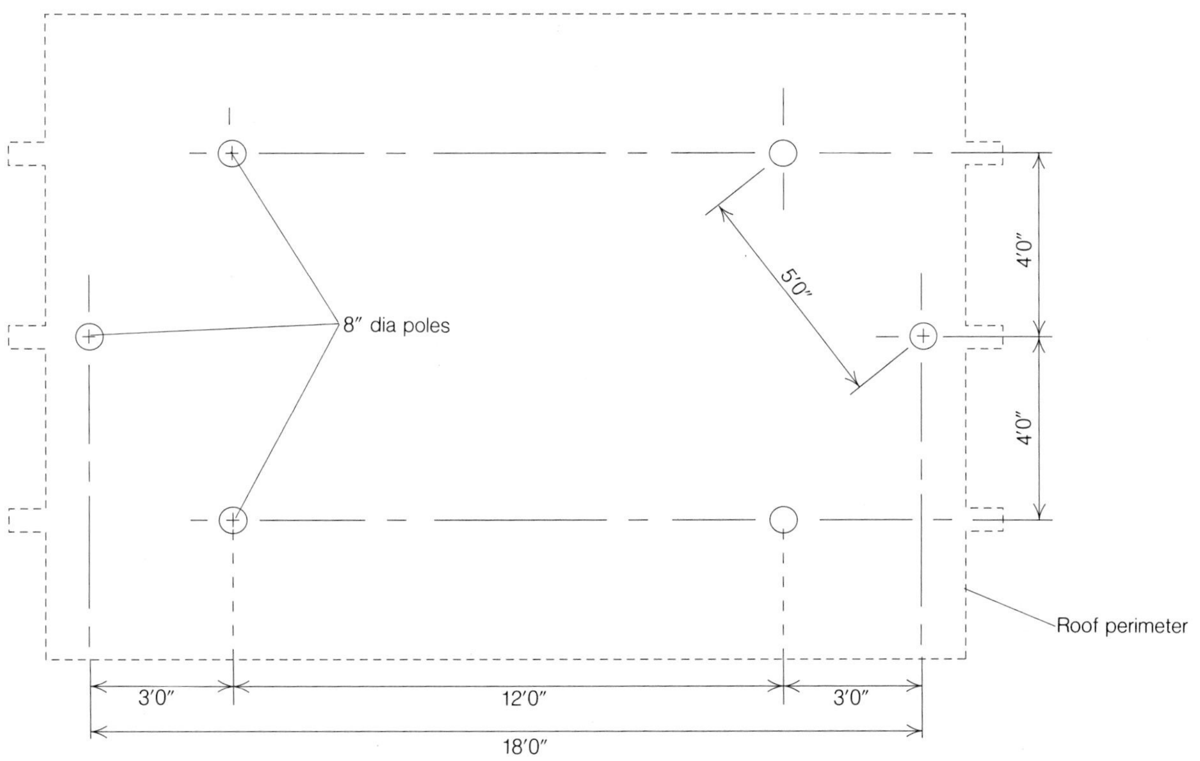

8″ dia poles
5′0″
4′0″
4′0″
Roof perimeter
3′0″
12′0″
3′0″
18′0″

When you are ready to install the poles, drive two or three long stakes cut from 2 by 4s along the wall of the first hole so that their ends protrude a foot or two above the ground. These stakes will brace the end of the pole as you lift it and will also prevent dirt from being inadvertently scraped off the sides of the hole.

With at least one assistant, place the butt end of the pole against the stakes and raise it Iwo Jima–style. Be careful—it will be heavy, and when it is nearly vertical it will drop into the hole suddenly. Remove the stakes and repeat the procedure with the other poles.

Next, install temporary bracing to hold the poles in position. Use a long 2 by 4 as a lever to get the bottom of the pole centered in its hole, then install two diagonal braces at a 90-degree angle to hold it plumb. This is a trial-and-error undertaking, so take the time to ensure that all the poles are plumb, parallel, and centered on the layout. A mistake here will cause problems when it's time to frame the roof.

When the poles are all set and securely braced, fill the holes with concrete. The concrete should extend above finished grade and slope away from the poles to drain water. For a cleaner finish, use short sections of cardboard forming tubes for forms at the bases of the poles.

## Pole Bracing

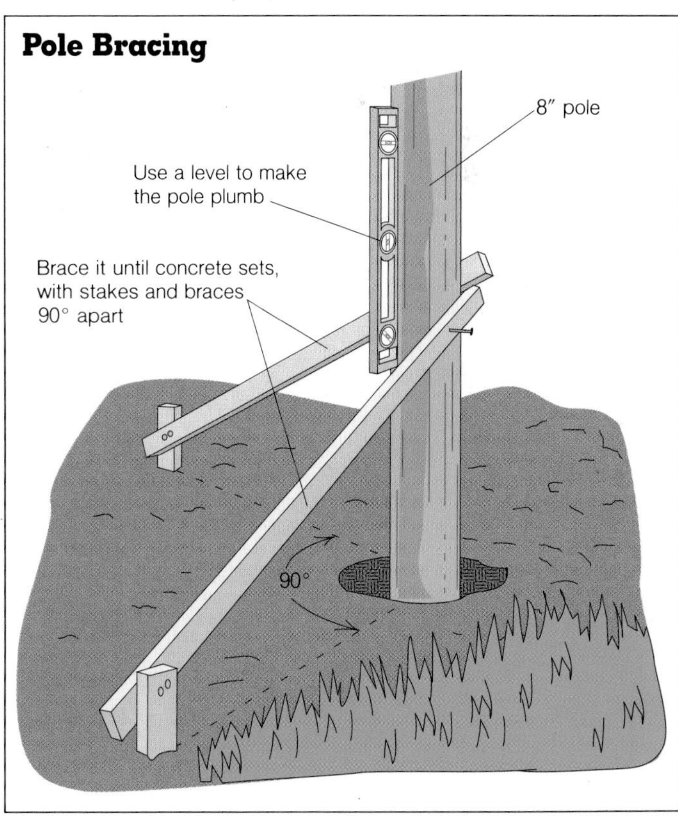

## Post Footing Detail

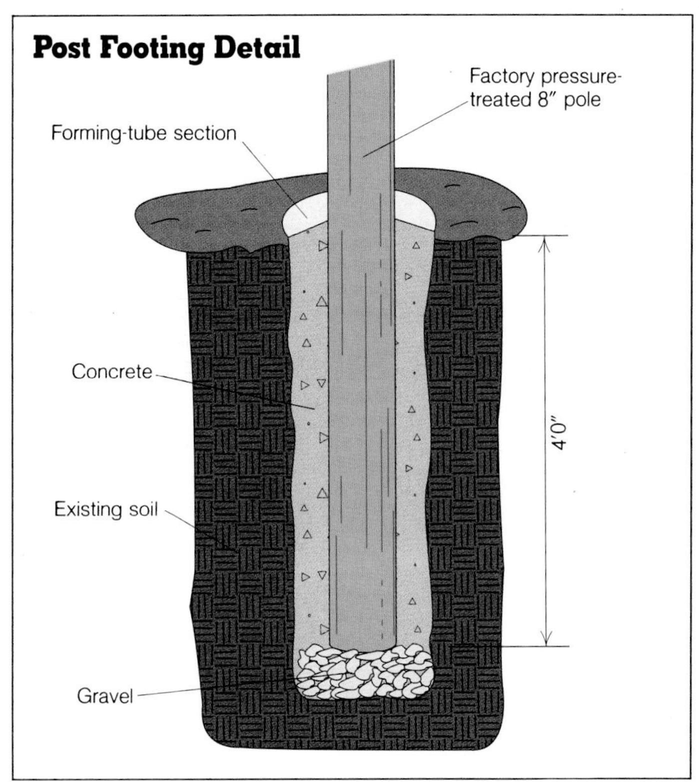


## Post Cap Detail

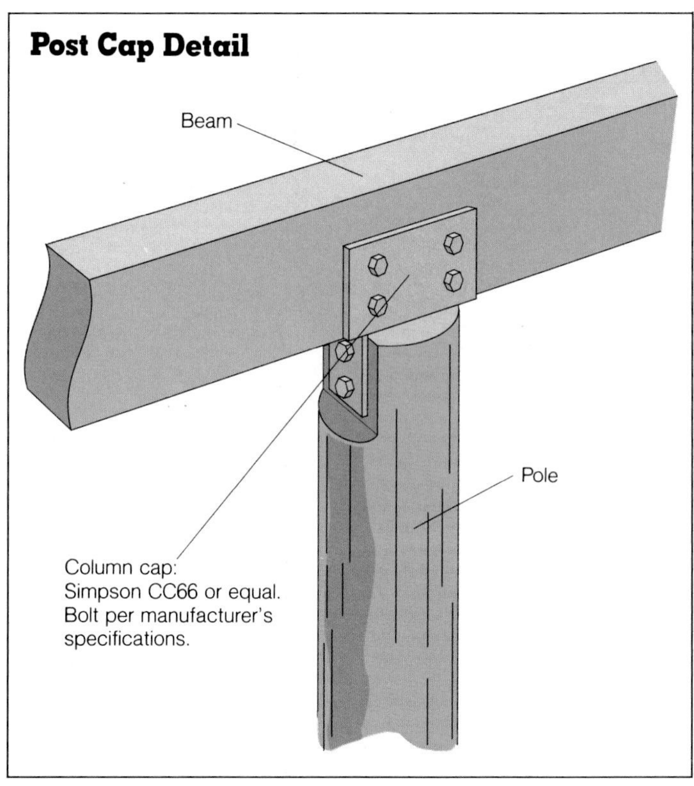


## Roof Framing

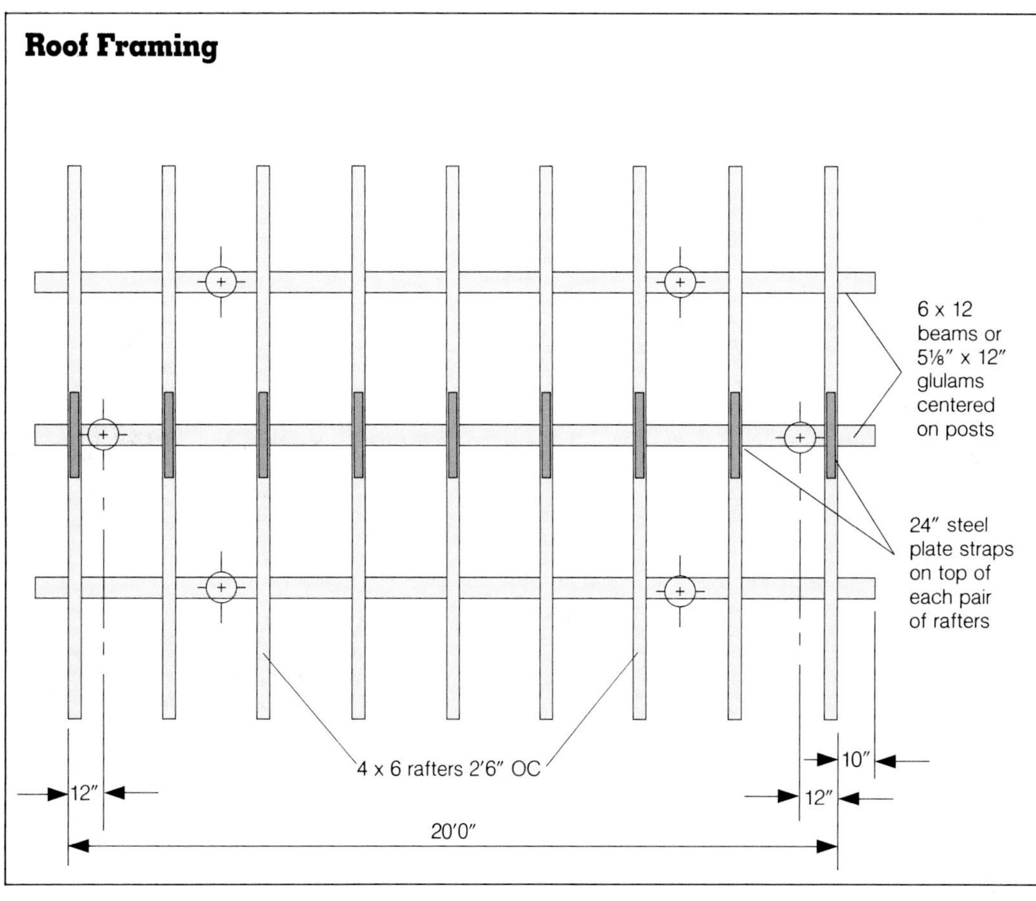


# Installing Beams

After the concrete has cured, cut the tops of the poles to their finished heights, using a water level or a builder's transit to mark the cuts. A strip of heavy paper or sheet metal wrapped around the pole will help to lay out a level cut line.

Use a chisel or chain saw to make flat spots on the sides of the poles to accept the straps of the beam saddle; then slip the saddle into place and drive 16d nails partway into the bolt holes to hold it in position. Do not install the bolts yet.

Cut the three main beams to length, and chamfer or round over their bottom edges so they will seat firmly in the brackets. If you are using glulam beams, this is done for you at the factory. With as many assistants as you can muster, raise the beams into position, with the crown side facing up. Make any adjustments necessary, and install all of the bolts.

Bolting up heavy hardware can be frustrating. The usual procedure is to drill halfway through from both sides with a bit ¹⁄₁₆ inch larger than the bolt diameter. No matter how careful your aim, however, sometimes the holes don't meet up in the middle and the bolt just won't go in. Reaming out the hole is rarely successful; it weakens the joint, and if the bit gets jammed, it's dangerous as well. The trick is to bend the bolt to fit the crooked hole. To do this, support the ends of the bolt between two blocks of wood on a solid surface and give it a firm blow in the middle with a heavy hammer. Try the fit and adjust the bend until you can drive it through.

## Roof Framing

Cut one of the 4 by 6 rafters as shown on page 32. Make sure it fits, then use it as a pattern to lay out and cut the others. Fasten the rafters to the beams at 30 inches on center with ½-inch by 10-inch lag screws. Lubricate the threads with wax or soap or you will risk breaking off the screw before it's fully driven. Countersink the screws at the ridge and install metal straps over the tops of opposing rafters to tie them together.

Next, install 2 by 4 purlins perpendicular to the rafters at 24 inches on center. Nail the purlins at each rafter with two 16d nails. Install flat blocking between the purlins on the end rafters to support the roof sheathing.

Nail down the roof sheathing, using ⅝-inch plywood or 1-by tongue-and-groove boards, with the face grain running perpendicular to the purlins. For plywood, use 6d nails at 6 inches on center on the edges and 12 inches in the field; for 1 by 6 boards, use three 6d nails at each support. Install a 1 by 3 trim board around the perimeter of the roof deck to cover the ends of the purlins and sheathing.

## Roofing

Cover the canopy with composition shingles applied according to the manufacturer's instructions. Be sure to use roofing nails that penetrate almost, but not quite, through the sheathing.

### Framing Detail

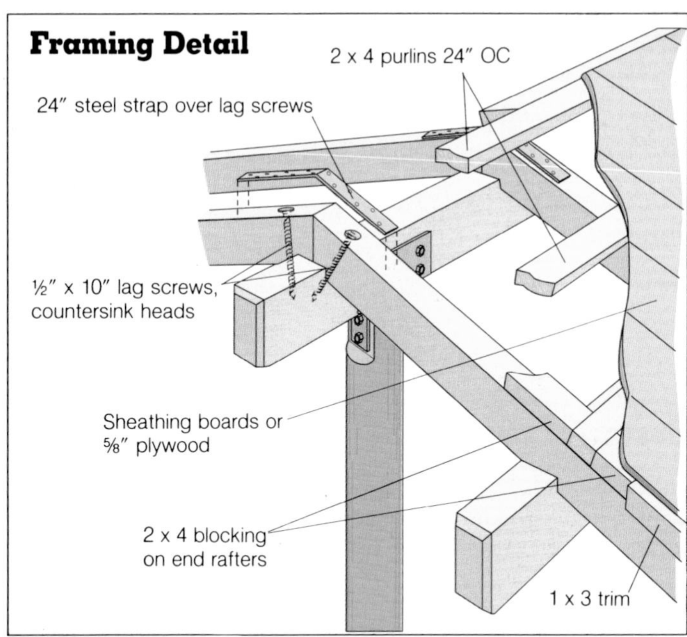


## Materials List

| Description | | Material/Size | Length | Quantity |
|---|---|---|---|---|
| Pole footings | Gravel | ¾″ gravel | — | 100 lb |
| | Concrete | — | — | 1½ cu yd |
| Lumber | Poles | 8″ dia PT pole | 12′ | 6 ea |
| | Beams | 6×12 or 5⅛×12 glulam beam | 22′ | 3 ea |
| | Rafters | 4×6 | 8′ | 18 ea |
| | Purlins/blocking | 2×4 | RL | 200 l.f. |
| | Sheathing | ⅝″ plywd or 1×6 or 1×8 T&G bds | 4′×8′ | 10 sh |
| | Eave trim | 1×3 rwd or cedar* | RL | 80 l.f. |
| Hardware | Column caps | heavy column cap | — | 6 ea |
| | Column-cap bolts | per mfg | — | — |
| | Rafter screws | ½″ lag screw (w) | 10″ | 36 ea |
| | Straps | std plate strap | 24″ | 9 ea |
| | Nails: purlins | 16d sinker | — | 5 lb |
| | sheathing | 8d sinker | — | 5 lb |
| | trim | 8d HDG | — | 1 lb |
| | Assorted metal fasteners as per text | | | |

*or other naturally durable species
See page 105 for materials list abbreviations.

# YARD SEPARATOR

*This whimsical little redwood trellis provides a graceful and distinct transition between separate areas of a yard. It is easy to build, requiring about a weekend's worth of work. The posts and shaped beams are made of rough-sawn lumber in order to give the structure more stiffness and improve the proportions of the whole.*

## Posts

The posts for this trellis are planted in the ground like fence posts, so they should be made from a naturally durable species of wood or pressure-treated wood suitable for ground contact. Heartwood of redwood, cypress, and some types of cedar are likely choices. Soaking the ends of the posts in a wood preservative will help to make them last even longer.

Install the posts just as you would if building a fence. Dig the holes at least two feet deep and place a few inches of gravel in the bottom for drainage. Plumb and brace the posts with 2 by 4s and backfill around them with tamped earth (or use concrete for a stronger installation). Cut the posts to length and chamfer the tops after they are installed.

## Cross-beams

Lay out the shaped cross-beams for cutting as shown on page 35. The easiest way to lay out the large curves is to construct two perpendicular lines in the form of a tee on a large flat surface (a garage floor, deck, or patio, for instance). Place one of the 2 by 12s on the crossbar portion of the tee, centered on the vertical line, and another board on the vertical line to complete the tee. Then use a piece of 1 by 2, with a nail in

## Rafter and Post Detail

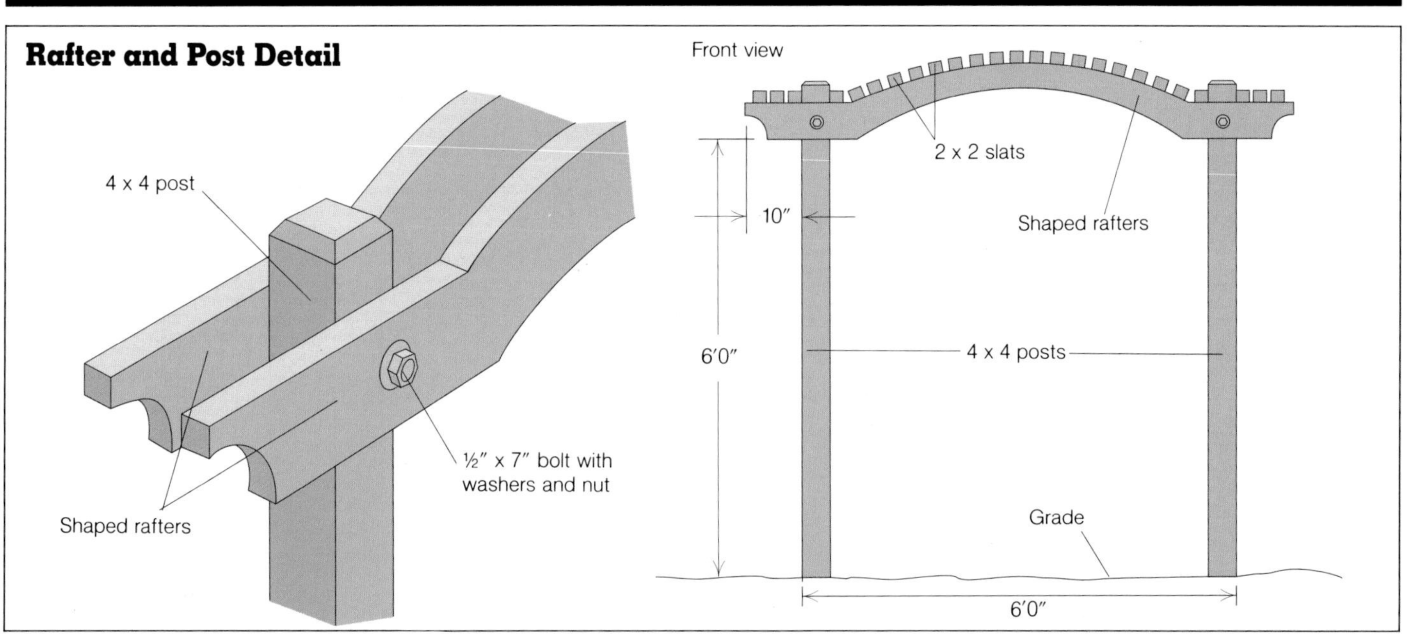


## Rafter Diagram

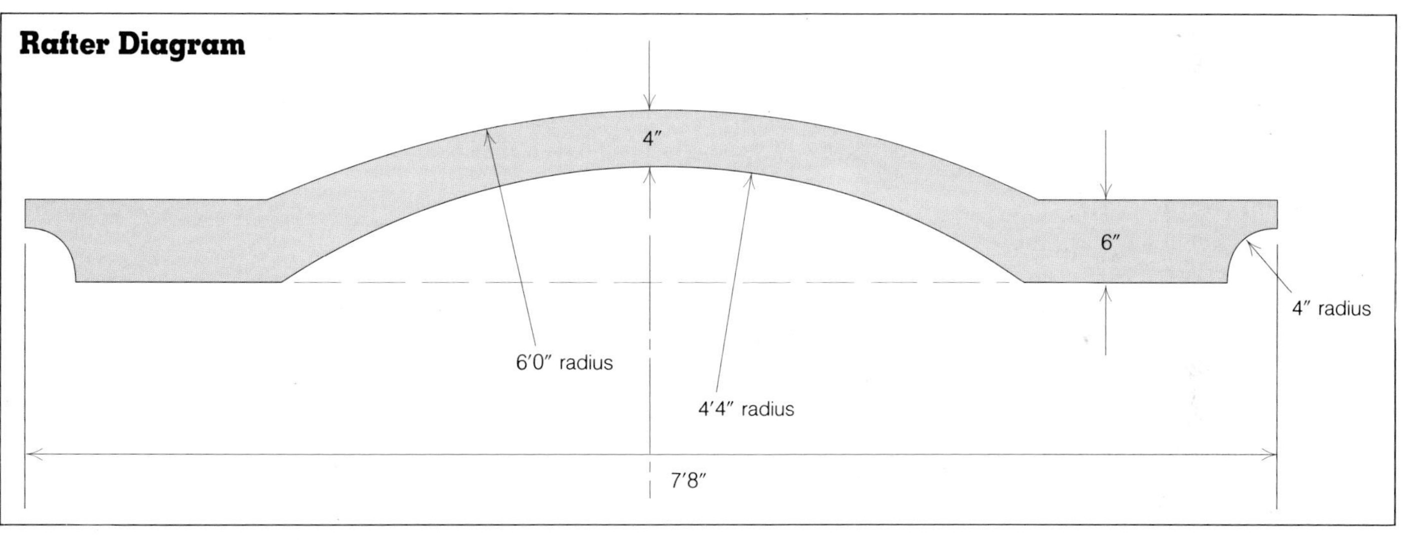


## Slats Detail

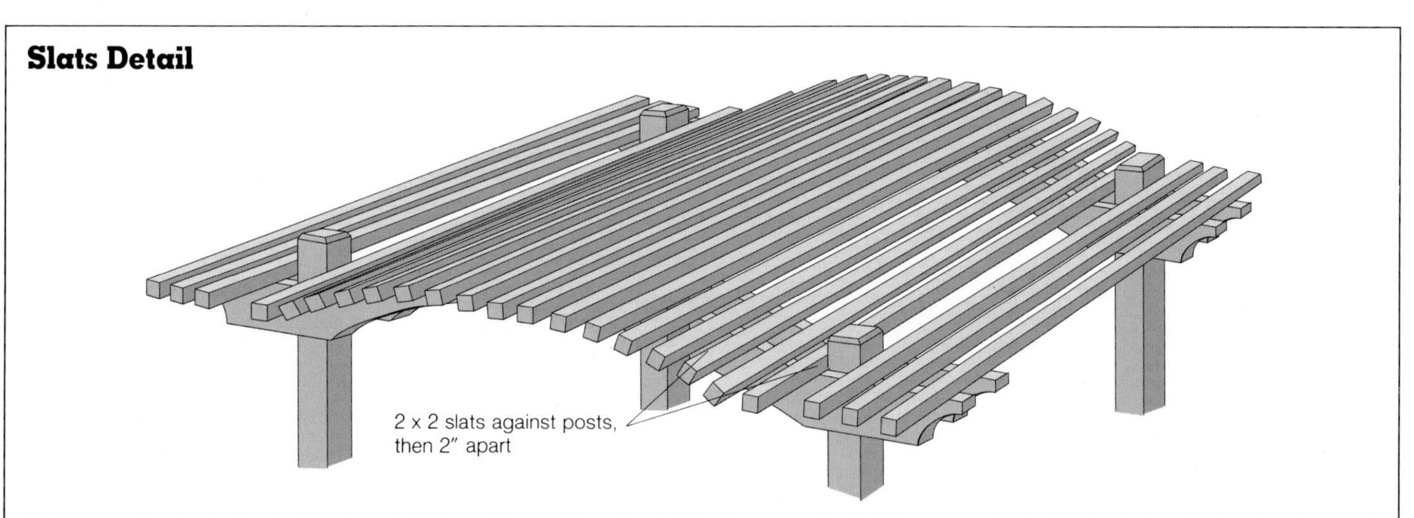

one end as a pivot, as a compass to scribe the arc. A reasonable approximation can also be made by laying out the centers and ends of the arcs on the board and bending a thin, flexible strip of wood around the layout marks.

Cut out the cross-beam with a saber saw or band saw and use it as a pattern to mark all of the others.

Nail two 2 by 4s (that you used for temporary bracing) across the posts to support the cross-beams while you install them. This will facilitate lining the cross-beams up just right before you install the bolts.

## Grille

Cut all of the 2 by 2s for the grille to length before installing them. Start with the four 2 by 2s that abut the posts, and fasten them to the posts as well as the cross-beams. Fill in the rest of the 2 by 2s, working from the posts toward the center; use 2-inch spacer blocks to keep the openings between the 2 by 2s consistent. Adjust the spacing as necessary as you approach the center so you don't end up with an odd gap in the middle.

Cutting the large curves in the cross-beams weakens them considerably. Although they are still strong enough to support the canopy, you run the risk of splitting them by pounding nails through all of those 2 by 2s. For this reason, it is better to use 3-inch coated deck screws, specially designed for outdoor use, to fasten the grille. Drill pilot holes first to avoid splitting.

### Framing Plan, Viewed from Below

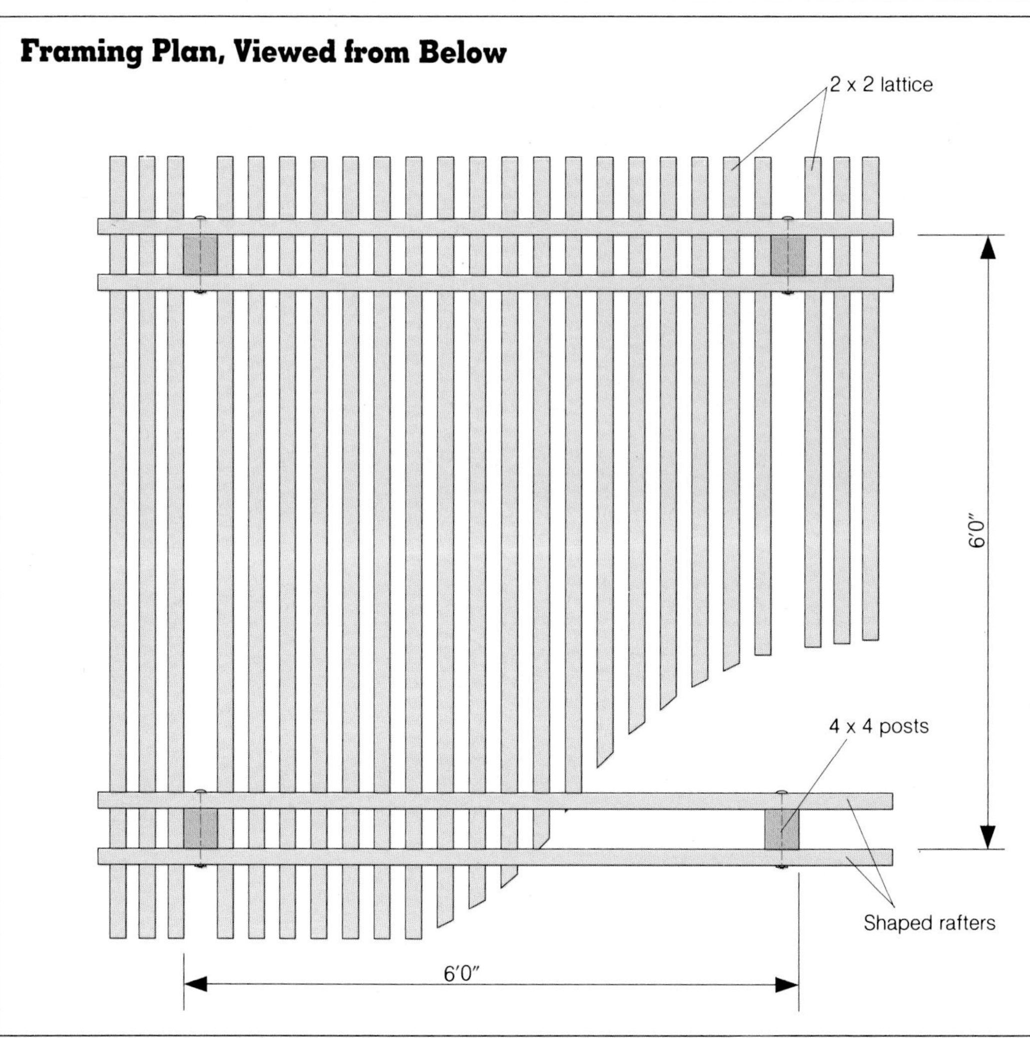


## Materials List

| Description | | Material/Size | Length | Quantity |
|---|---|---|---|---|
| Footings | Concrete around posts | 60-lb sacks concrete mix | — | 8 sacks |
| Lumber | Posts | 4×4 rough-sawn rwd or cedar* | 8′ | 4 ea |
| | Cross-beams | 2×12 rough-sawn rwd or cedar | 8′ | 4 ea |
| | Grille | 2×2 rwd or cedar | 8′ | 25 ea |
| | Misc. scrap lumber for temporary bracing as per text | | | |
| Hardware | Cross-beam bolts | ½″ MB (n/2w) | 9″ | 4 ea |
| | Screws | Coated deck screw | 3″ | 2 lb |

*or other naturally durable species

See page 105 for materials list abbreviations.

## Alternate Version

While the yard separator just described serves to define the passage from one area to another, this alternate version is meant to be an end in itself, a special retreat. With its cantilevered canopy, it lends a dramatic focus to the yard, and is ideal for a spa cover or, incorporated into a deck, as an awning over a table and chairs.

### Structure

The basic structural difference between this version and the yard separator is the addition of two pairs of 2 by 8 beams that support the cantilevered portion of the canopy. These beams are supported by posts at one end and, near their midpoints, by 18-inch 4 by 4s suspended from the center pair of shaped cross-beams. The forward pair of posts has been spread apart and the cross-beams have been correspondingly lengthened to provide a roomier area under the trellis.

### Dimensions

|  |  |
|---|---|
| Length of 2 × 8 beams | 8′0″ |
| Length of shaped beams | 4 @ 8′0″<br>2 @ 10′8″ |
| Length of 2 × 2 grille pieces | 8′0″ |
| Distance between main posts (measured from outside of post to outside of post) | Front pair 6′0″<br>Rear pair 9′0″ |
| Minimum height of shaped beams, to lowest point | 6′0″ |
| Length of short 4 × 4s | 1′6″ |

### Side Elevation

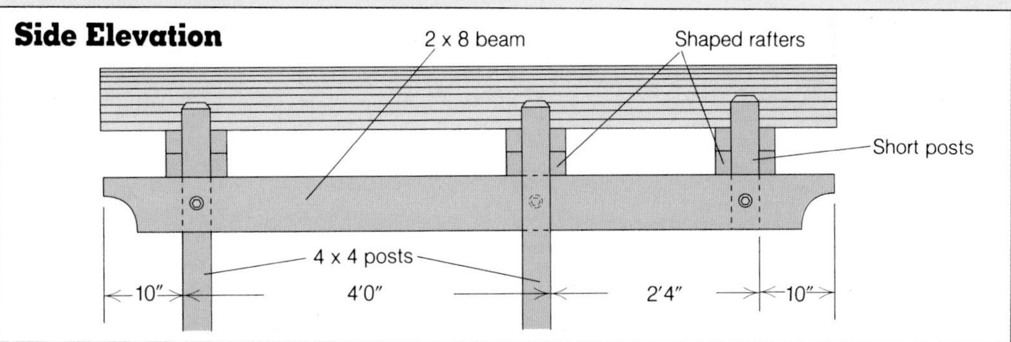


### Framing Plan

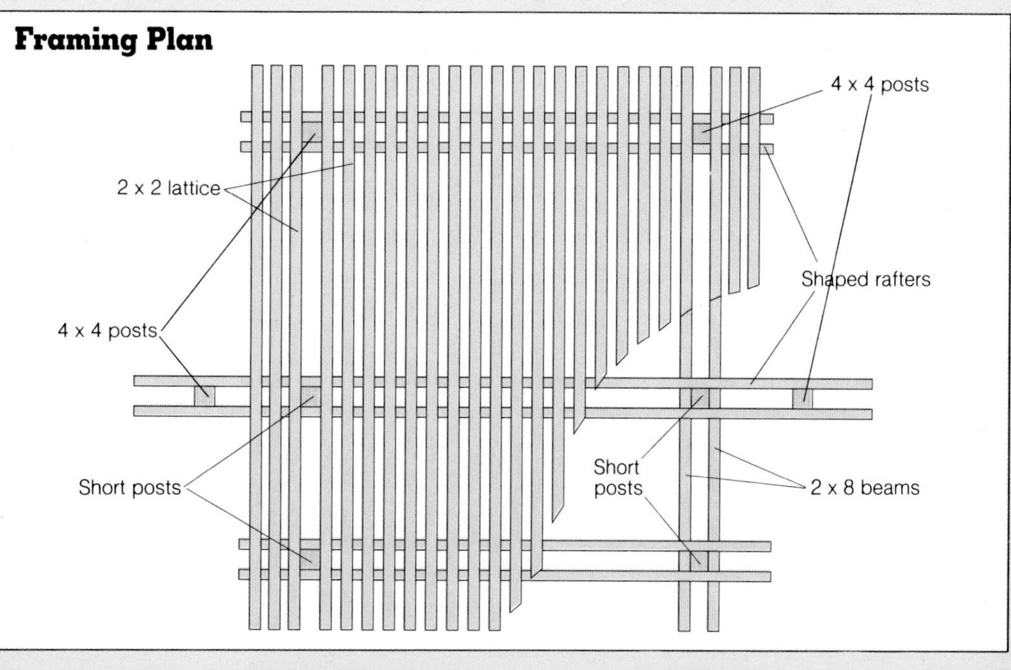

# ENTRY TRELLIS ON PRECAST COLUMNS

*This elegant entry trellis utilizes precast concrete columns over structural pipe columns, topped by rough-sawn corbels and beams, with a split-grapestake lattice of redwood or cedar.*

## Columns

Before you do anything else, order the concrete columns. Tuscan-style columns have been used for this trellis because of their simple, uncluttered lines. They are available from most manufacturers in various lengths and diameters. Two basic materials are generally used: precast concrete and glass-fiber reinforced concrete (GFRC). Precast-concrete columns are the least expensive, but they weigh about three times as much as GFRC columns, so any savings may be negated by additional freight charges if they must be shipped long-distance. Check with your supplier for recommendations and actual price comparisons.

Most types of columns come in two pieces so they can be assembled over structural posts. Overall height, shaft diameter, and plinth size vary among manufacturers, so you will need to know these dimensions to set up the footings and have the pipe columns fabricated.

Once you've obtained the columns, have a welding shop that specializes in structural-steel work make up the pipe columns as shown on page 40. The length of the shaft from the top of the base plate to the bottom of the beam saddle should be equal to the length of the precast column plus an additional 6½ inches.

The greatest amount of work involved in this project is in setting up and installing the columns. Careful attention to detail is critical when pouring the footings, installing the pipe columns, and assembling the concrete columns over them.

## Footings

Like the tree trunks they resemble, the columns must be firmly rooted in the ground, which means construction of a substantial footing. Excavate a hole for each column, 14 inches in diameter and 4 feet deep, and then enlarge the upper 12 inches or so of the hole to accommodate the form for the column pier. Build the form from 2 by 12s or ¾-inch plywood and install it (oriented at 45 degrees to the axis of the trellis) so that it protrudes about 6 inches above grade. The tops of all the pier forms must be at the same elevation.

Next, make reinforcing-bar cages that go into the footings. These consist of four No. 5 (⅝-inch-diameter) vertical bars tied together with three rings made from No. 2 bars (also known as ¼-inch pencil rod). Assemble them on the ground and suspend them in the holes with wires attached to nails in the tops of the pier forms. There should be at least 3 inches of clearance between the rebar and the sides of the hole.

The anchor bolts that support the pipe columns must be located precisely to fit the holes in the base plate. This is accomplished by suspending the anchor bolts from a block of wood, which simultaneously forms a recess in the top of the pier when concrete is poured around it. Cut the blocks from 2 by 12s, 10 inches square, and bevel the edges 10 to 15 degrees so you can remove them later after the concrete has cured. Place each block against the base plate of a pipe column, trace the holes onto it, and drill it with a bit $^{1}/_{16}$ inch larger than the anchor bolts. Hang it on the pier form as shown below, slip the anchor bolts up from underneath and thread on the nuts to hold them. You are ready to pour concrete.

It will take about 1 cubic yard of concrete to fill the four

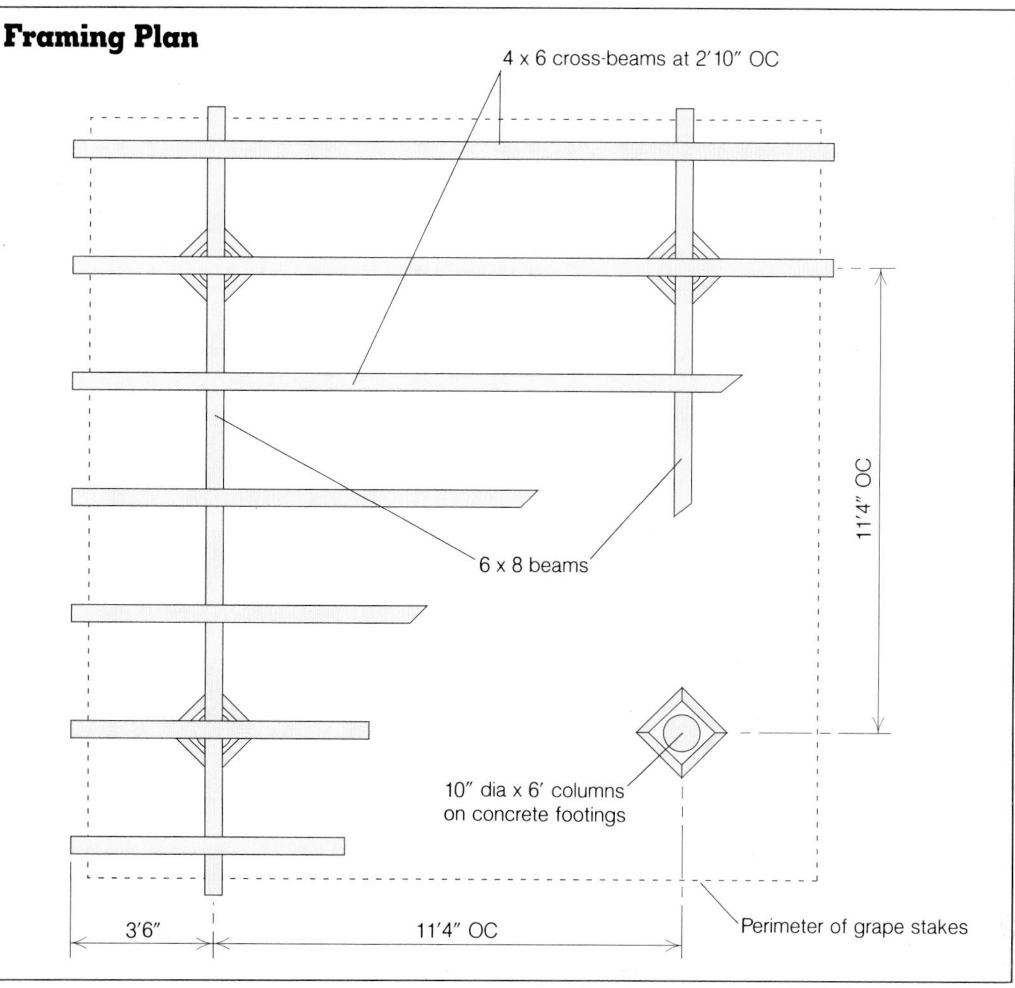


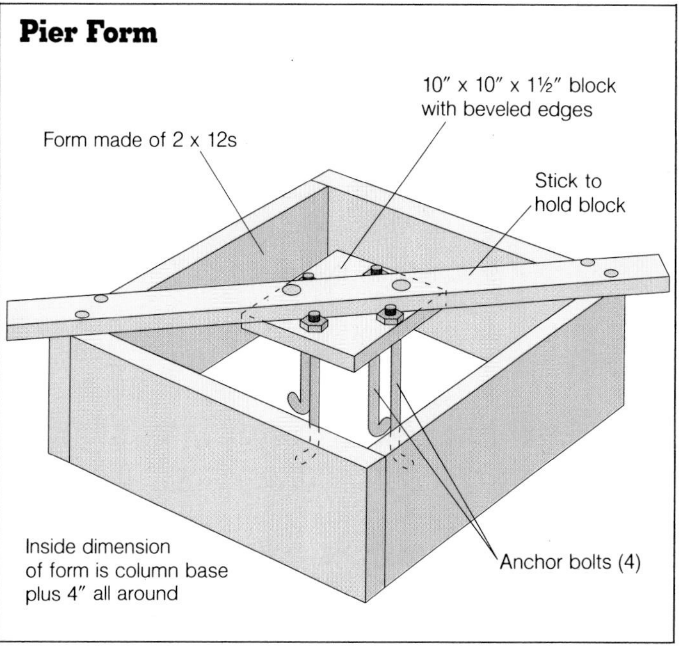


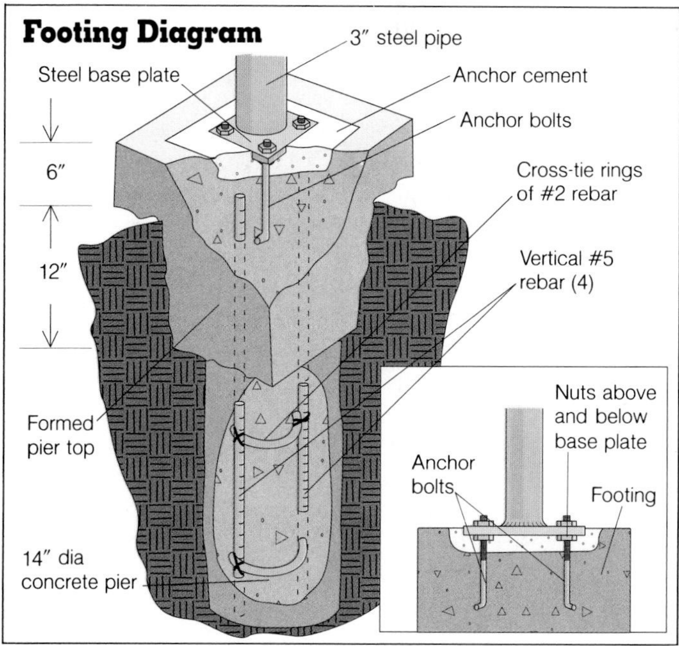

footings for this trellis. There won't be much room around the edges of the anchor-bolt blocks for pouring the concrete, but a makeshift funnel made of scrap wood will make this job a little easier. As you pour, work the concrete in to the hole with a shovel handle or a piece of rebar, and make sure the area under the anchor-bolt block is filled completely. Trowel the tops of the piers smooth as the concrete starts to set, and round over the corners with an edging tool.

After the concrete has cured, strip off the pier forms and pry out the anchor-bolt blocks. If a block won't come out easily, drive a large screw partway into its center and pull it up with a claw hammer. If that doesn't work, just split it out piece by piece with a chisel.

## Installing Pipe Columns

If the piers came out well, installing the pipe columns will be easy. Thread nuts onto the anchor bolts, nearly to the bottom of the threads. Slip the pipe column over the bolts so the base plate rests on the nuts, and thread another set of nuts loosely onto the bolts. Plumb the column by adjusting the nuts up and down until it is just right, and then cinch the nuts tight.

Sometimes, in spite of all your efforts, the anchor bolts will not quite line up with the holes in the base plate of the pipe column. If the fit is close, you may be able to bend a bolt a little to make it fit; but if not, you will have to take the pipe column back to the welder and have one or more holes enlarged with a cutting torch. If you do this, use washers with the nuts when you reinstall the column.

When all the pipe columns are set, fill the recesses in the tops of the piers with anchor cement—a quick-setting portland-cement product that is mixed to the consistency of heavy cream and poured into place. This locks together the whole pier-and-column assembly permanently.

## Beams and Corbels

Install the two 6 by 8 main beams next. Precut the ends to the stepped shape shown on the opposite page. Each step is 4 inches wide and one-third the depth of the beam. Cut ¼-inch-deep recesses in the bottom of the beam where it seats in the beam saddle. This makes the bottom of the beam flush with the bottom of the beam saddle and allows you to snug the corbels tightly to the bottom of the beam.

Get plenty of help when you install the main beams, because they will be heavy and awkward to handle. If you've already cut the 4 by 6 crossbeams, your assistants can go ahead and help you put those up at the same time.

The 6 by 6 corbels that mount to the underside of the main beams are put up in two pieces, with their ends notched to fit around the pipe columns. If you make up the corbels full length, then cut them in two and cut the notches, they can be reassembled with the grain matching, and the joint between the halves will be nearly invisible.

**Pipe Column**

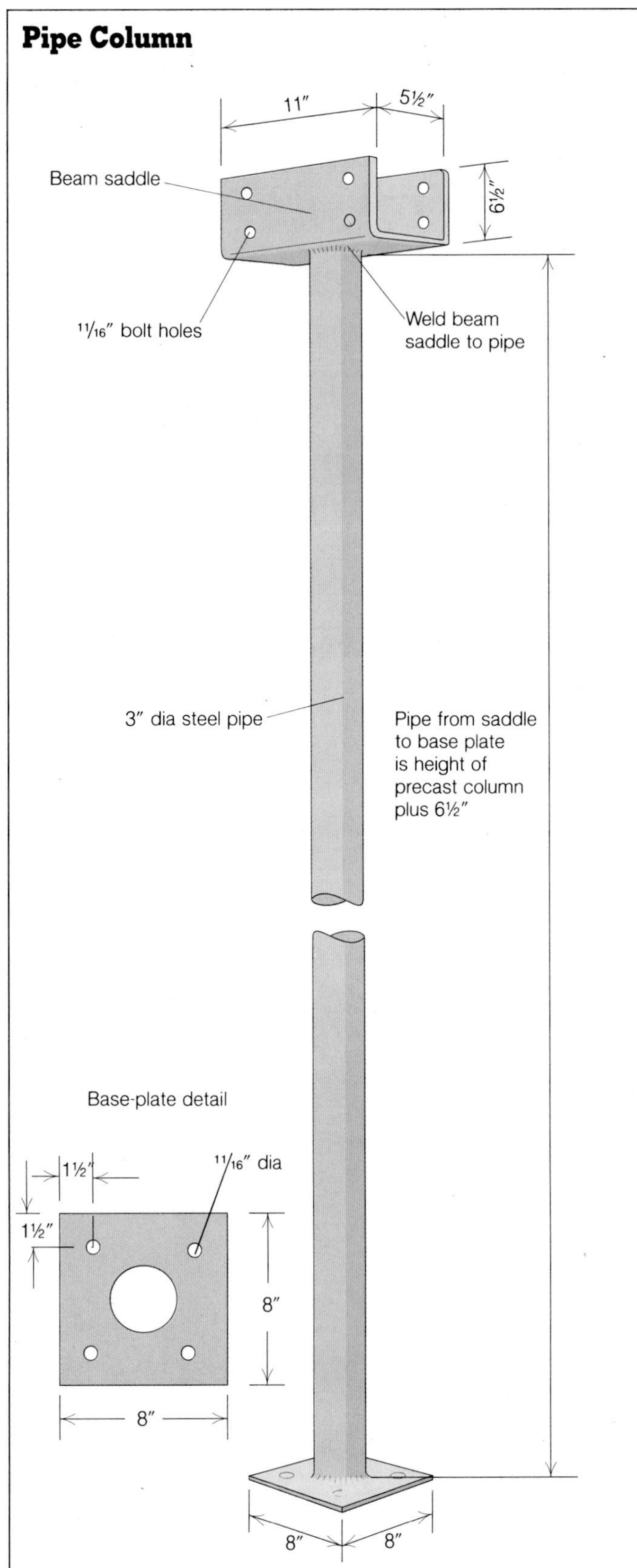

## Installing Precast Columns

Once the beams and corbels have been bolted in place, you are ready to install the precast-concrete columns. The installation procedure outlined here will work for most columns, but refer to the manufacturer's instructions as well; there is always more than one way to do a job, and the factory may recommend a method that works better with its product.

Stand up both halves on top of the footing—there should be a slight gap at the top between the column and the corbel. Next, pry the column up until it touches the corbel and drive wooden shims under the base to hold it. Separate the halves of the column just enough to apply a bead of construction adhesive to the mating surfaces, then press them together and secure band clamps around the shaft.

Allow the adhesive to cure for a few days before grouting the columns. Use a mixture of one part cement to three parts sand, with just enough water to make a dry, crumbly mix that will form a ball when squeezed in the palm of your hand. Pour this mix down the top of the column until it is full. It is not necessary to pack it down. Use the same mortar to fill in the space under the base of the column, only this time pack it firmly with a piece of scrap wood. After it hardens, remove the shims and fill the holes with more mortar.

The columns can be completed with either paint or a finish coat of stucco, which will more effectively hide the seams in the columns. If you want to use stucco, hire a professional to do the job.

### Roof and Column Tops

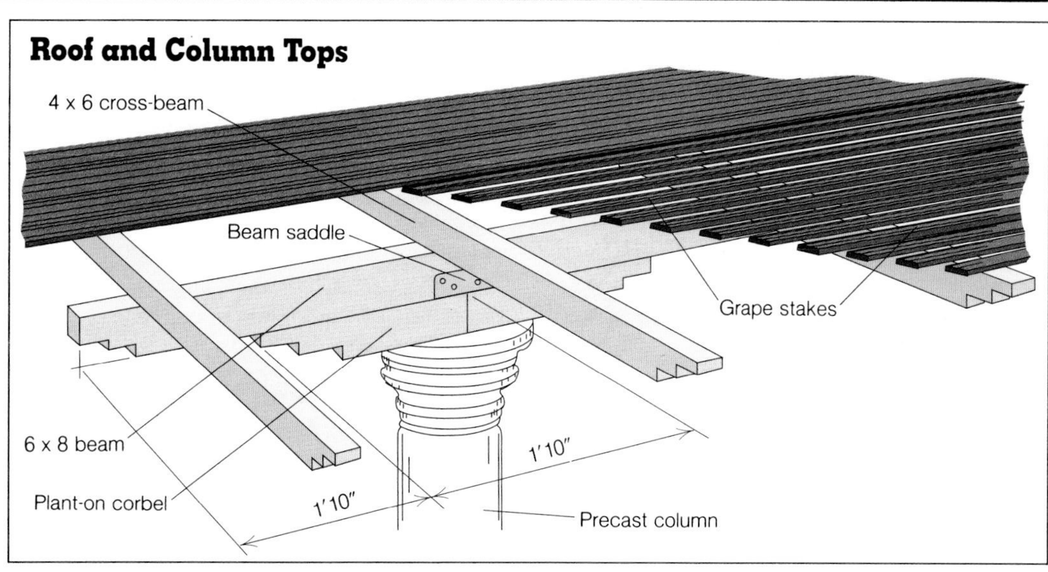


### Materials List

| Description | | Material/Size | Length | Quantity |
|---|---|---|---|---|
| Column footings | Pier forms | 2×12 | RL | 40 l.f. |
| | Anchor bolts | ⅝″ × 12″ (n) | — | 16 ea |
| | Reinforcing steel | #5 rebar<br>#2 rebar | —<br>— | 50 l.f.<br>30 l.f. |
| | Concrete | — | — | 1 cu yd |
| Pipe columns | (see drawings and text) | — | — | 4 ea |
| Lumber | Main beams | 6×8 rough-sawn | 20′ | 2 ea |
| | Cross-beams | 4×6 rough-sawn | 20′ | 7 ea |
| | Corbels | 6×6 rough-sawn | 8′ | 2 ea |
| | Lattice | 1×3 split grapestake | RL | 800 l.f. |
| Concrete columns | Columns | 10″ dia×6′ tall split column | — | 4 ea |
| | Adhesive | 28-oz tubes const adhesive | — | 2 ea |
| | Grout | ready-made mortar mix (60-lb sacks) | — | 15 sacks |
| Hardware | Beam-saddle bolts | per mfg | — | 16 ea |
| | Corbel screws | ⅜″ lag screw (w) | 5″<br>9″ | 8 ea<br>8 ea |
| | Nails: cross-beams<br>lattice | 16d HDG<br>8d HDG | —<br>— | 2 lb<br>7 lb |
| | Assorted metal fasteners as per text | | | |

See page 105 for materials list abbreviations.

# DAPTING OVERHEAD STRUCTURES

*Most overhead structures are designed to fit a specific situation in a specific site. You may want to accent a particular corner of the yard, shade an existing patio, or define and separate a certain spot from surrounding areas. Here are a few tips on how to adapt an overhead design to suit your special needs.*

## Changing Size

To make an overhead wider, you will either have to increase the length of its joists or add another beam and more posts. Longer joist spans may require larger framing members, especially if the structure must support a heavy load, such as that imposed by winter snow. If you use larger joists, increase the size of beams and posts accordingly to maintain the proportions of the whole.

To make a patio roof longer, increase the length of ledgers and beams and add more joists. You may have to add posts, too. Check the table on page 43 for maximum recommended spans.

## Changing Shape

All of the overhead plans shown in this book are rectangular in design, but you may require one that is L-shaped, U-shaped, or offset in the middle. Usually, this is just a matter of constructing the overhead as though it were two separate structures; where the two parts join, the beams for one portion can be supported in metal hangers attached to the beams of the other, or they can rest on top. The second method results in a stepped canopy, which can add depth and visual interest to the structure. Wherever two sections meet, they should be securely fastened with bolts, straps, or metal framing anchors.

*The possibilities for adapting an overhead to your site are limitless. Use long, narrow trellises to cover walks, protect windows from unwanted sunlight, or provide shelter for shade-loving plants. Raised portions of the canopy will focus attention on the area below. Cover an expansive area, such as a large patio or deck, by adding more posts, beams, and joists. If you'd like to leave some areas sunny, you can usually use the same post-and-beam arrangement as for the rest of the overhead, but omit the lattice covering.*

## Maximum Recommended Beam Spans

| | Spacing Between Members | | |
|---|---|---|---|
| | 4′ | 8′ | 12′ |
| 2×6 | 7′11″ | 7′0″ | 6′3″ |
| 2×8 | 10′6″ | 9′6″ | 8′0″ |
| 2×10 | 13′4″ | 12′0″ | 10′6″ |
| 2×12 | 16′3″ | 14′6″ | 12′9″ |
| 4×4 | 6′11″ | 6′0″ | 5′3″ |
| 4×6 | 10′10″ | 9′6″ | 8′3″ |
| 4×8 | 14′4″ | 12′6″ | 11′0″ |
| 4×10 | 18′3″ | 16′0″ | 14′0″ |
| 4×12 | 22′2″ | 19′6″ | 17′0″ |
| 6×6 | 14′2″ | 11′3″ | 9′6″ |
| 6×10 | 19′8″ | 17′1″ | 15′3″ |

Note: Figures in this table have been adapted for lightweight outdoor structures using naturally durable species of lumber (redwood, cedar, cypress) or pressure-treated lumber. They are based on combined live and dead loads of 30 pounds per square foot. Longer spans may be possible using stronger grades and species of lumber. Check local codes.

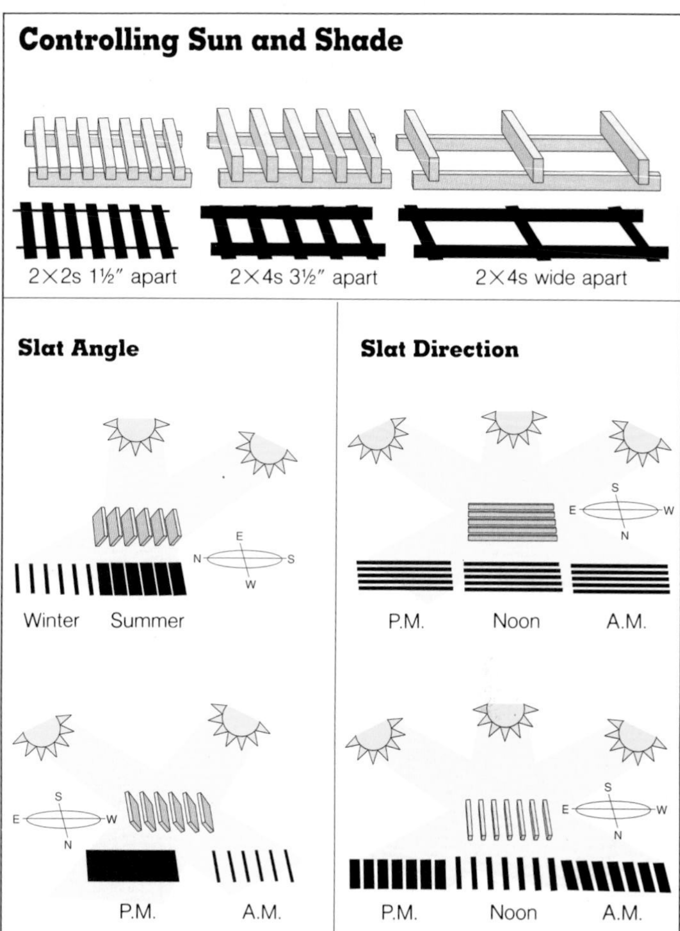


## Changing Post Layout

In most cases, posts for a patio roof are located at the corners, with intermediate posts that are equally spaced between. Sometimes, though, it's necessary to shift the post layout around in order to frame a view, accommodate traffic patterns, or avoid obstacles such as underground utilities or established plantings.

In general, posts should be located 6 to 10 feet apart, with the spaces between them more or less equal. Longer spans require larger beams to support roof loads without sagging. As a rule of thumb, a beam can safely span one foot for each inch of depth; that is, a 4 by 6 will span 6 feet; a 4 by 8 will span 8 feet, and so on. Avoid beam spans that are greater than 12 feet whenever possible.

The table above lists maximum recommended spans for wood beams. If you live in an area that is subject to heavy winds or snow loads, consult your local building official or an architect to ensure a safe design for your structure.

## Controlling Sun and Shade

Overhead structures with open-lattice type of coverings can be designed to take advantage of patterns of light and shadow. By varying the size, spacing, and orientation of framing members, it's possible to control the amount of sunlight that reaches the sheltered area. Because there are so many variables, it's best to experiment. Try different lattice sizes and spacings over a small area to judge the effect and find the best pattern for your particular application.

Typically, lattice slats are set so that the space between them is approximately equal to their depth. Thus, 2 by 2s are spaced 1½ to 2 inches apart; 2 by 4s on edge are spaced 3 to 4 inches apart. This arrangement makes for an attractive patio cover that provides a comfortable level of shading.

For maximum sunlight, use just a few lattice members and wide spacing. Patio roofs of this type are generally designed to define an area rather than to create shade. Be warned, though; such a structure will look weak and spindly unless the framing members are substantial enough to give it some strength and muscle.

Lattice slats that are oriented east to west will provide shade during most of the day. A north-south orientation will provide shade in the morning and evening but allow some sunlight through during the midday hours.

Climbing vines are a time-tested way to control the amount of sunlight under an overhead structure. Deciduous varieties, such as clematis, wisteria, or grapevines, provide cool shade in summer and allow warm sunlight through in winter.

# SIX SHED PLANS

*Most people who have lived in the same home for any length of time will eventually require additional work and storage space. When the attic, garage, and closets are filled to capacity, it's time to consider the benefits an outdoor shed can bring to a household.*

*In addition to providing needed storage space, a shed can serve as a work space, playhouse, potting area, or simply a place to keep ungainly equipment out of sight. The photos on the following pages show that when done well, sheds are not only enormously useful but can enhance their surroundings as well.*

*Six varied shed plans begin on page 50. No matter which shed you may choose to build, the first plan, or Basic Shed (page 50), should be reviewed for overall shed-building construction techniques. Although the other plan designs vary in size, materials, and configuration according to the purposes they serve, you may want to refer back to the Basic Shed for some construction details.*

*Each plan is fully illustrated and contains a complete materials list. Some provide alternate plans for similar structures that may more closely fit the needs of individual households.*

*Firewood and garden equipment are efficiently stored in this attractive low shed that fits snugly along a fence. The shed blends unobtrusively into its location by utilizing the same color scheme and boards as the fence; the fence also serves as the back wall of the shed. The flooring of 2 by 6 slats spaced slightly apart keeps stored firewood away from ground moisture and provides ventilation.*

*Shaped fascia and scalloped door trim are two decorative touches that convert this simple shed into what looks like a charming country cottage nestled into the garden.*

*This shed, styled like a classic barn, has plenty of room inside for a riding mower and other ungainly yard items. Its dark green color helps it blend into the landscape of lawn and trees. The windows allow light in and a vent provides air circulation. The area under the gambrel roof can serve as overhead storage space for items used infrequently.*

*This finely crafted redwood shed has been carefully built to fit among the existing boulders and trees, making the most of the available space without disturbing the natural surroundings. The custom double doors, vertical grain redwood siding, and cedar shingles complete the finished look.*

*Following the design of a classic New England cottage, this lap-sided building serves as two sheds in one. The various doors allow direct access to specific storage and work areas. A louvered vent incorporated into the gable provides ventilation inside.*

*Vines clamber up the trellis siding of this multigabled structure, effectively incorporating the shed into its garden surroundings. There is plenty of room inside for equipment storage, benches, and work space. The pitched concrete floor makes it easy to roll equipment in and out, and can be hosed down to wash refuse from potting and other garden tasks into a drain located inside.*

*These whimsical playhouses have been developed from basic shed designs embellished with details to create the most desirable of fantasy play areas.*
*Top left: A simple shed has been spruced up with a gable over a Dutch door; trim on the windows and corners; and even a planter box. Brick steps tie into the outdoor play area.*
*Top right: Set out in a field ideal for game playing, this elevated playhouse on stilts doubles as a climbing structure. The entrance from the railed-in balcony is simply a round hole to clamber through.*
*Bottom: Ornate details create a fairy-tale setting for imaginative play, while borrowing design elements, such as siding, from surrounding buildings. An attached overhead and rails protect the little porch area. Small dormer roofs add charm, and open windows are embellished with trim and planter boxes. Note that planters should be set away from the wall by at least 1 inch to prevent the siding from rotting.*

# THE BASIC SHED

*This is the fundamental shed design, a light-wood-framed structure on skids with a gabled roof. The only unusual feature is the cantilevered eave beams, which complicate the wall framing to some extent, but not much. Otherwise, this shed is constructed with standard stick-framing techniques.*

## Foundation

The foundation for the Basic Shed consists of a pair of built-up skids resting on a bed of crushed gravel. Begin by excavating a shallow recess, more or less flat, in the ground where the shed will be; remove any plant material or organic debris. Put down a layer of coarse gravel at least 4 inches deep, and grade it off so that it is as level as possible. A layer of sheet plastic under the gravel will prevent weeds from growing under the shed.

Build up the skids from three 2 by 8s, pressure treated to resist rot and termites. Treated wood rated for ground contact will last longer than wood approved for above-grade use only. Nail the 2 by 8s together with 16-penny (16d) hot-dipped galvanized (HDG) nails, two every 12 inches, or use 3-inch coated deck screws. The skids here are shown with a curve cut into the ends to repeat the shape of the eave beams and rafter tails; it is easiest to cut this profile into the individual 2 by 8s prior to assembling them.

Place the completed skids on the gravel bed with their outer edges 8 feet apart. Level them carefully, individually and to each other, by wiggling the high ends deeper into the gravel or raising the low ends and packing more gravel underneath them.

## Floor

Assemble the two rim joists and the two end joists on top of the skids. Use pressure-treated lumber for extra protection. Measure across the diagonals of the assembly to make sure it is square, and tack the corners of the skids with 8d nails. Fill in the rest of the joists, 16 inches on center, with three 16d nails into each end through the rim joist and two 16d toenails into the skid; then toenail the rim joists to the skids with 16d nails every foot.

Use ⅝-inch or ¾-inch plywood for the shed floor. It's advisable and worth the trouble to use plywood with exterior glue so that if the floor gets wet, the plywood won't delaminate. Space the sheets $\frac{1}{16}$ inch apart on the ends and ⅛ inch at the edges to allow for expansion, and stagger the end joints in adjacent courses. Fasten the panels with 8d nails every 6 inches on the edges and 10 inches in the field.

## Perspective View

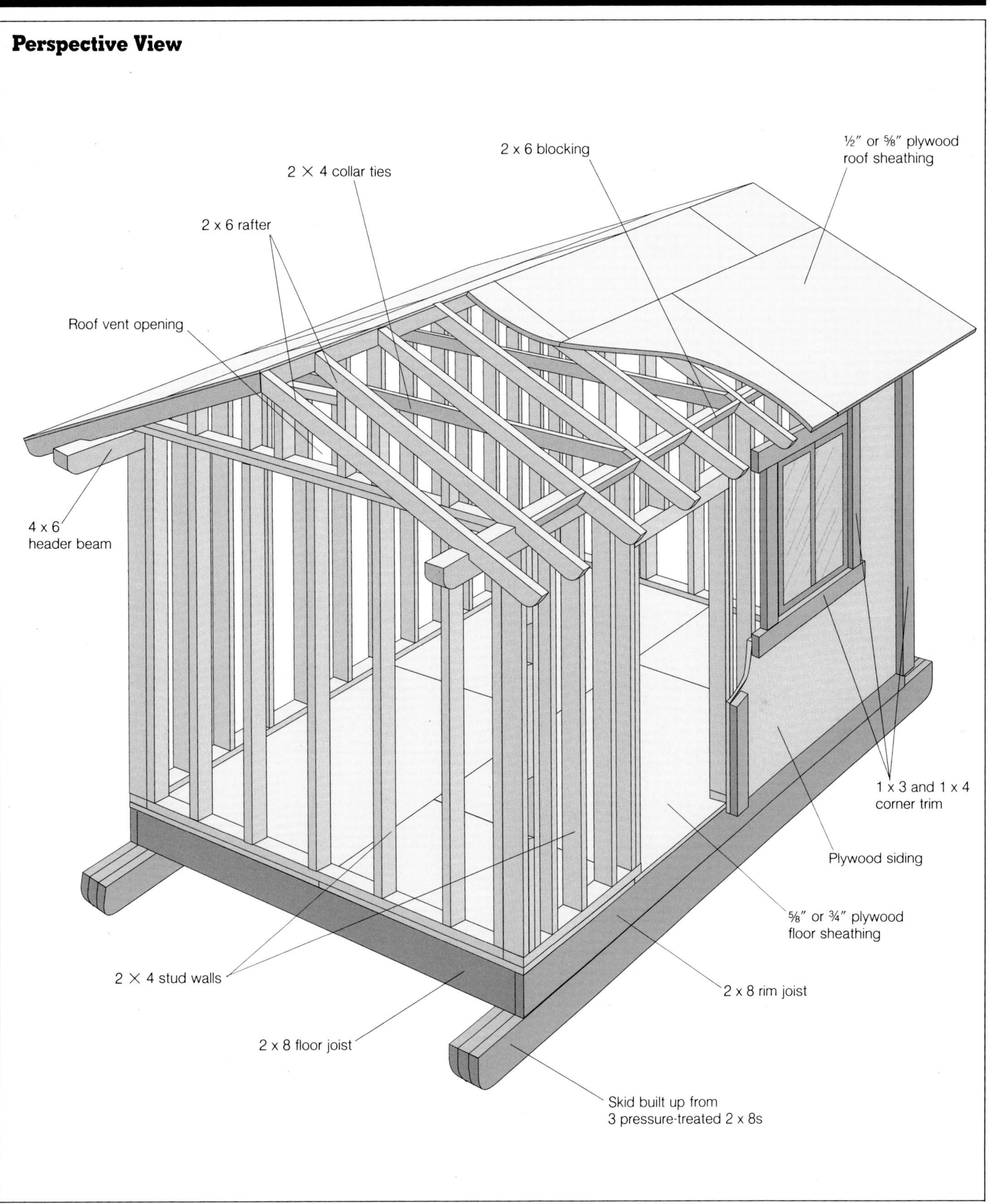

## Walls

Cut the top and bottom plates for the walls in pairs, with the long walls running the full length of the building and the end walls cut to fit in between. Lay out the locations of the studs, 16 inches center to center, and locate all door and window openings. Getting the exact rough-opening sizes for windows (and doors, too, if you will be using manufactured units) from your supplier before you frame the walls is necessary, since most manufacturers have slightly different requirements. Every door or window opening will have two studs on each side: a king stud, which runs from plate to plate, and a shorter trimmer stud, which supports the header beam over the opening.

With the stud locations marked out on the plates, shorten the top plates of the long walls back to the second stud from the corner for the 4 by 6 notched eave beams, as shown on page 53. Assemble one of the long walls first, flat on the floor, with two 16d nails into the end of each stud. Remember, the studs under the eave beams will be 2½ inches shorter than the others. After the wall is nailed together, install the cap plate over the top plate; this piece laps onto the eave beam, but stops 3½ inches short of the end of the notch to allow the cap plate from the end wall to tie in at that point. Nail the cap plate to each eave beam with five 16d nails, and to the top plate with 16d nails every 24 inches, staggered.

With an assistant, stand the completed wall up, nail it to the floor joists below the plywood, and brace it temporarily with two 2 by 4s. Frame the other walls in a similar fashion, nailing the corners together as you go.

Once all the walls have been erected and the cap plates for the end walls installed, nail temporary diagonal braces on the inside of each wall to hold it plumb. This bracing will remain until after the roof has been framed and the siding installed. If the upper ends of the braces protrude above the top

### Floor Framing

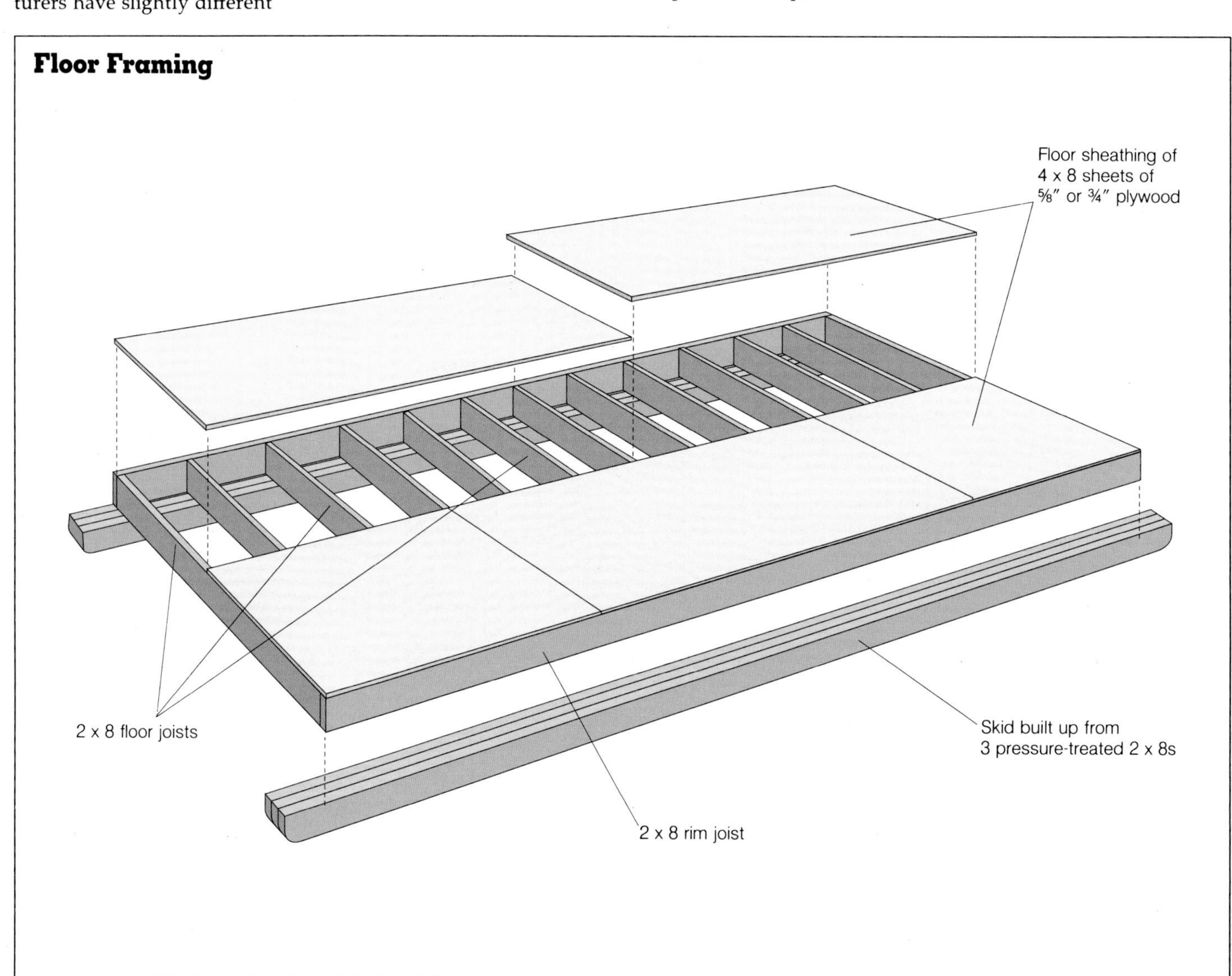

## Eave Detail

Eave beam built into side stud wall before erection
4′7¼″
2′0″
2′7¼″
1½″
4½″ radius
4 x 6 board
Top plate
Top plate
Cap plate
Studs
Studs
Corner post


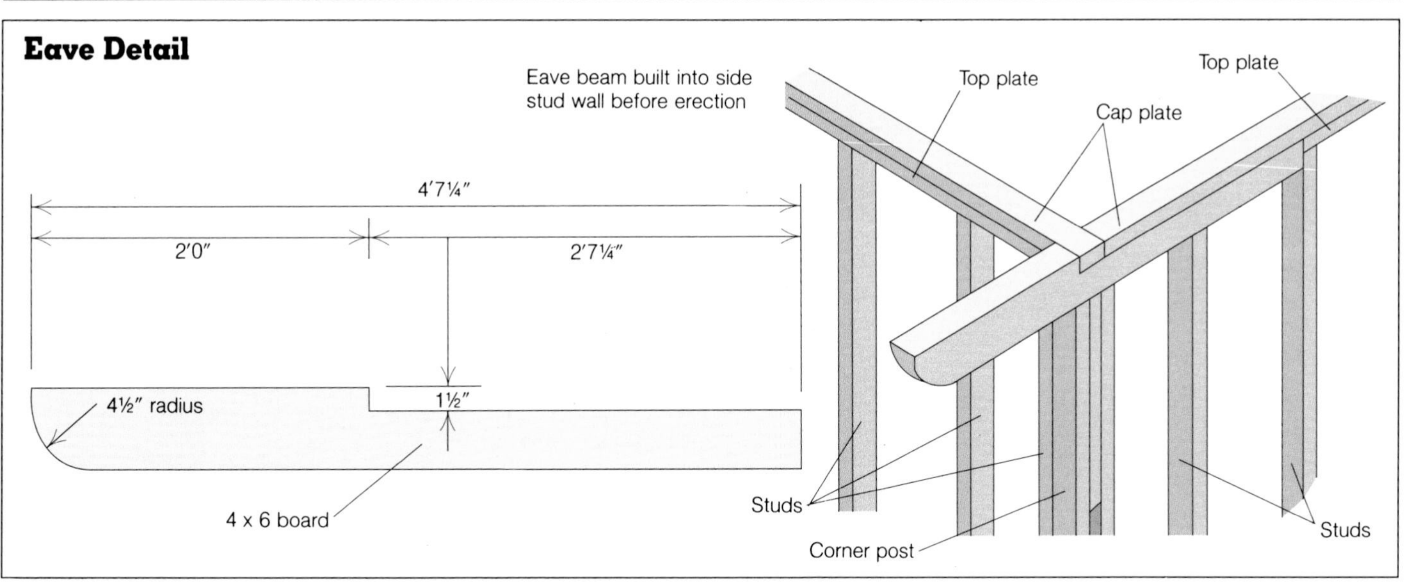

## Wall Framing

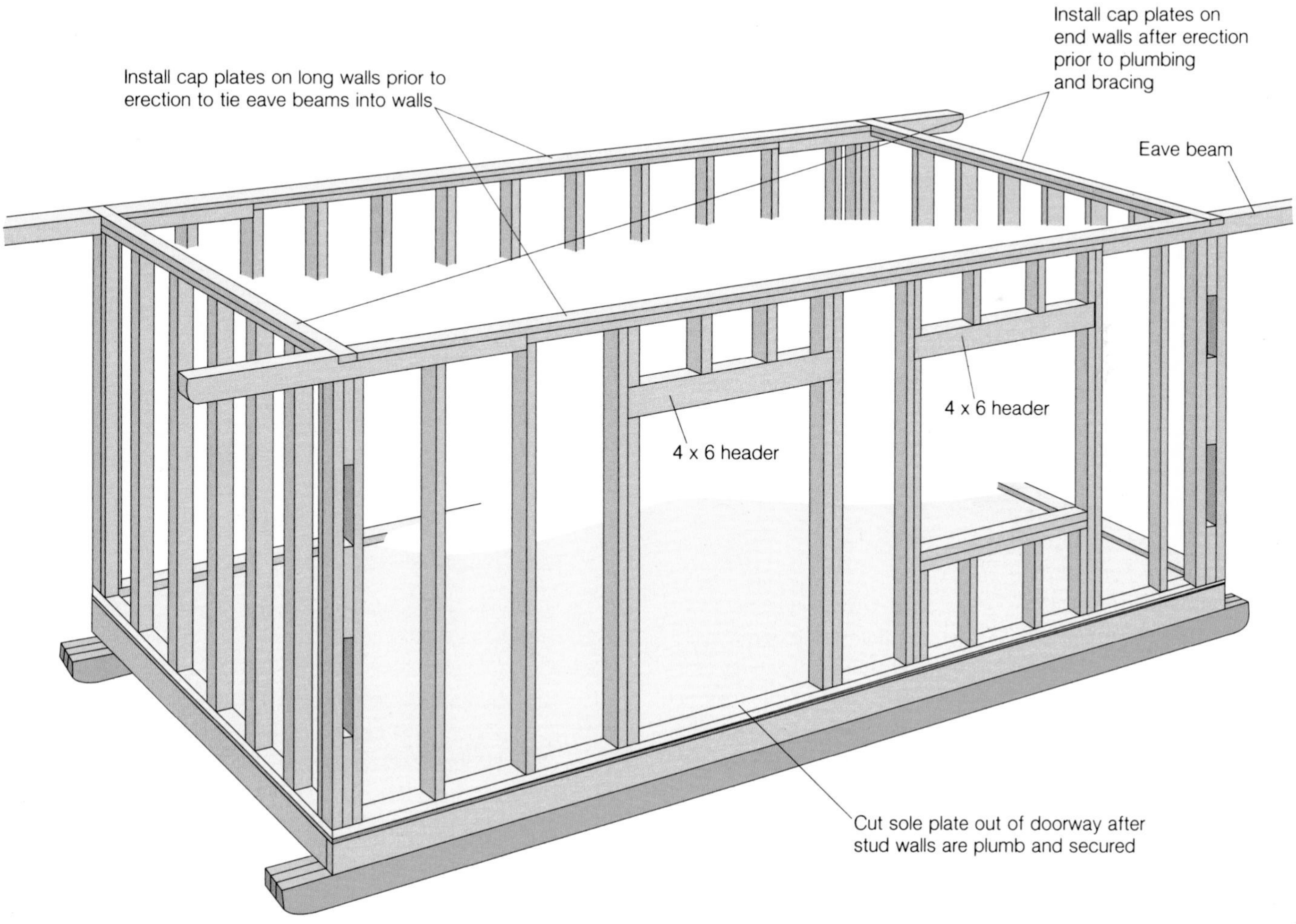

Install cap plates on long walls prior to erection to tie eave beams into walls
Install cap plates on end walls after erection prior to plumbing and bracing
Eave beam
4 x 6 header
4 x 6 header
Cut sole plate out of doorway after stud walls are plumb and secured

## Roof Framing

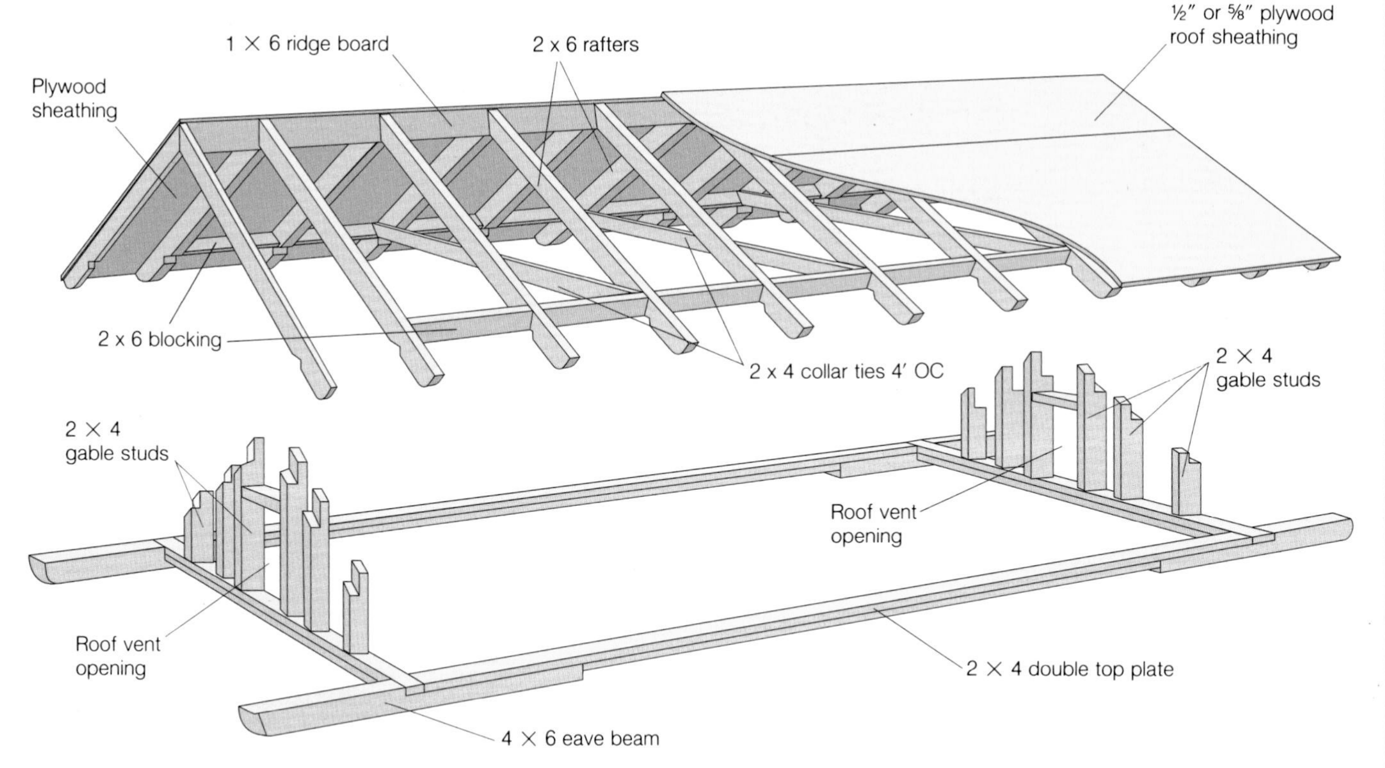

1 × 6 ridge board
2 x 6 rafters
½" or ⅝" plywood roof sheathing
Plywood sheathing
2 x 6 blocking
2 x 4 collar ties 4' OC
2 × 4 gable studs
2 × 4 gable studs
Roof vent opening
Roof vent opening
2 × 4 double top plate
4 × 6 eave beam


plate, cut them off so they won't interfere with the roof framing.

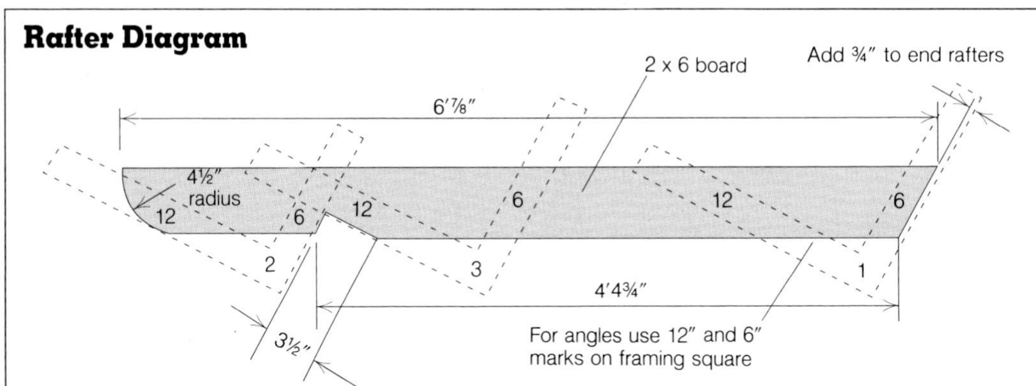

## Roof

Lay out one of the 2 by 6 rafters according to the rafter diagram at right; double-check all your angles and dimensions, and cut it to shape. Use this rafter as a pattern to cut a second one, and hold them up on the building to check the fit, with a scrap block between them to represent the thickness of the ridge. All the cuts should fit snugly. If they don't, go back and recheck your layout. If all is well, proceed with cutting the rest of the rafters, keeping in mind that the four end rafters must be cut longer so they will cover the ends of the ridge board.

## Rafter Diagram

2 x 6 board
Add ¾" to end rafters
6'⅞"
4½" radius
12
6
12
6
12
6
2
3
1
4'4¾"
3½"
For angles use 12" and 6" marks on framing square


Next, cut the ridge to length. It should extend past the end walls 16½ inches on each end. Lay out the positions of the rafters on the ridge and on the walls of the shed. The outside face of the first rafter should be flush with the outside of the shed wall; the center of the next one will be 24 inches in from that point, and the intermediate rafters of the roof are spaced 24 inches center to center.

Cut the 2 by 6 blocks that fit between the rafters. The four blocks that butt against the end-wall rafters will be 20¾ inches long; the others should be cut at 22⅜ inches.

Assembling a roof frame can be tricky until the first few rafters have been installed. You need to hold up about five pieces at once and try to nail them all together at the same time. Enlist the aid of another pair of hands, follow the procedure outlined below, and your headaches will be minimal.

First, prop the ridge up to the proper height. This can be difficult to calculate, but for

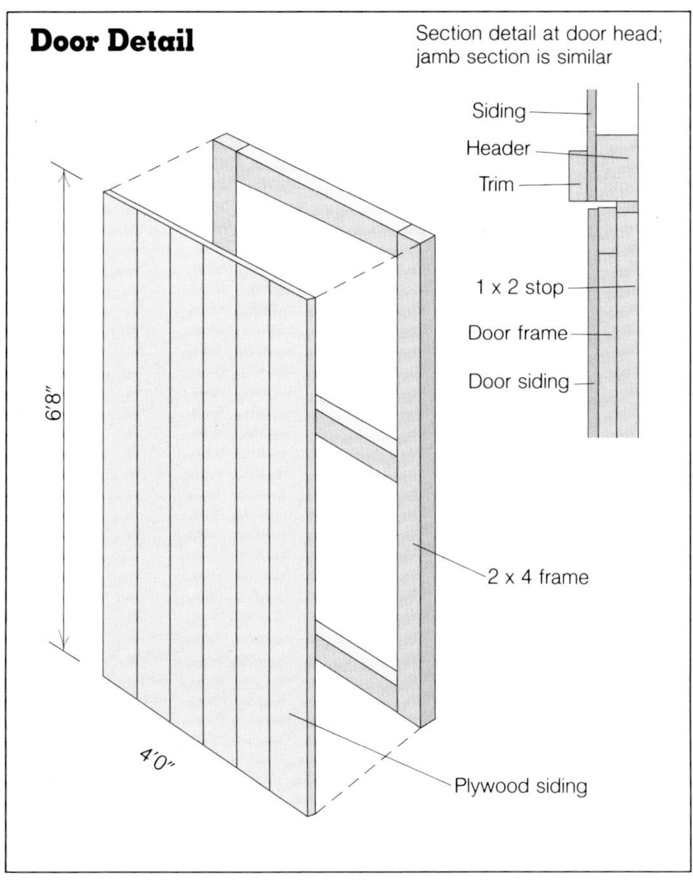


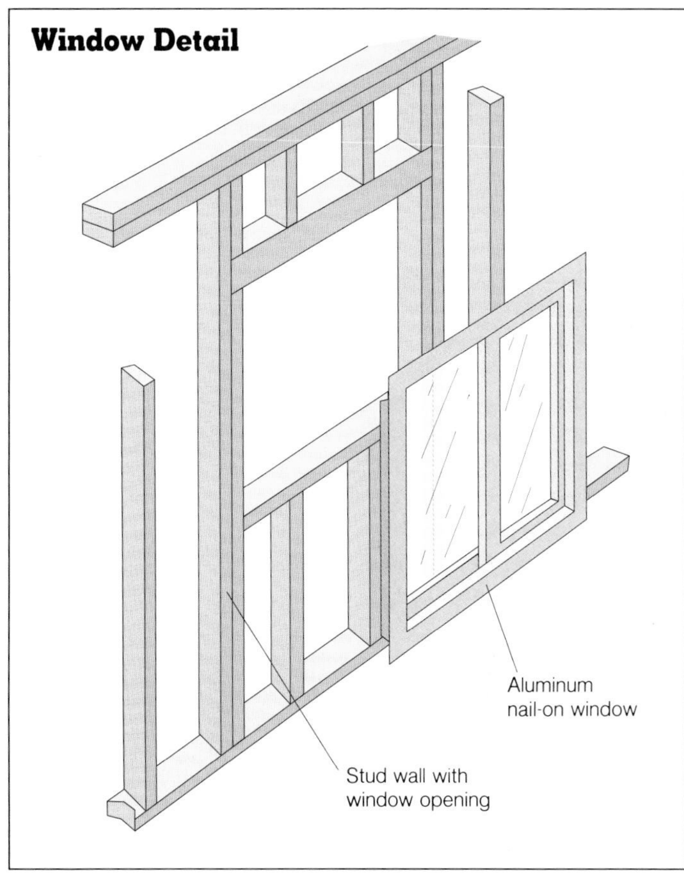


this building the top of the ridge should be 28 inches above the top of the walls. Use 2 by 4s nailed to the outside of the end walls as temporary supports.

Install the rafters over the end walls first. While your assistant supports the upper end of the first rafter, toenail it to the wall with two 16d nails, and then facenail the upper end through the ridge with two more 16d nails. Install the opposing rafter the same way, then the pair at the other end of the shed. You may need to adjust the height of the ridge slightly to get everything to fit properly. Once the first rafters are in, the rest are easy. Install them in pairs, putting in the blocking at the walls as you go. Install 2 by 4 collar ties across the rafters every 4 feet, with three 16d nails in each end; without these the weight of the roof will spread the walls apart.

The roof sheathing goes on next. Use ½-inch or ⅝-inch plywood. It is easier to keep the points of the shingle nails from penetrating through the sheathing if you use the ⅝-inch thickness. Space the panels just as you did for the floor, and stagger the end joints. Nail them down with 8d nails every 6 inches on the edges and 12 inches in the field. As an alternative to plywood for roof sheathing, you may also use OSB (oriented strand board). This material expands more than plywood, however, so you should increase the gaps between panels to ⅛ inch at the ends and ¼ inch along the edges. Install it with the textured side up—the smooth side can be extremely slippery, especially if there is a little sawdust on it.

Finish off the edge of the roof with 1 by 2 cedar or redwood eave trim, which covers the edge of the plywood and adds support between the rafter tails.

## Shingles

Cover the roof with roofing material as soon as the framing is done to protect the shed from the weather. Composition shingles are the most common type of roofing and are fairly easy to install. Follow the manufacturer's instructions printed on the bundle wrapper.

## Siding, Doors, and Window

Install the window first. Aluminum nail-on windows are relatively inexpensive and easy to install. With an assistant on the inside of the structure to help center the window in the rough opening, tack one edge of the window to the framing with 1½-inch roofing nails. Measure the diagonals of the window to make sure it is square; if it's not, pry one corner over gently until the diagonal measurements are equal, then nail off the rest of the window. Install the two louvered gable vents, and you are ready to put up siding.

The siding for this shed is rough-sawn plywood, which provides structural bracing as well as a finished wall surface. Use 4 by 9 sheets so you can completely cover the shed walls all the way to the bottom of the floor framing.

Install the siding with 8d HDG nails, 6 inches apart on the edges and 12 inches in the field. Leave a ⅛-inch gap between the siding and the window, and fill it with caulk before you install the trim.

The figure on page 55 shows a simple door with a 2 by 4 frame and a plywood face. Be sure to assemble it on a flat surface, and run a bead of construction adhesive on the frame before you nail the plywood to it.

Install the trim at the corners and around the door and window, and the shed is nearly finished. The corner trim will fit better if you nail the two pieces together before you nail them to the building.

## Finishing Touches

When you paint or stain the shed, help it blend into the landscape by using a color scheme that harmonizes with existing buildings. Oil-based paints and stains used to be the products of choice for outdoor use, but in recent years paint manufacturers have greatly improved the quality, durability, and selection of their water-based products. These are easy to use, clean up with soap and water, and are healthier for you and the environment.

You'll need to build some kind of access to the shed door—either steps or a ramp. A ramp is a must if you will be rolling the lawn mower or other large objects in and out.

## Materials List

| Description | | Material/Size | Length | Quantity |
|---|---|---|---|---|
| Gravel bed | | ¾″ gravel | — | 2 cu yd |
| Framing lumber | Floor: skids | 2×8 PT | 18′ | 6 ea |
| | floor joists | 2×8 (PT optional) | 16′<br>8′ | 2 ea<br>13 ea |
| | Floor sheathing | ⅝″ or ¾″ exterior plywd | 4×8 sh | 4 ea |
| | Wall framing: eave beams | 4×6 | 10′ | 2 ea |
| | studs | 2×4 | 92¼″ | 54 ea |
| | plates | 2×4 | 16′ | 9 ea |
| | headers | 4×6 | 8′ | 1 ea |
| | Roof framing: rafters/blocking | 2×6 | 14′ | 11 ea |
| | ridge | 2×6 | 20′ | 1 ea |
| | collar ties | 2×4 | 8′ | 3 ea |
| | roof sheathing | ½″ or ⅝″ plywd or OSB | 4×8 sh | 7 ea |
| | eave trim | 1×2 | RL | 72 l.f. |
| Roofing | | comp shingles | — | 133 s.f. |
| Finish materials | Window | aluminum window | 4′×4′ | 1 ea |
| | Door frame | 2×4 | 8′<br>12′ | 2 ea<br>1 ea |
| | Gable vents | 14″×14″ louvered vent | — | 2 ea |
| | Siding | rough-sawn plywd siding | 4×9 sh | 13 ea |
| | Trim | 1×4 | RL | 120 l.f. |
| Nails | | 16d HDG<br>16d sinker<br>8d sinker<br>8d HDG | —<br>—<br>—<br>— | 2 lb<br>12 lb<br>5 lb<br>5 lb |
| | Assorted metal fasteners as per text | | | |

See page 105 for materials list abbreviations.

## Concrete-Slab Foundation

As an alternative to the wood floor on skids, a concrete slab offers some advantages. Having the floor close to the ground lowers the overall height of the shed and facilitates moving things in and out.

Most building codes require that slab footings be excavated below the frost line; however, this is not practical for small outbuildings if you live in an area where the frost line may be as far down as 6 feet. You may be able to dispense with footings altogether and pour a thicker slab (6 inches or so) over a bed of gravel. Check with the local building department to see if this type of foundation is permitted.

You will need a level, well-drained site for the slab. Dig the footing trenches about 3 inches outside the building line to allow enough room for the forms and stakes. Set the 2 by 12 perimeter forms level and square, and use them as a guide to grade off the inside area to a depth 8 inches below the top of the forms. Put down a 2-inch layer of sand, followed by a vapor barrier, which keeps the finished slab from wicking away ground moisture, then another 2-inch layer of sand.

Install the footing reinforcing bars, bending them around the corners. Overlap splices at least 18 inches and tie them together with wire. Roll out 6 by 6 reinforcing mesh over the sand, and you're ready to pour.

If you can't back up a concrete truck to the site, use wheelbarrows or hire a concrete pumper. Fill the forms to the top, pulling the reinforcing mesh up into the fresh concrete as you go. Level the concrete by dragging a 2 by 4 across the forms with a sawing motion, and smooth the surface with a wood float.

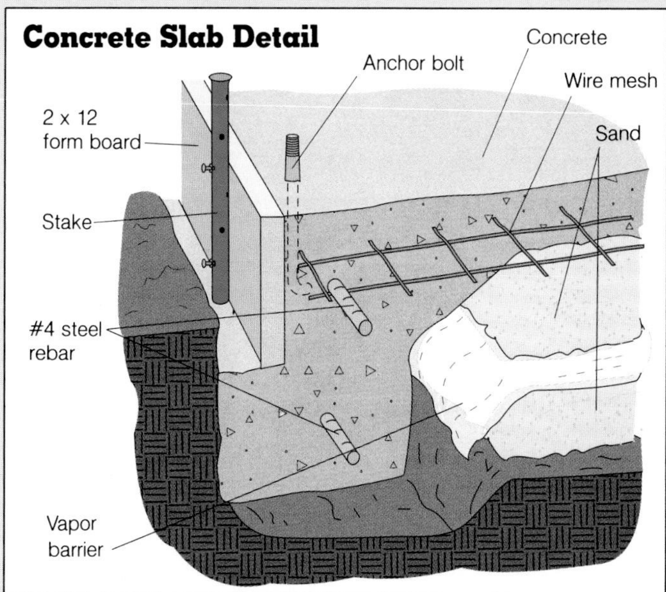


Install the anchor bolts while you wait for the concrete to set up enough to trowel. Bolts should be placed within 12 inches of corners and door openings, and no more than 6 feet apart.

When troweling concrete, timing is everything. Keep testing the surface with the trowel—as soon as it stops bringing water to the surface, it's time to get to work. If you want a smooth surface, re-trowel the slab when the concrete has hardened a little more; for a nonskid finish, drag a push broom over the almost-hardened concrete.

## Customizing Sheds

You can soup up the shed—and improve its usefulness—by tailoring it to your specific needs. An attached awning and deck can increase the usable area around the shed. (See page 18 for details on how to build an awning.) Added windows and skylights will brighten the interior. You may want to use wide sliding doors or the roll-up type to expand the interior and improve accessibility for equipment, such as a lawn tractor.

The overall dimensions of the shed can be modified as necessary to accommodate specific storage needs and the space available. To maximize the use of standard materials, it's best to make adjustments in increments of 4 feet.

Plan the layout of the shed interior before you start to build. Consider what will be kept there, traffic patterns inside, and what goes where; this will help you determine the amount of space you need, and the placement of windows, doors, and storage areas, and will ensure that everything remains accessible.

# HALLOW YARD STORAGE SHED

*If all you require is a small storage shed, this design will fulfill your needs and is easy to build as well. Basically, it utilizes fence construction, with a quick and easy roof. It will fit into a narrow sideyard and hold up to four trash cans, a lawn mower, and assorted yard tools and garden supplies.*

## Fasteners

Because this shed is designed for simplicity, with the fewest possible framing members, screws are preferable to nails for fasteners. Deck or coarse-thread wallboard screws hold better than nails, won't loosen over time, and are easily driven with a Phillips bit in a drill motor or cordless screwdriver. Although they are more expensive than nails, you will need only three or four pounds for the whole shed.

## Posts

This shed depends on its posts for lateral stability, so they should be well planted, otherwise the weight of the gates will cause the shed to lean to one side. Install the posts just as you would for a fence: Locate the holes with string lines; dig them a little more than 2 feet deep and 8 or 9 inches in diameter. Put a few inches of gravel in the bottom of each hole, set the posts to the strings, and temporarily brace them plumb and parallel. Fill the holes with concrete.

After the concrete cures, cut all the posts to the same height, about 6 feet, 4½ inches above the ground. Then install the two long 2 by 4 plates on top of the posts. If some posts are a little out of place, you can pull them into line as you fasten the plate. Use three 3-inch screws per connection.

## Roof

Make up four roof trusses as shown on page 59. The arc cut in the bottom chord is optional, but it gives the roof a light, springy look. Use two 3-inch screws through each rafter into the bottom chord, and two screws driven at an angle through the peak. Screw the trusses to the top plates, directly over the posts. Measure across the plates as you go to make sure they remain parallel.

Cut the six 2 by 2 purlins to length, 18 inches longer than the overall dimension of the shed, and then screw them to the trusses.

The roof of this shed is covered with inexpensive ribbed fiberglass panels, but plywood

## Framing Plan

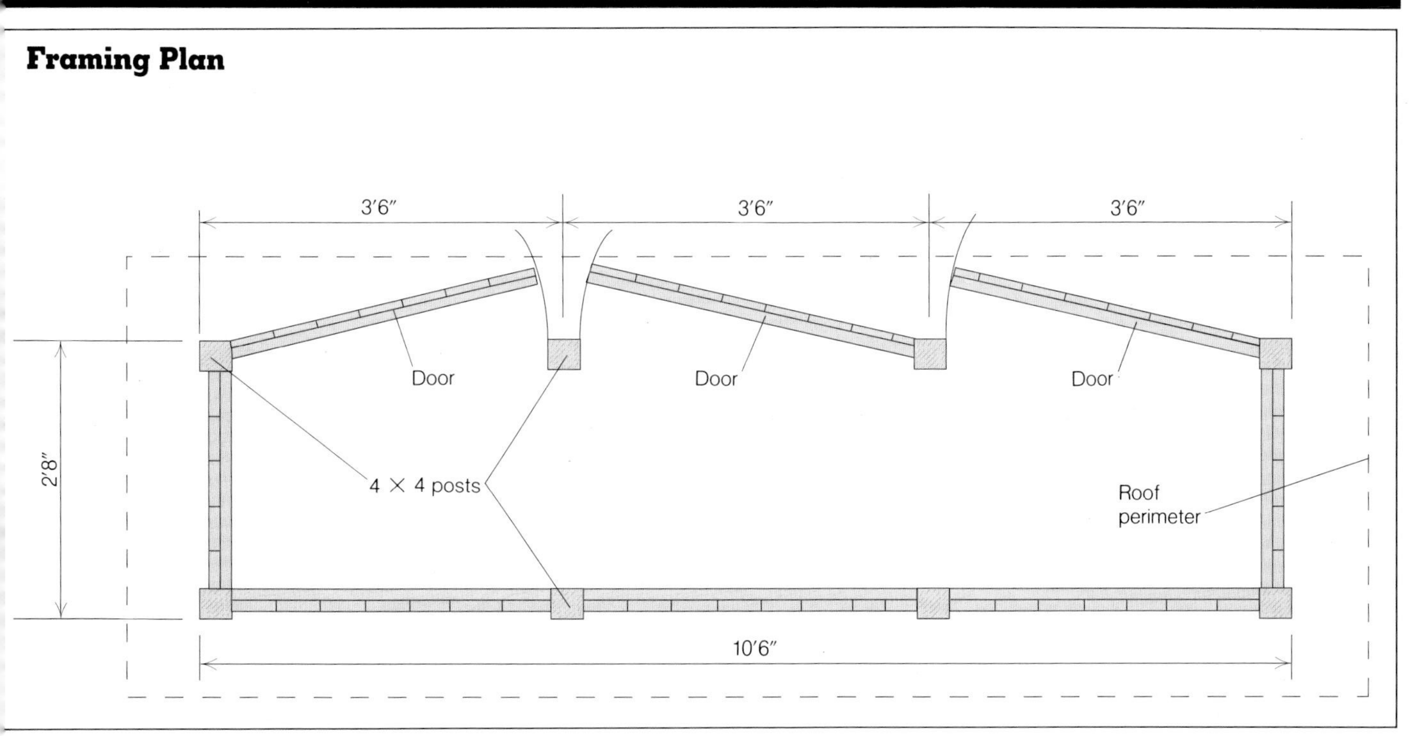


## Section View

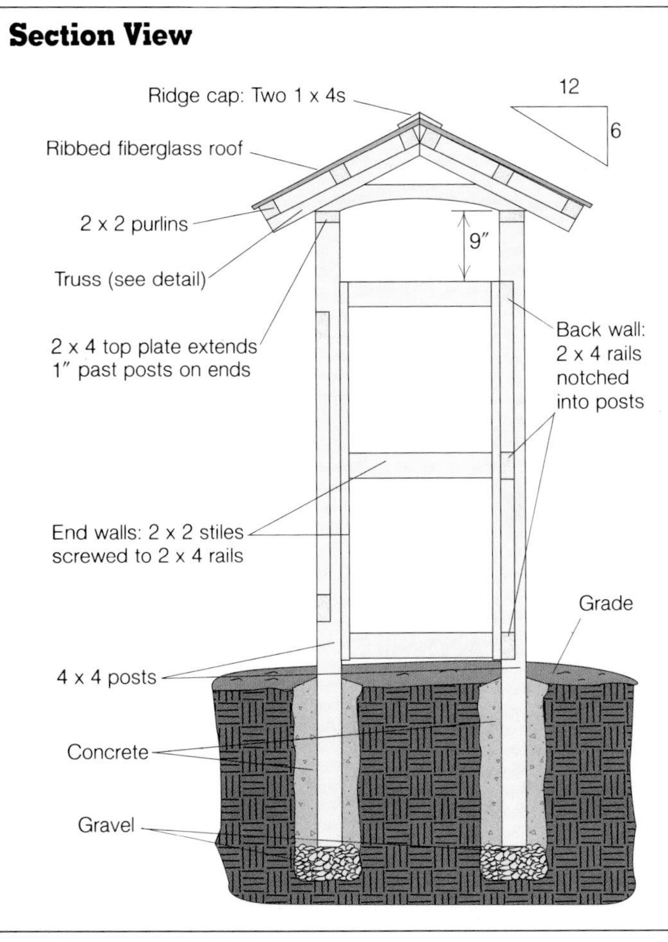


## Truss Diagram

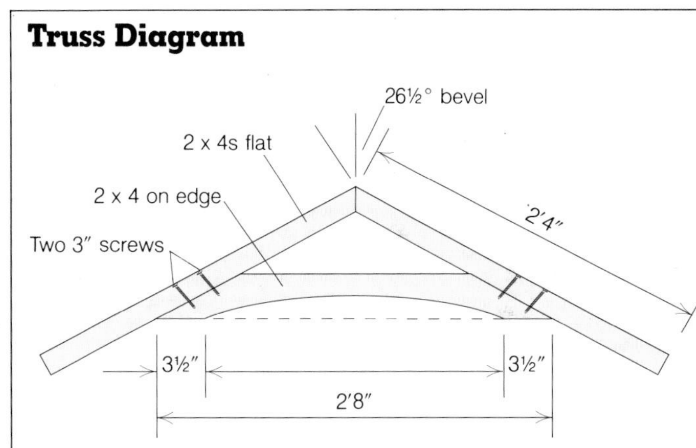


## Roof Detail

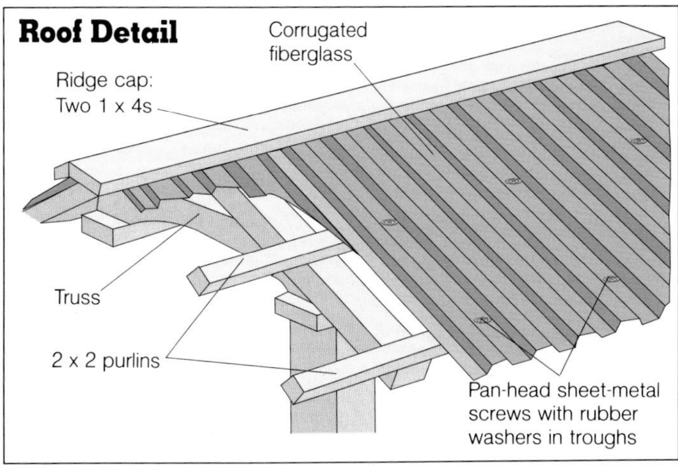

and conventional shingles would also work well. The shed is dimensioned so that the panels can be used full width—you only have to cut the pieces to length. Cut them so they will overhang the lower purlin by about an inch; use a handsaw or a fine-tooth plywood blade in your circular saw. If you stack the panels together you can cut several pieces at the same time.

Lay two sections of the roofing panels side by side, with the edges overlapping by one corrugation. Measure the overlap. Half this dimension will be the amount the panels overhang the purlins at each end of the roof. Screw the panels to the purlins with ¾-inch by No. 8 pan-head sheet-metal screws. If you can find them, washers with a rubber gasket on one side will seal against leaks under the screw heads. Place the screws in the bottom of the corrugations, every 8 inches or so; be sure to put screws where the sheets overlap.

Cover the ridge of the roof with a wood cap made from two 1 by 4s. Bevel one edge of each board at a 26½-degree angle, and toenail them together with 5d HDG finish nails. Cut the completed cap to length so that it overhangs the roof by about 2 inches on each end; angle the corners back 15 or 20 degrees. Fasten the cap through the fiberglass panels to the purlins with pairs of 3-inch screws about 18 inches apart.

## Materials List

| Description | | Material/Size | Length | Quantity |
|---|---|---|---|---|
| Post footings | | concrete | — | ⅓ cu yd |
| Lumber | Posts | 4×4 rwd, cedar*, or PT | 10′ | 8 ea |
| | Rails and roof trusses | 2×4 | 12′ | 5 ea |
| | Gate frames | 2×4 | 8′ | 13 ea |
| | Purlins | 2×2 | 12′ | 6 ea |
| Roof | Roofing panels | 2′×8′ fiberglass | — | 4 pcs |
| | Ridge cap | 1×4 rwd or cedar* | 14′ | 2 ea |
| Siding | | 1×6 | 6′ | 58 pcs |
| Hardware | Screws | 3″ coated deck screw | | 1½ lb |
| | | 1⅝″ coated deck screw | | 2 lb |
| | | ¾″×#8 SMS | | 100 ea |
| | Assorted metal fasteners as per text | | | |

*or other naturally durable species
See page 105 for materials list abbreviations.

## Walls

The walls of the shed are open at the top and bottom for free ventilation—an important consideration for trash-can storage—but if this is not a concern for you, or if you need to keep critters out, the walls can be completely enclosed by extending the siding boards from ground to roof.

Put up the back wall of the shed first. Cut three 10-foot, 6-inch, 2 by 4 rails. The top of the top rail is 9 inches below the top of the top plate; the bottom rail, 4 inches above the ground. Notch the posts for the rails by making a series of cross-grain saw cuts 1½ inches deep; knock out the waste with a hammer and then smooth the bottom of the notch with a chisel. Fasten the rails with two 3-inch screws at each post.

You can cover this shed with almost any kind of siding lumber—shiplap, tongue and groove, or ordinary fence boards are fine. Fasten the siding with two 2-inch screws at each support for 1 by 6 boards; use three screws for 1 by 8 or wider. Arrange the boards so

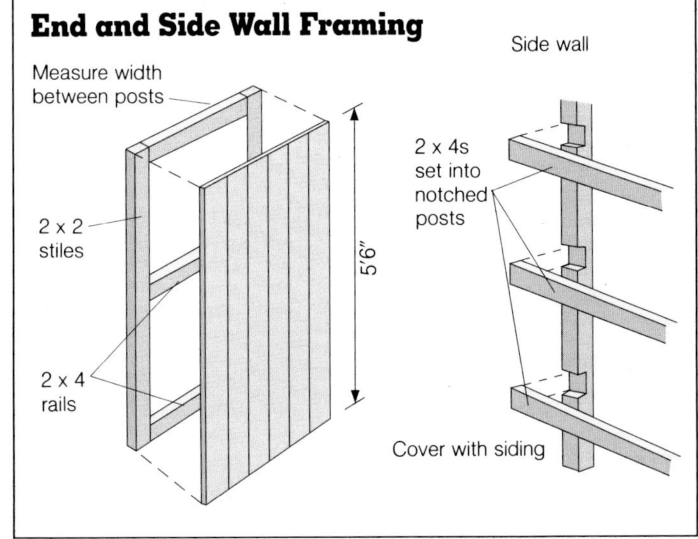


the first and last pieces in each bay are at least a half-board wide. If you're building the shed against a fence or an existing building, apply the siding on the inside of the shed instead of the outside.

The end walls are easier to build if you construct them on sawhorses and install them as completed units, making sure to measure the width carefully. Screw the 2 by 2 stiles to the three 2 by 4 rails and apply the siding to this framework. Set the completed panel in place, prop it up to the right height, and screw through the 2 by 2s into the posts.

## Doors

The doors to this shed are built like fence gates, with siding boards over a simple Z brace. When you install the siding, be sure to screw it to the diagonal brace as well as to the horizontal rails. Hang the doors with T-hinges and gate latches. Mount the hinges to the door first; then prop it into position and screw the hinges into the posts. Allow about a ½-inch clearance on the latch side for expansion of the siding boards. This type of door has a tendency to warp, so mount a 1 by 2 stop on the inside of the post on the latch side to help hold it flat.

## Finishing Up

Think about how you plan to use your shed, and set it up to serve your needs. Here are a few suggestions for starters.

- For a floor that won't get muddy, put down concrete garden pavers over a gravel bed.
- Install shelving in the upper half of the shed to provide extra storage space for small items, and leave the bottom open for bulky things such as trash cans or bicycles.
- Put up wall hooks to keep shovels, rakes, and other long-handled tools from getting tangled up in a corner.

## Poolside Dressing Room

This efficient little shed can be adapted for a variety of uses. One possibility is shown here: a four-post version that's an outdoor changing room, with a bench and clothing hooks inside. A small cabinet on the back wall holds extra towels.

There are a few structural differences between this room and the Basic Shed. The door is on the end of the building, so the 2 by 4 rails are notched into the posts on the side walls instead of the back. This shed is wider, so the side overhangs have been widened, too, and an extra truss has been added between the posts. If your area receives snow in the winter, add a short section of 2 by 2 under the middle truss to prevent the top plate from sagging.

If you will be building the dressing room over an existing patio or pool deck, it may not be practical to use posts in post hole footings. You can use shorter posts mounted in standard post holes, but the side and back walls must be braced for lateral stability with plywood siding or diagonal bracing.

To build the bench, first mount two 2 by 4 cleats to the side walls, 14 to 16 inches off the ground. Use 2-inch screws driven through the siding from the outside of the shed. Then screw three 2 by 6s to the cleats for the bench seat.

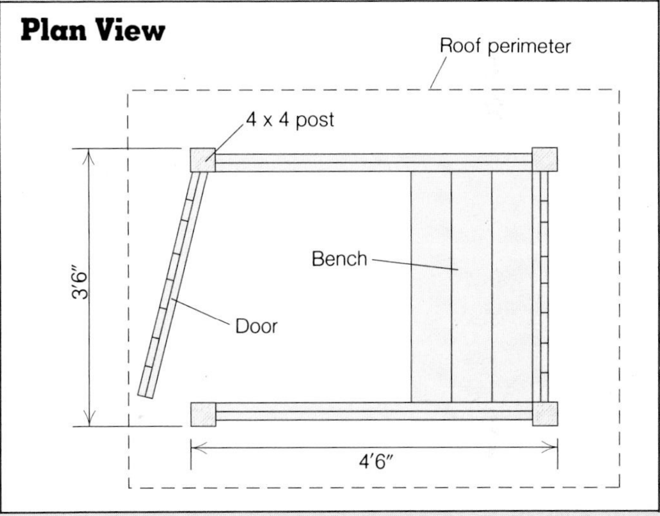


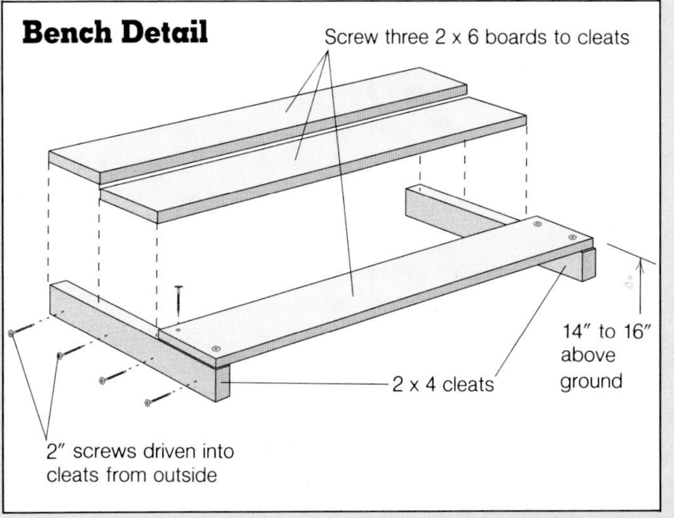

# LOW-PROFILE YARD STORAGE

*At just 7½ feet tall, this sturdy little storage shed can be built close to a property line and stay within most zoning requirements. A pyramid-shaped hip roof and a raised floor keep its contents dry; and a band of screening just under the roof admits light and air while keeping insects out.*

## Posts and Rails

Begin by setting the four corner posts in 2-foot-deep postholes with a small amount of gravel in the bottom of each. The posts should consist of naturally decay-resistant wood or pressure-treated lumber suitable for ground contact. Use 2 by 4s to temporarily brace the posts plumb; then fill the holes with concrete.

When the concrete has cured, level the area under the shed with a shovel and spread out 2 or 3 inches of coarse gravel, which will provide drainage under the floor and help to support the floor joists.

Nail the 2 by 6 rim joists to the outside faces of the posts at the sides and back of the shed, resting them directly on the gravel. Use three 16d nails for each post. Then install the remaining joists, spaced approximately 18 inches on center, with three 16d nails in each end. Note that the joist at the front of the shed is set back 1 inch from the face of the posts to accommodate the gates that will be installed (see page 65).

Put a little more gravel in around the floor joists and work it under each one with the tip of a shovel; then install the floor boards. You will need to notch the boards around the posts at the corners.

Cut the posts to length, 4 feet, 10 inches above the floor. Nail 2 by 4 top plates onto the posts, mitering them at the corners, with two 16d nails in each end; then install another 2 by 4 around the outside of the top plates, again with mitered corners.

Next install the intermediate 2 by 4 rails at the sides and back of the shed; the upper rail is mounted 6 inches below the built-up top plates, and the second halfway between the upper rail and the floor. The ends of these rails should be flush with the face of the posts at the front of the shed.

## Roof Framing

Cut the rafters for the roof according to the rafter diagrams on page 64. There are a couple of details you should pay special attention to as you cut.

To lay out the plumb and level cuts on a hip rafter, set the framing square so that the

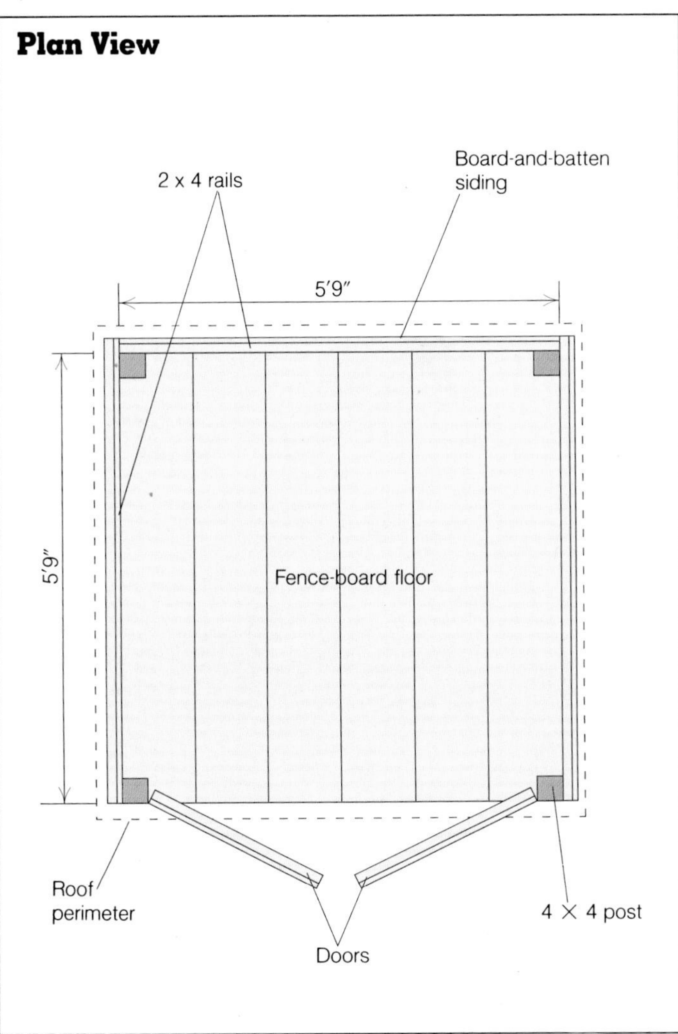


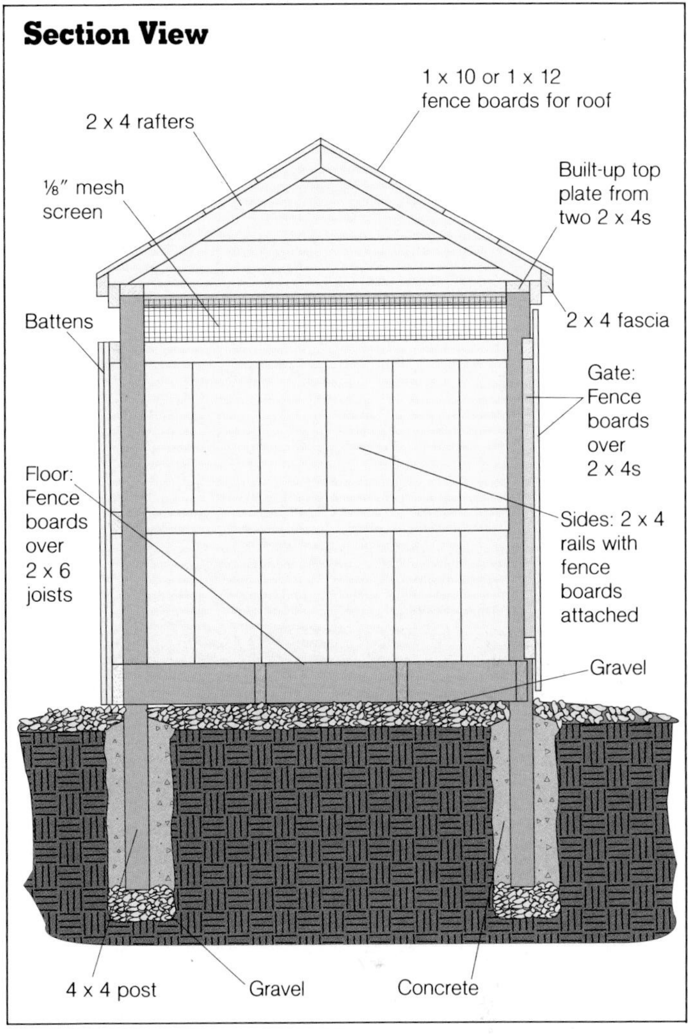


edge of the rafter lines up with the 7-inch mark indicated on one leg of the square and the 17-inch mark on the other leg. For jack rafters, use the 7-inch mark on one leg and the 12-inch mark on the other.

The bevel cuts at the top of jack rafters are cut in opposite directions on either side of the hips, making each jack either "left-handed" or "right-handed." Be sure to cut equal numbers of each as they are not interchangeable.

To assemble the roof, first nail the beveled 2 by 4 fascia to the built-up top plates. The top edge of the fascia should be set 2 inches above the plates, forming a ledge that will support the bottom ends of the rafters as you assemble them.

Set the two primary (longer) hip rafters in place and toenail their top ends together with 8d nails; toenail the bottom ends to the plates with two 16d nails. Install the secondary (shorter) hips in the same way. Nail the jack rafters to the hips with two 8d nails in the top and two 16d toenails down at the bottom.

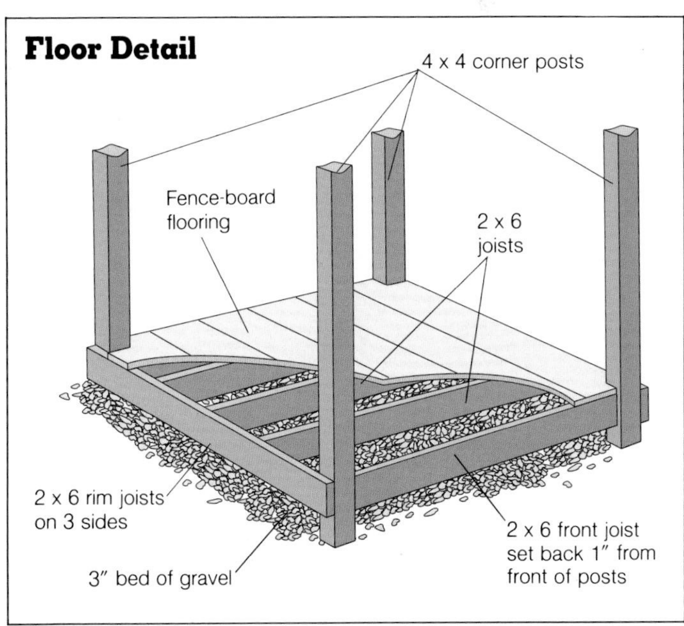

## Roof Framing

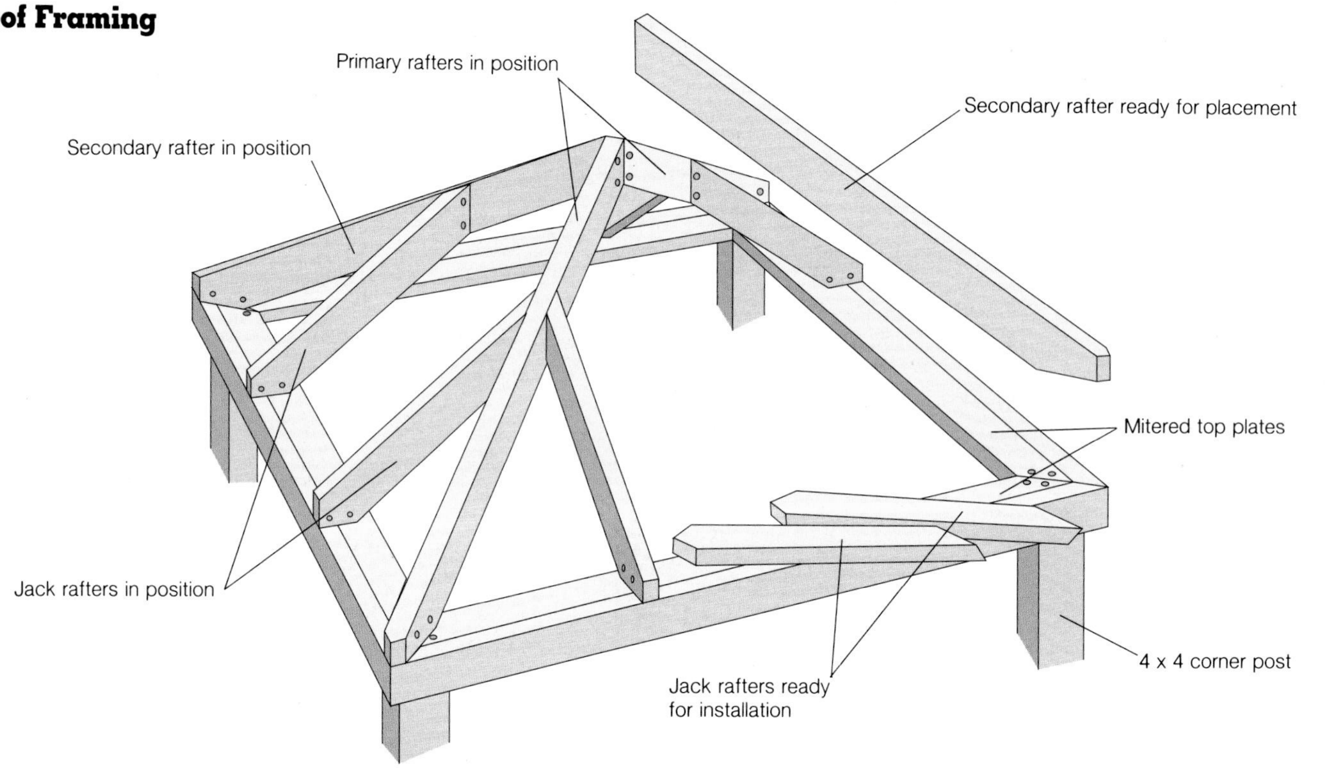

Primary rafters in position

Secondary rafter ready for placement

Secondary rafter in position

Mitered top plates

Jack rafters in position

4 x 4 corner post

Jack rafters ready for installation

## Rafter Diagrams

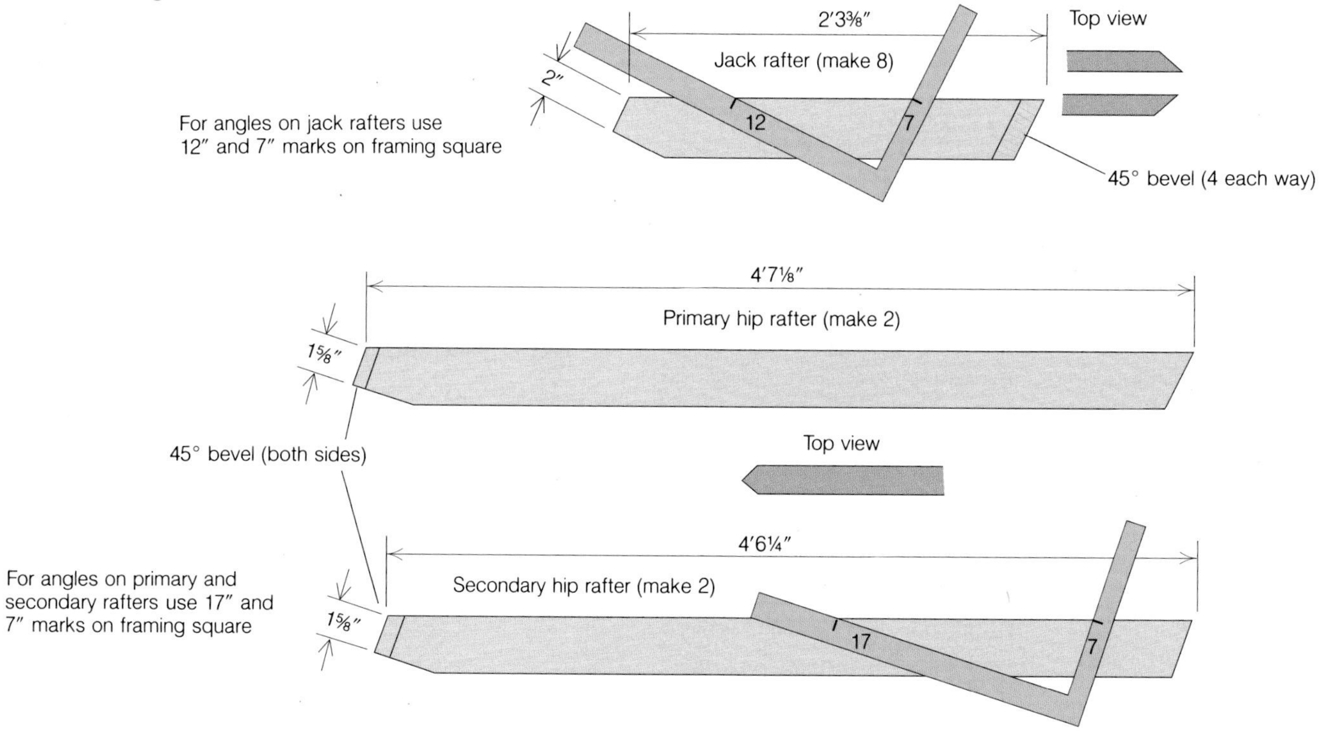

2′3⅜″

Top view

Jack rafter (make 8)

2″

For angles on jack rafters use 12″ and 7″ marks on framing square

12

7

45° bevel (4 each way)

4′7⅛″

Primary hip rafter (make 2)

1⅝″

45° bevel (both sides)

Top view

4′6¼″

For angles on primary and secondary rafters use 17″ and 7″ marks on framing square

Secondary hip rafter (make 2)

1⅝″

17

7

Install the fence-board roof sheathing with three 8d nails into each rafter. (If you prefer, plywood can be used for sheath roofing if it's pressure treated, and for the wall siding and floor as well.) Run the sheathing about halfway up the roof and trim the boards in place; use the cutoffs to finish the roof up to the peak. Don't forget to predrill for the nails in the shortest pieces to keep the wood from splitting.

Cover the roof with composition shingles or other suitable roofing material, applied according to the manufacturer's specifications.

## Siding and Gates

Cover the walls with 5-foot fence boards, with 1 by 2 battens over the joints, and install 1 by 3 and 1 by 4 trim on the corners as shown above. Use 8d HDG nails to prevent rust stains.

Assemble the gates with more board-and-batten siding over 2 by 4 Z braces, making sure to place the bottom rail high enough to clear the floor when the gates are closed. Hang the gates with T-hinges. A cane bolt mounted to one gate, and a gate latch or slide bolt on the other, completes the hardware installation.

Finally, staple ⅛-inch mesh hardware-cloth screening over the space between the siding and the top plates. The completed shed can be finished with the paint or stain of your choice, or left unfinished to weather naturally.

### Siding and Gate Detail

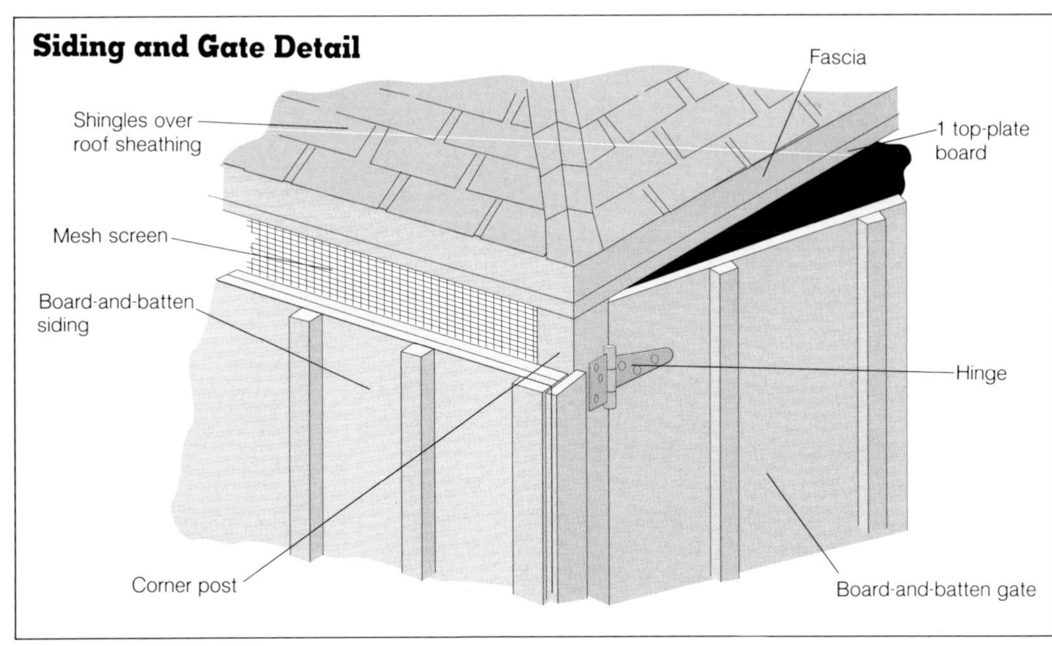


### Materials List

| Description | | Material/Size | Length | Quantity |
|---|---|---|---|---|
| Post footings | | 60-lb sacks concrete mix | — | 8 sacks |
| | | gravel | — | ½ cu yd |
| Framing lumber | Posts | 4×4 PT or heart rwd or cedar* | 8′ | 4 ea |
| | Floor joists | 2×6 PT | 6′ | 7 ea |
| | Top plates, rails, rafters, and fascia | 2×4 | 6′ | 30 ea |
| | Floor sheathing, roof sheathing, and siding | 1×12 rough-sawn fence | 6′<br>5′ | 18 ea<br>24 ea |
| | Trim | 1×2 battens<br>1×4 corner | 5′<br>5′ | 20 ea<br>8 ea |
| Roofing | | comp shingles or type as chosen | — | 67 s.f. |
| Hardware | Miscellaneous | gate hinges, latches, cane bolt | — | as required |
| | Screen | ⅛″ hardware cloth | — | 12 s.f. |
| | Nails | 16d sinker<br>8d HDG<br>roofing | —<br>—<br>— | 5 lb<br>5 lb<br>as required |

*or other naturally durable species

See page 105 for materials list abbreviations.

# SMALL BARN

*This miniature barn is basically two sheds linked by a raised roof that hovers over an open center bay. The open bay is an ideal place to keep large objects, such as a lawn tractor or rowboat; the six side bays can be used as work space and to securely store bicycles, lawn furniture, tools, and garden items.*

**Foundation Detail**

Note: Reinforcement may be required in slab area. Check local code.

## Structure

This shed utilizes classic barn construction: Two rows of posts support a truss-and-purlin roof structure, with shed roofs on each side. It is a post-and-beam structure that uses some light metal framing connectors. These connectors are much stronger than nails alone and tie the building together at the critical joints. Be sure to use all the specified fasteners when installing them.

The posts, beams, and rafters are all constructed from 4 by 4 stock. Because they will be exposed, it's advisable to pick them out yourself if you can, as 4 by 4s are particularly prone to warping and twisting. Examine the end grain carefully; avoid pieces with "boxed

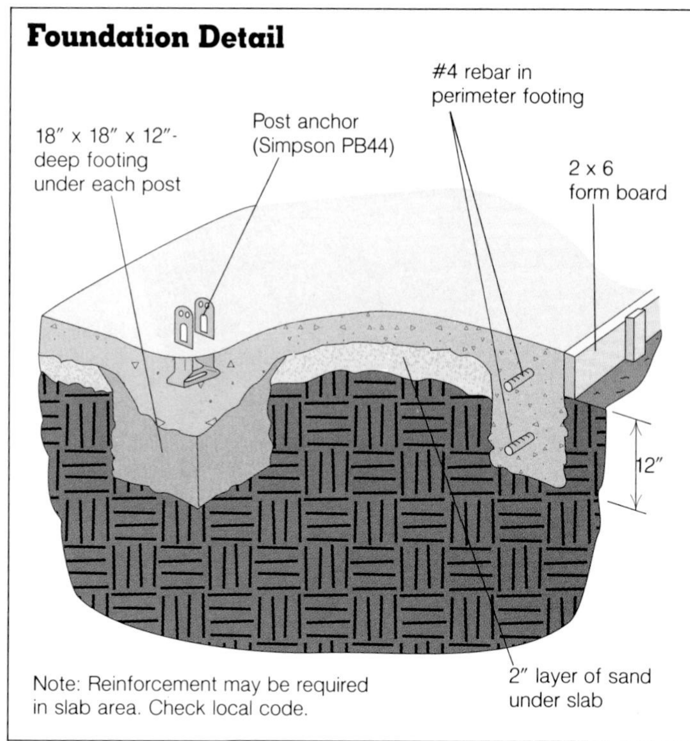

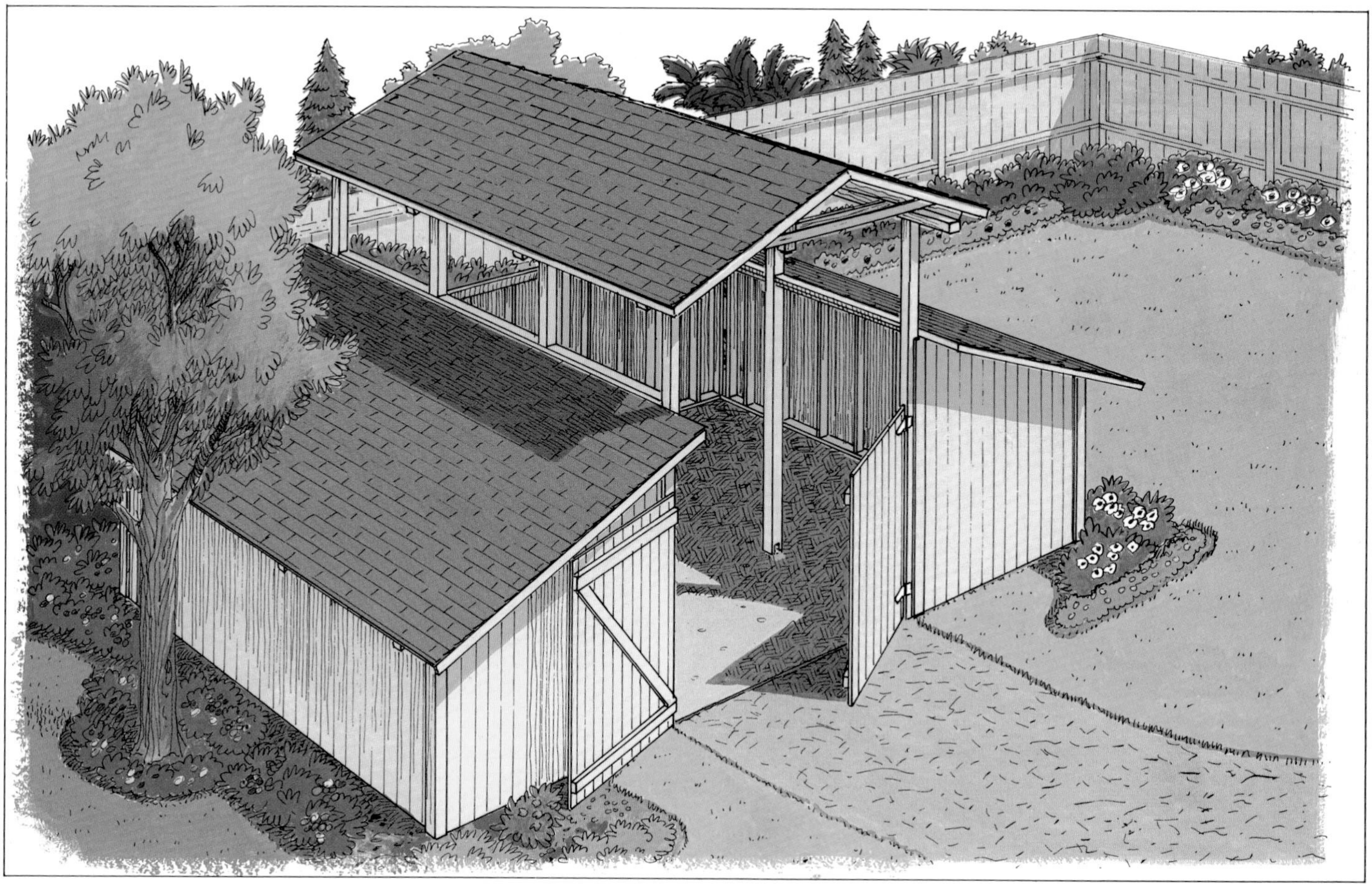

## Perspective View

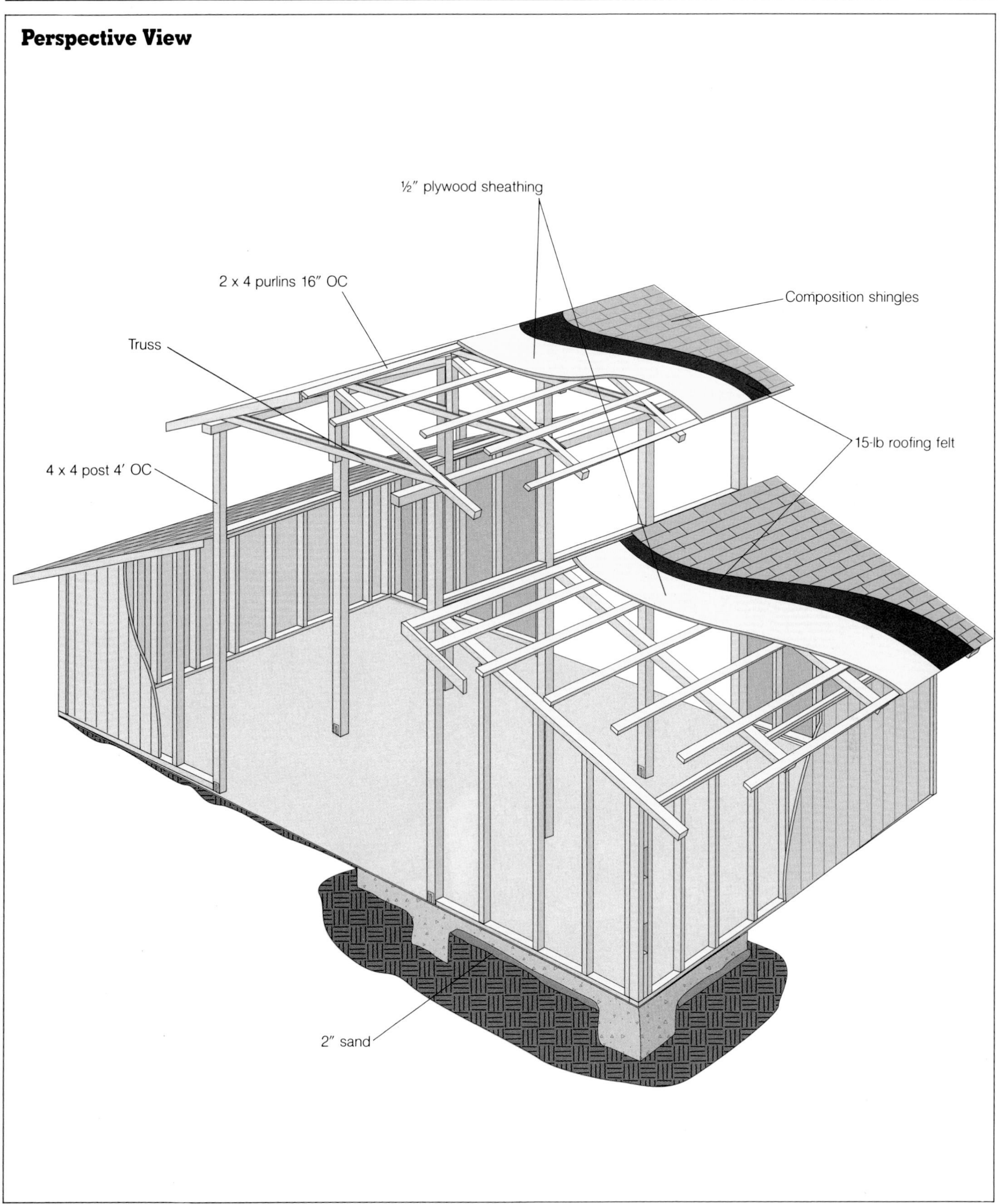

## Plan View

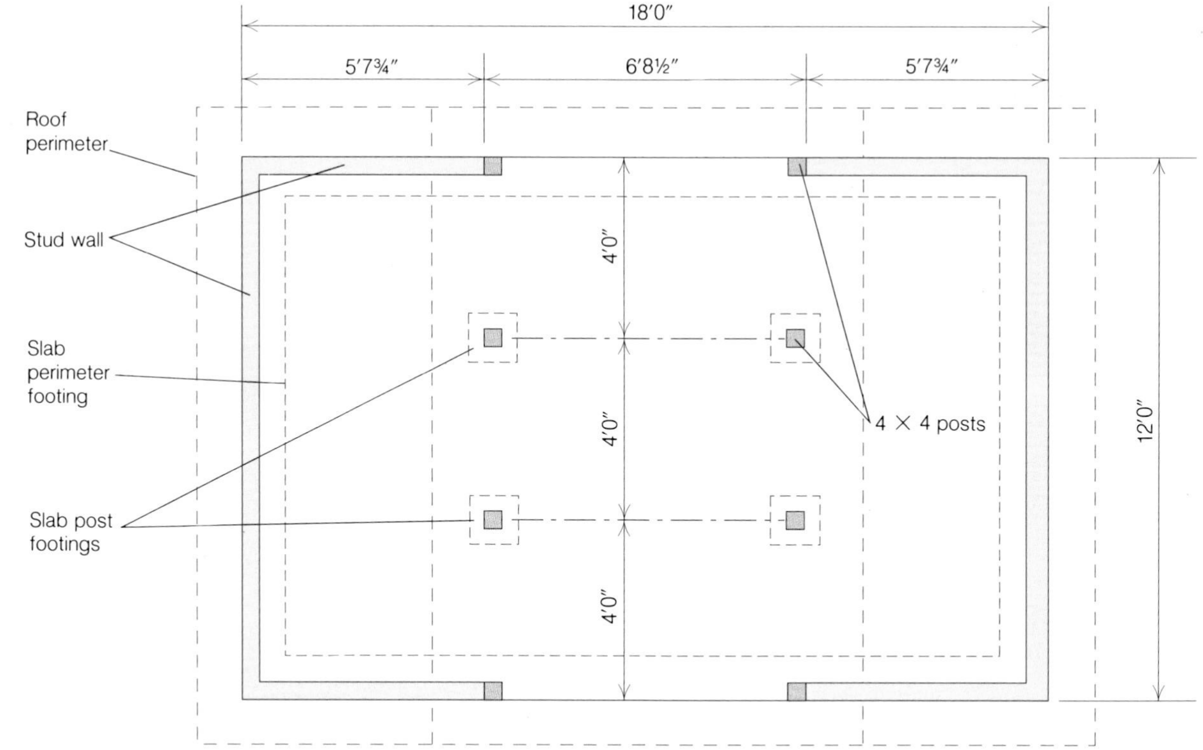

18'0"
5'7¾"
6'8½"
5'7¾"
Roof perimeter
Stud wall
Slab perimeter footing
Slab post footings
4'0"
4'0"
4'0"
4 × 4 posts
12'0"


## Truss Detail

4 x 4 rafters
For angle at top of truss use 6" and 12" marks on framing square
6
12
1'10"
7'0"
1 × 4 collar ties
4 x 4 king post, bevel bottom edges
Seat-cuts 7'0" apart

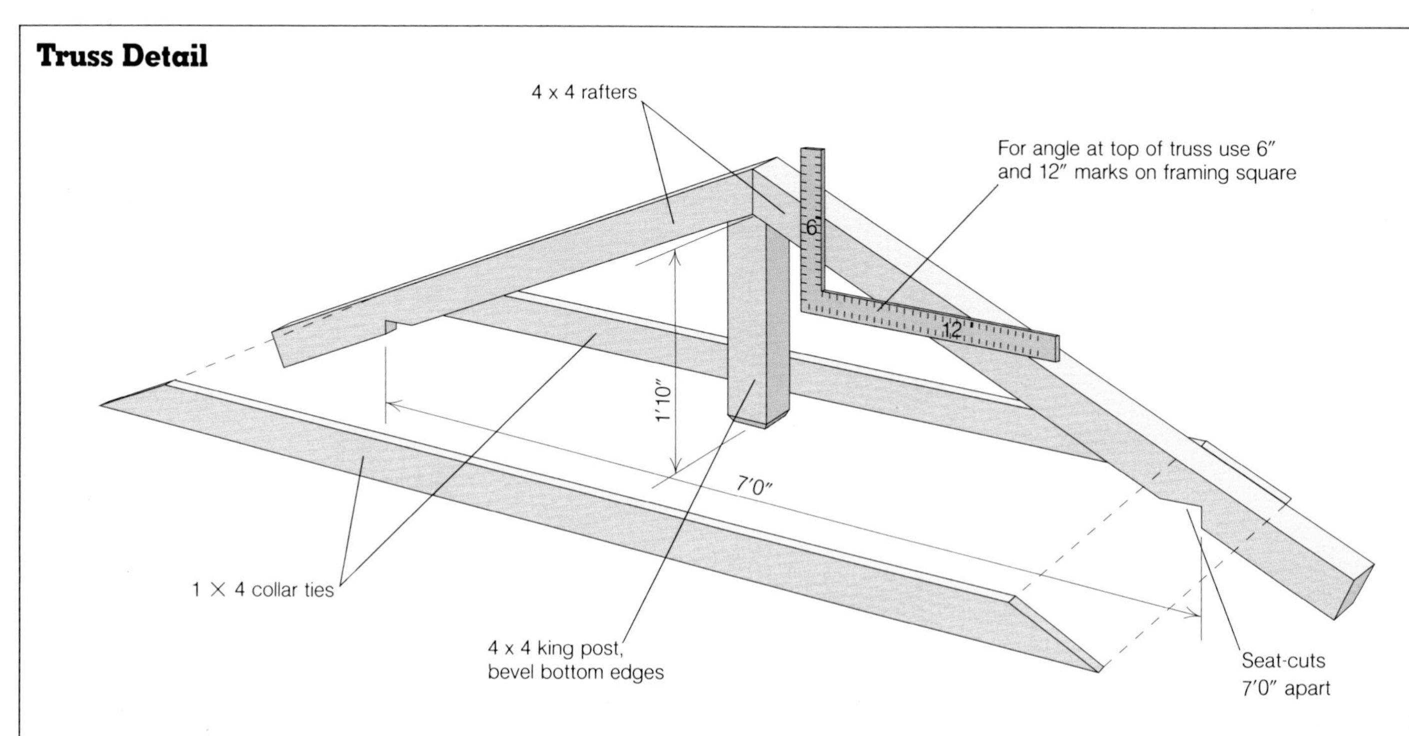

heart" (the center of the tree) showing, because they will definitely split and twist as they dry. If you can't pick your own material, ask for one of the lumberyard's better grades when placing your order.

## Foundation

This barn rests on a concrete slab, which gives it a durable, easy-to-clean floor. The slab is not especially difficult to form up and pour, but it's not a project to pick as a first-time concrete job. You'll have to place the concrete and screed it level, locate and set the anchor bolts and post bases, and float and trowel the slab smooth—all in the space of two or three hours before the concrete hardens. Unless you're experienced and confident in your abilities, you are better off hiring a professional for this part of the work. You can save some money by doing the digging and setting the forms yourself, but have a pro on the job when pour day comes around.

## Wall Framing

The two low outside walls are the first part of the barn to go up. The walls are 5 feet tall, so cut the studs 4 feet, 7½ inches each. Cut the pressure-treated 2 by 4 bottom plates to length (12 feet) and drill them for the anchor bolts. Frame each wall flat on the floor, with double top plates and studs 16 inches on center. Tilt the completed wall up, lift it onto the anchor bolts, and brace it plumb with scrap 2 by 4s.

Next, install the eight posts that form the center bay. You'll need to cut them all to length (10 feet, 2½ inches) and install the post caps on top before raising them. Nail each post into its metal post base, then quickly brace it before the post tips over.

Once the posts are all plumbed and securely braced, the two 4 by 4 beams can be set (this is a job for two people). Cut them long enough so that they extend about 6 inches past the post at each end. Place the beams in the post caps, double-check to see that the posts are spaced the same top and bottom, and nail off the brackets. Tack scrap 2 by 4s from beam to beam to maintain the proper spacing.

**Rafter Diagrams**

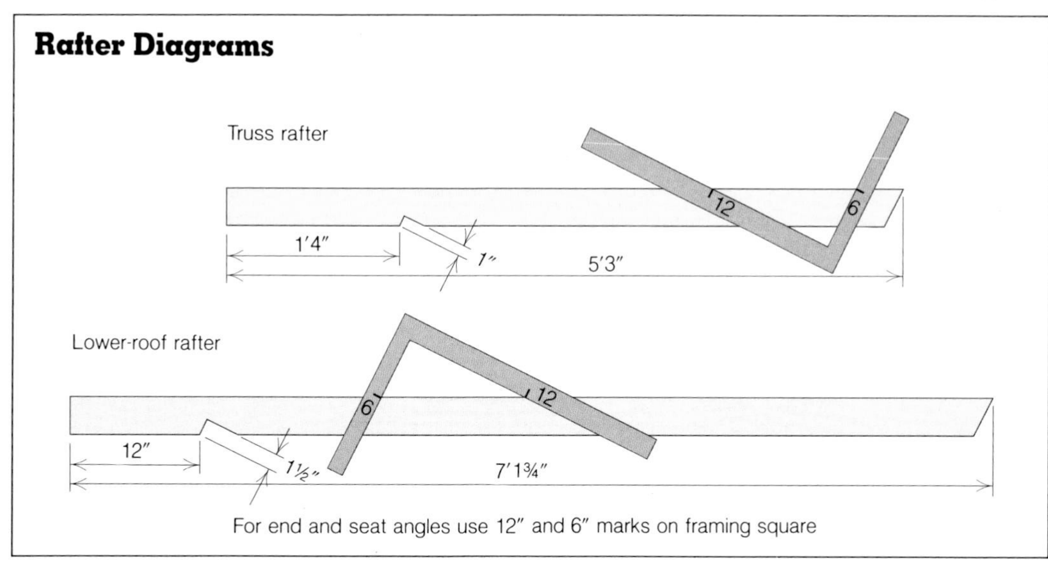


**Lower Roof**

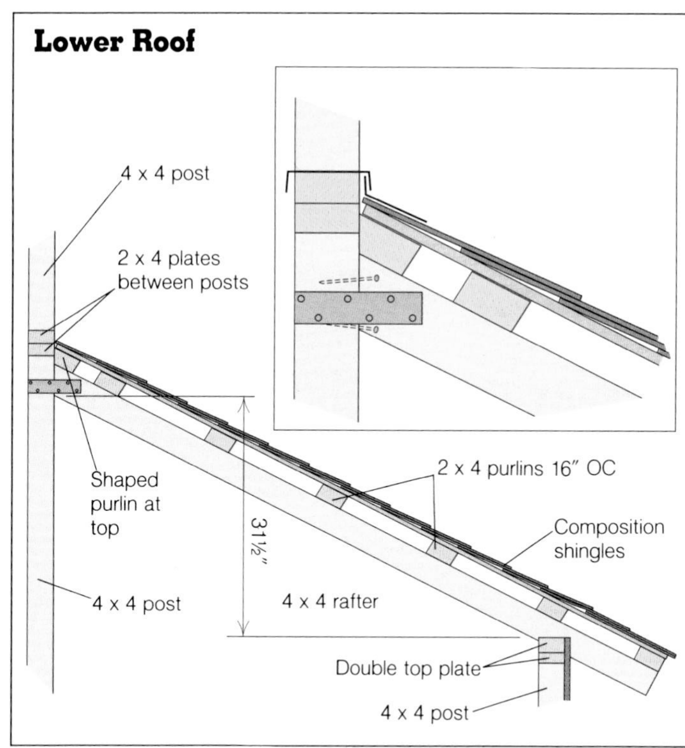


## Trusses and Rafters

Lay out and cut the 4 by 4 rafters for the lower roof and the parts for the trusses according to the diagram above. If you're worried about making a mistake, draw the roof out full size on the floor and check your measurements directly from the drawing.

Assemble the trusses on the floor. Toenail the two rafters together first with four 16d nails. Place one of the collar ties across the rafters with its bottom edge even with the seat cuts (the distance between seat cuts should be 7 feet), and nail it on with three 8d nails at each end. Take an extra minute to predrill for the nails—this is a primary connection and you don't want to split the wood. Install the short 4 by 4 king posts with two 8d toenails to the rafters and two more at the collar tie. Flip the truss over and install the other collar tie.

## Lower Roof

Install the rafters for the low shed roofs first. The bottom of the rafters should be 31½

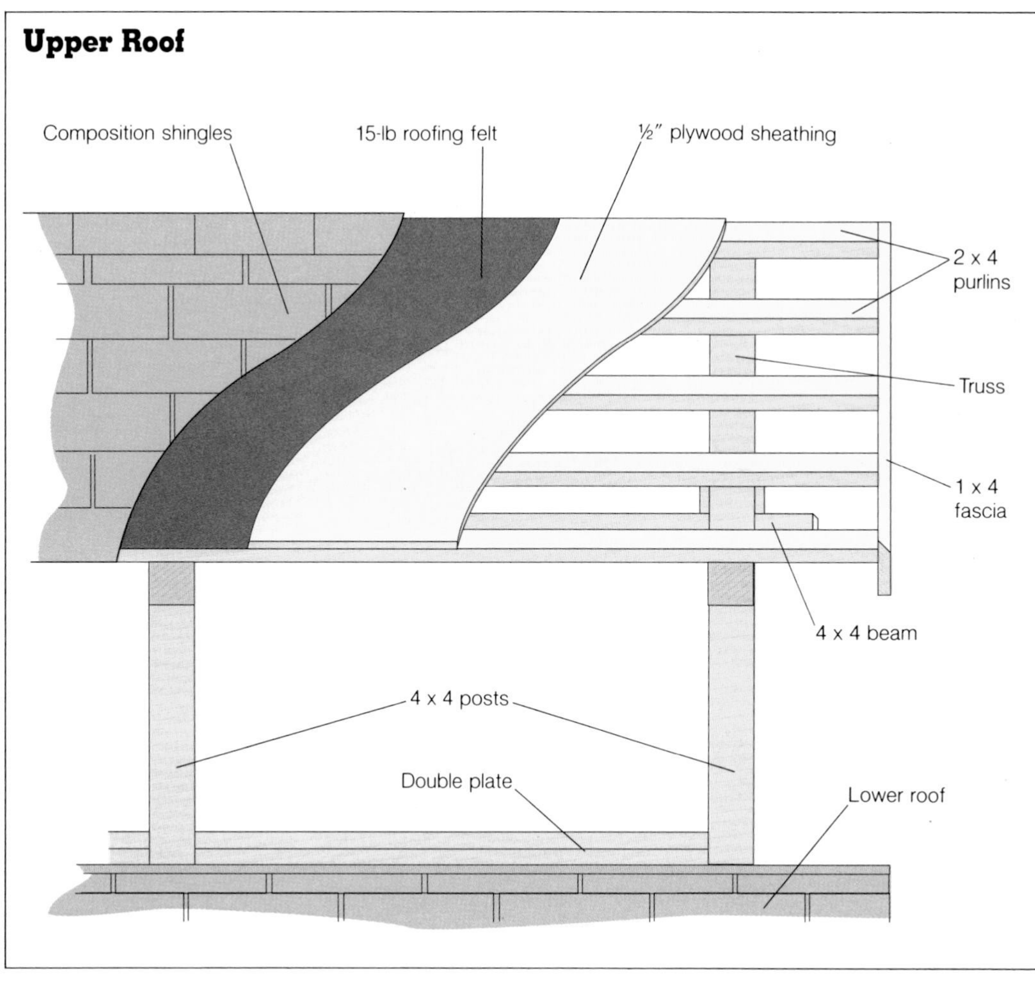


inches above the outer walls. Snap a chalk line across the posts at this height. Toenail the rafters to the posts with four 16d nails. If they don't quite fit on the line, don't worry about it; just nail them where they do fit. Wrap plate straps around the posts and onto the rafters and fill in all the nails.

Once the rafters are up, you can fill in the studs for the end walls. Bolt down the pressure-treated 2 by 4 sill and lay out the stud locations. Place a stud on a layout mark, plumb it with a level, and mark the top of the stud along the bottom of the rafter. Then cut it to length at a 26½-degree bevel.

When all the studs are installed, proceed with the plywood siding. This will brace the structure enough to make it safe to work on the roof.

Nail down the 2 by 4 purlins, 16 inches on center, with two 16d nails to each rafter. Install the plywood roof sheathing with the face grain

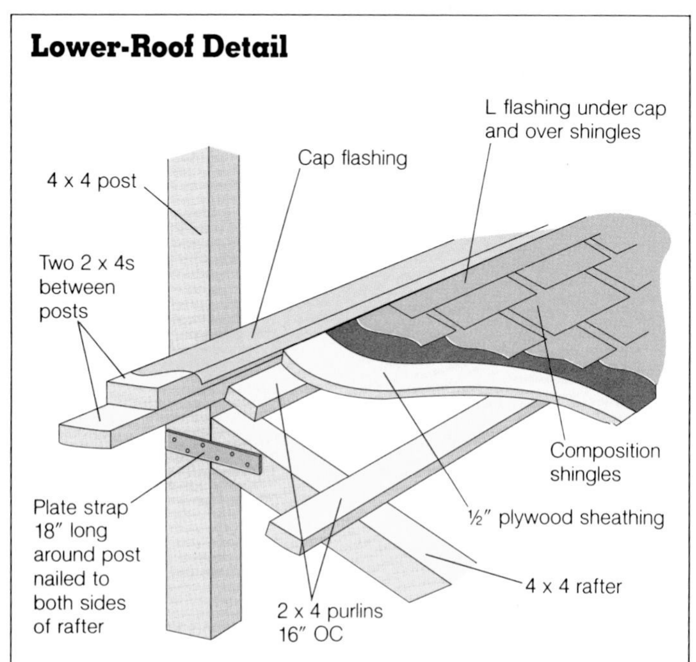


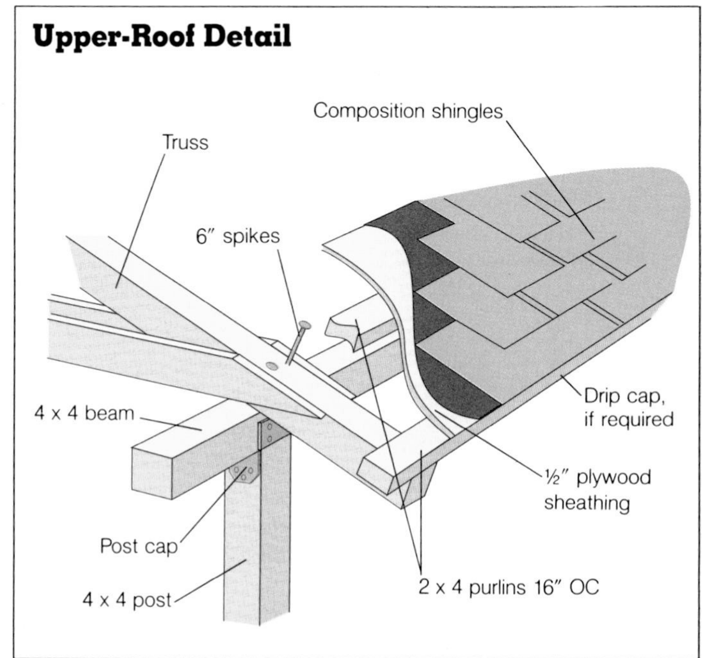

perpendicular to the purlins, using 6d common nails 6 inches apart on the edges and 12 inches in the field.

## Upper Roof

Installing the trusses is not a job for the lone carpenter. Two people are needed to lift the trusses up onto the beams, then one to hold them steady while the other installs the fasteners. The trusses are attached with 6-inch spikes, which hold the roof down in high winds (½-inch by 6-inch lag screws will also do). It will be necessary to predrill first with a bit somewhat smaller than the spike.

Install the purlins and plywood just as you did for the lower roof, and nail the 1 by 4 fascia boards to the ends of the purlins.

The final step before putting on the shingles is to install double 2 by 4s between the posts along the top of each lower roof so that they form a curb about 3 inches high above the plywood.

Cover the roof with a layer of 15-pound felt and composition shingles applied according to the manufacturer's instructions. At the upper edge of the low roofs, install flashing as shown; this keeps water from getting under the shingles and causing rot. Be sure to notch the cap flashing around the posts and caulk all joints thoroughly.

## Finishing Up

Install plywood siding and corner trim, hang a couple of simple gates at each end of the center bay, and your barn is complete. If you need secure storage, close off some of the side bays with plywood-covered stud walls and locking doors. When open to the outside, the side bays can be used for such varied purposes as firewood storage or an open-air chicken coop.

## Materials List

| Description | | Material/Size | Length | Quantity |
|---|---|---|---|---|
| Foundation | Sand base | washed concrete sand | — | 1½ cu yd |
| | Concrete | — | — | 3 cu yd |
| | Reinforcing steel | #4 rebar | — | 140 l.f. |
| | Post bases | 4×4 light post base | — | 8 ea |
| | Anchor bolts | ½″×10″ | — | 16 ea |
| Framing | Sill plates | 2×4 PT | 12′ | 4 ea |
| | Top plates | 2×4 | 12′ | 4 ea |
| | Studs | 2×4 | 10′ | 20 ea |
| | Posts | 4×4 | 12′ | 8 ea |
| | Beams | 4×4 | 14′ | 2 ea |
| | Rafters/trusses | 4×4 | 14′ | 8 ea |
| | Collar ties | 1×4 | 8′ | 8 ea |
| | Purlins | 2×4 | 14′ | 24 ea |
| | Roof sheathing | ½″ plywd | 4×8 sh | 14 ea |
| | Fascia and trim | 1×4 | 12′ | 10 ea |
| | Siding | T-111 plywd siding | 4×10 sh<br>4×8 sh | 3 ea<br>10 ea |
| Roofing | | type as chosen | — | 400 s.f. |
| Hardware | Post caps | light base/cap | — | 8 ea |
| | Plate straps | 1½″×18″ | — | 4 ea |
| | Nails | 16d sinker<br>8d sinker<br>6″ spikes<br>8d HDG | —<br>—<br>—<br>— | 15 lb<br>8 lb<br>16 ea<br>8 lb |
| | Assorted metal fasteners as per text | | | |

See page 105 for materials list abbreviations.

# GARDEN STORAGE WITH SHADE ROOF

*This little garden structure is a miniaturized version of a similar building at the Daitokuji Monastery in Kyoto, Japan. It has a small storage room and some open shelving for tools and supplies. Mainly, though, this is a place to rest—a quiet shady spot where you can relax after a productive day in the garden.*

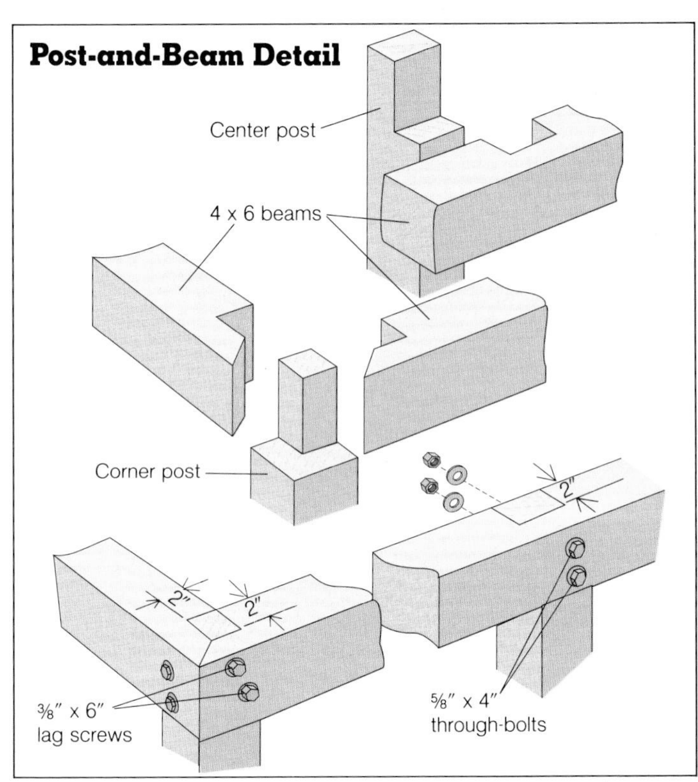


## Foundation and Posts

This shed gets its lateral stability from its posts, which are buried 2 feet into the ground. The posts should be of pressure-treated or decay-resistant wood. Set them in concrete, taking care to get them plumbed and aligned before you pour, but don't cut them to length until after the concrete cures.

Level the ground where the storage room and shelving recess will be, and set 2 by 4 perimeter forms for the L-shaped floor slab. Footings are not necessary, because the roof loads are carried by the posts, but deepen the slab edge a little to key it to the ground. The slab requires only about ¼ cubic yard of concrete, so it is possible to mix it yourself in a wheelbarrow or a rented

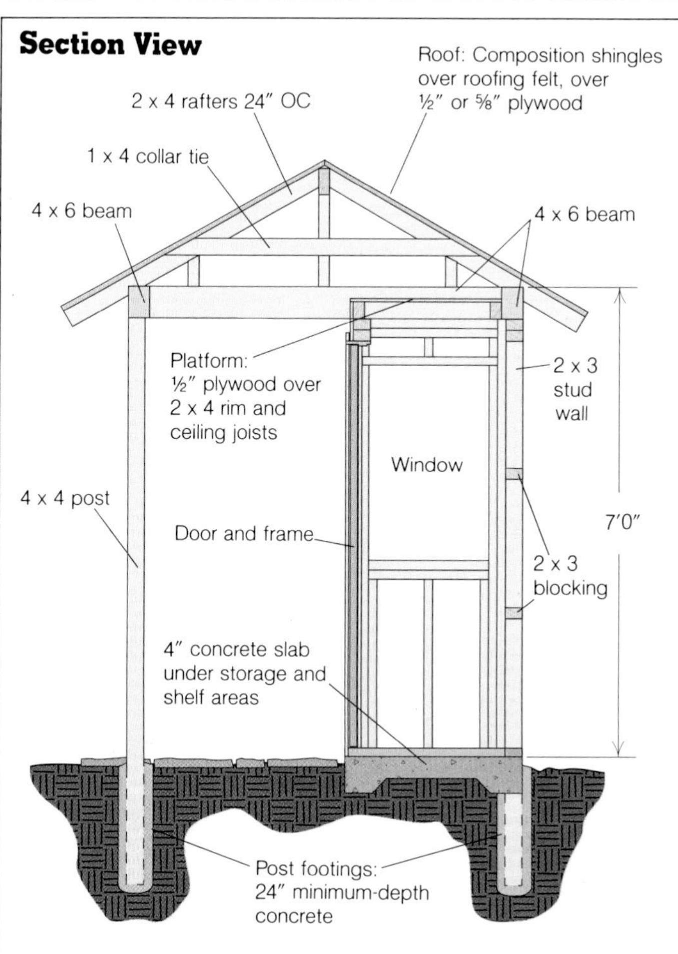


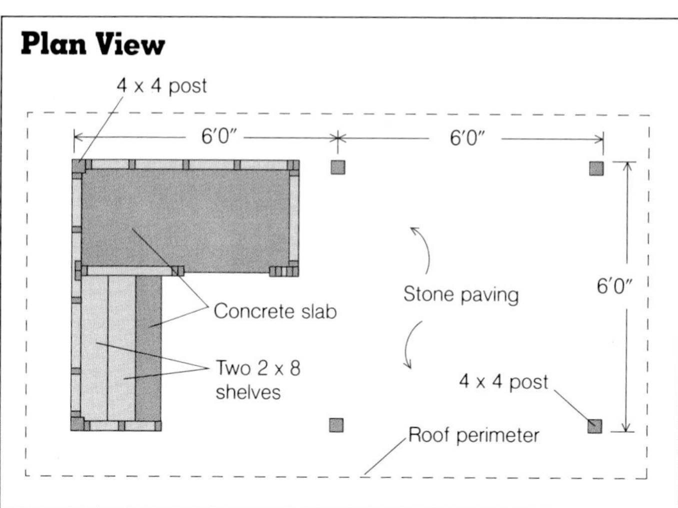


concrete mixer. Use a mix of one part portland cement, two parts sand, and three parts gravel. Give the slab a light broom finish after an initial troweling.

## Post-and-Beam Joinery

The post-to-beam joints for this shed are meant to provide a secure, interlocking connection while maintaining a simple and uncluttered look. Cutting these joints involves notching both the posts and the beams, as shown in the illustration on page 72. The same basic procedure is used to make the notches in the center of the beams and the ends of the posts.

The tops of the posts must be cut to length and shaped after the posts are installed, which means you will be working on them from a ladder or scaffold. This calls for extra caution, because you will be using the tools in an awkward position, close to your face. Wear eye protection and a dust mask when sawing, and be absolutely sure your work platform is stable and at a comfortable height.

Level across all the posts and cut them off at the top-of-beam elevation. Notch the four corner posts on two faces; notch only the outside faces of the center posts. Cut the 4 by 6 beams as shown on page 72 and fasten them in place at the corners with ⅜-inch by 6-inch lag screws; use ⅜-inch by 4-inch through-bolts at the center post connections.

Check the beam assembly for squareness by measuring the diagonals from corner to corner. If the dimensions are off by more than ¼ inch or so, you can square up the beams by tying a loop of rope diagonally across two posts just under the beams, inserting a stick into the loop, and twisting the rope until the beams have been pulled into square. Then nail a temporary 2 by 4 diagonal brace on top of the beams in a position that won't interfere with your rafter framing later.

## Shed Framing

The walls for the storage room and shelving recess are framed with 2 by 3 lumber, which ensures adequate strength while providing a little more interior room than a 2 by 4 stud wall would. If your lumberyard doesn't stock 2 by 3s, you can rip them from 2 by 6s, or substitute 2 by 4s.

Frame the walls on the ground, using pressure-treated lumber for the bottom plates. Nail the walls securely to the posts, the beams, and to each other; then run a bead of construction adhesive under the bottom plates to secure the walls to the slab. Note that it's a lot easier to set the walls in place under the beams if you build them about ¼ inch short. Just insert shims between the beam and the top of the wall when you nail it in place.

If you'll be using board-and-batten siding as shown here, install two rows of horizontal blocking in the walls so you'll have something to nail the boards to; blocking is not required for plywood siding.

Frame a ceiling over the storage room with 2 by 4 joists and a plywood deck. This will serve to close off the room and provide some extra storage space for seldom-used items.

## Roof Framing

Now comes the fun part—framing the hip roof. The roof assembly consists of four basic elements: the ridge, which forms the peak of the roof; common rafters, which run from the perimeter beams to

## Roof Framing

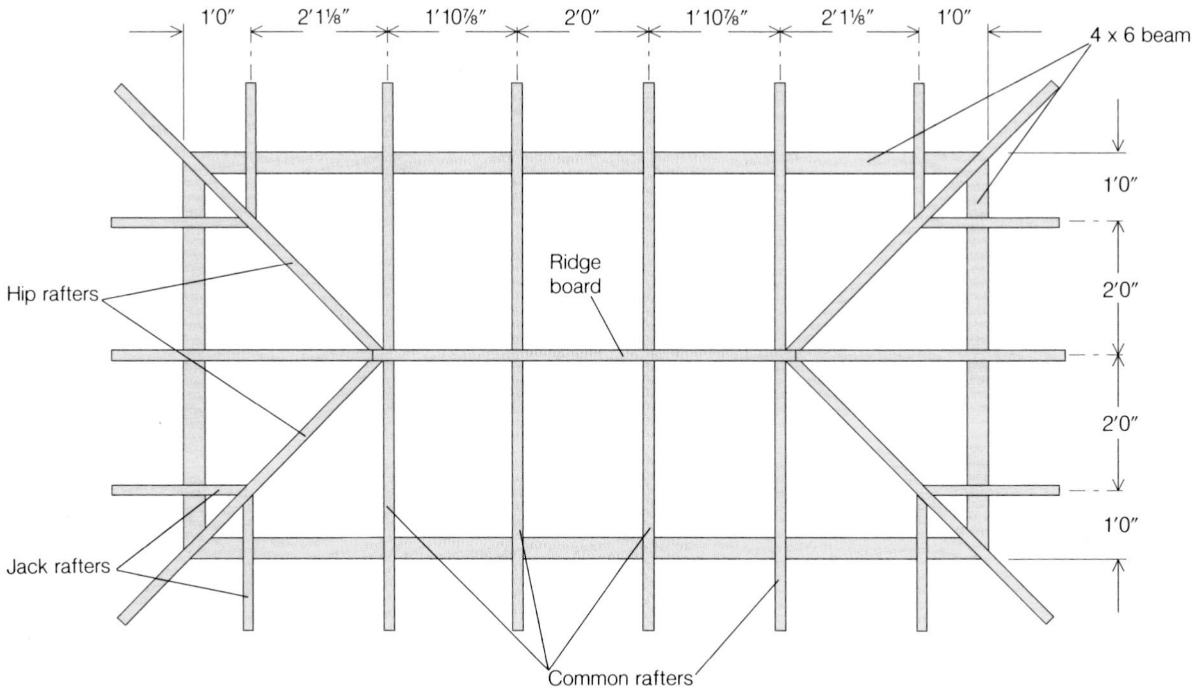

1'0" 2'1⅛" 1'10⅞" 2'0" 1'10⅞" 2'1⅛" 1'0"
4 x 6 beam
1'0"
2'0"
2'0"
1'0"
Ridge board
Hip rafters
Jack rafters
Common rafters

the ridge; hip rafters, which connect the building corners to the ends of the ridge; and jack rafters, which go from the beams to the hip rafters. Note that hip and jack rafters are either "left-handed" or "right-handed," that is, the compound miter on a left-hand rafter is the mirror image of that on a right hand rafter. You'll need equal numbers of both when you assemble the roof.

Cut the ridge board 6 feet, 3⅝ inches long. Here are a few things to keep in mind when you cut hip-roof rafters.

• Hip rafters are cut at a lower pitch than common or jack rafters; this is because the hip travels a longer distance as it rises to meet the ridge.

• The seat cut on a hip rafter is made deeper than on the other rafters. This is done so the top edges of the hip will align with the rest of the roof.

• The two common rafters that butt against the ends of the ridge are shorter than the other common rafters; this is because the ridge is extended at the ends to provide better nailing for the hips.

To cut the compound miter on a hip or jack rafter, first lay out a plumb line on the side of the rafter (7 in 12 for jacks; 7 in 17 for hips); then cut along the line with the bevel gauge on the saw set at 45 degrees. Remember to cut both left- and right-hand rafters.

To assemble the roof frame, first nail the ridge to all the common rafters on one side. Then, while an assistant holds up the ridge, install the opposing common rafters. Next put up the two common rafters that meet the ends of the ridge; their top edges should be ⅝ inch below the top corners of the ridge. Install 1 by 4 collar

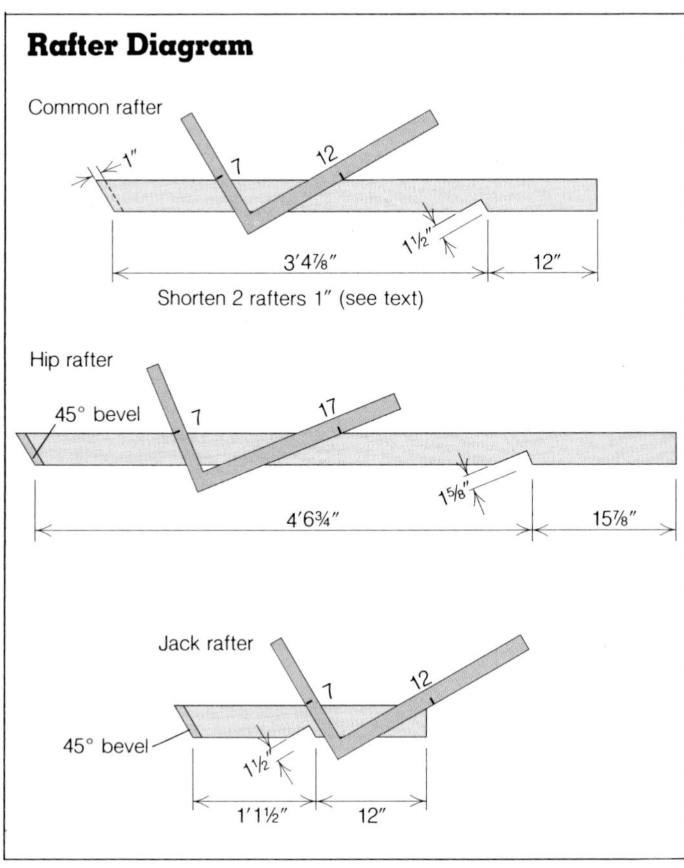

ties across the pairs of rafters at the ends of the ridge.

Once the common rafters are up, install the hips. Toenail them to the ridge and the 4 by 6 beams with two 16d nails in each end. The jack rafters go up last, also with two 16d nails top and bottom.

In an ideal world, all these parts would fit together perfectly, just as you cut them. Don't count on it; something—an out-of-square corner or an out-of-level beam—is bound to conspire against you to make misfits of one or more of your rafters. Make minor adjustments by shaving a little off the cut at the top of the rafter or opening up the seat cut at the bottom. If you have to remove more than ½ inch or so, however, you've probably made a mistake somewhere and should go back and check your work.

Install the plywood roof sheathing in full sheets, without cutting the corners at the hips. When one slope of the roof is covered, snap chalk lines over the centerlines of the hips and trim the plywood in place. Save the cutoffs—you can use them on the next side.

## Roofing and Finish Work

You can use virtually any kind of roof covering on this shed. Choose the type that best fits in with your landscape and existing structures. Whichever kind you choose, install it according to the instructions provided by the manufacturer.

Finish up the shed by installing the door, window, siding, and shelving. In keeping with the small scale of this shed, the 2-foot-wide door is only 6 feet, 2 inches tall, so if you are buying a standard-sized door you will have to cut it down. Get a solid-core door and cut the excess off the top. This will leave the bottom edge, where the door may be exposed to water, intact.

If you'll be storing fertilizer (or other odorous materials), put screened vents in the storage-room walls near the floor and ceiling. Protect children from hazardous garden chemicals with a lock on the door or a lockable cabinet inside.

There is one last detail: Don't forget to set up your shed with a bench and a little table—these are as much a part of the building as beams, rafters and walls.

## Materials List

| Description | | Material/Size | Length | Quantity |
|---|---|---|---|---|
| Foundation | Storage slab and post footings | concrete | — | ½ cu yd |
| Framing | Posts | 4×4 PT or heart rwd or cedar* | 10′ | 6 ea |
| | Beams | 4×6 | 12′ | 3 ea |
| | Sill plates | 2×3 PT | 12′ | 2 ea |
| | Walls: plates, studs, blocking | 2×3 | 8′ | 34 ea |
| | Ceiling framing | 2×4 | 10′ | 2 ea |
| | Rafters | 2×4 | 10′ | 10 ea |
| | Ridge | 2×6 | 8′ | 1 ea |
| | Collar ties | 1×4 | 10′ | 1 ea |
| | Roof sheathing | ½″ or ⅝″ plywd<br>or 1×6 bds | 4×8 sh<br>RL | 8 ea<br>310 l.f. |
| | Miscellaneous scrap lumber for temporary bracing per text | | | |
| Roofing | | shingles, type as chosen | — | 167 s.f. |
| Finishes | Door | 2′0″×6′2″ s.c. door and frame (w/hardware) | — | 1 ea |
| | Window | 1′6″×3′0″ window | — | 1 ea |
| Siding | | 1×12 rough-sawn | 8′ | 20 ea |
| Trim | | 1×2 battens<br>1×3 corner | 8′<br>8′ | 14 ea<br>12 ea |
| Shelving | | 2×8 | 8′ | 4 ea |
| Hardware | Post-to-beam bolts | ⅜″ lag screw (w)<br>⅜″ MB (n/2w) | 6″<br>4″ | 16 ea<br>4 ea |
| | Nails | 16d sinker<br>8d sinker<br>8d HDG | —<br>—<br>— | 5 lb<br>5 lb<br>3 lb |
| Miscellaneous | Const adhesive | 10-oz. | — | 1 tube |

*or other naturally durable species

See page 105 for materials list abbreviations.

# CHILDREN'S PLAYHOUSE

*This versatile playhouse is packed with possibilities. The lower room, with its open counter, could be a grocery store, a ticket booth, or a puppet theater. The floor above could be a stage, a ship's deck, or the terrace of a mansion. A firehouse pole allows for a quick exit, with a sandbox below for a soft landing.*

## Setting Posts

Seven 4 by 4 posts form the basic framework around which the playhouse is constructed. The two posts at the back of the structure, and the center post at the front, need only be as tall as the top of the deck; the four forward posts, which form the corners of the downstairs room, extend through the deck to support the guardrail above.

Locate the posts with string lines and set them in postholes at least 2 feet deep. In most cases, tamped earth will be adequate to secure the posts, but pouring concrete around them will result in a stronger, stiffer installation. As with any wood in contact with the ground, the posts should be either pressure treated or made from heartwood of a decay-resistant wood species. Redwood or cedar would be good choices.

If the posts have sharp corners, round them off with a rasp or router to minimize splinters.

## Deck Framing

The framing for the deck consists of a double rim joist (2 by 6 and 2 by 8), which wraps around the posts, and 2 by 6 floor joists, which are secured to the rim joists with metal hangers and angle clips. Use special hangers, designed for double 2 by 6 lumber, for the double joist that supports the front wall of the playhouse.

Install the 2 by 8 fascia joists first. Fasten them to the posts with two ⅜-inch by 4½-inch lag screws at each joint (offset the screws at the corner posts so they won't interfere with each other). The inner 2 by 6 rim joists are mounted 1½ inches below the top of the 2 by 8s and are fastened to the posts with metal angle clips. Nail the 2 by 6 and 2 by 8 together with pairs of 10d nails every 12 inches.

Install the floor joists and frame around the openings for the ladder and firehouse pole as shown on page 78.

## Perspective View

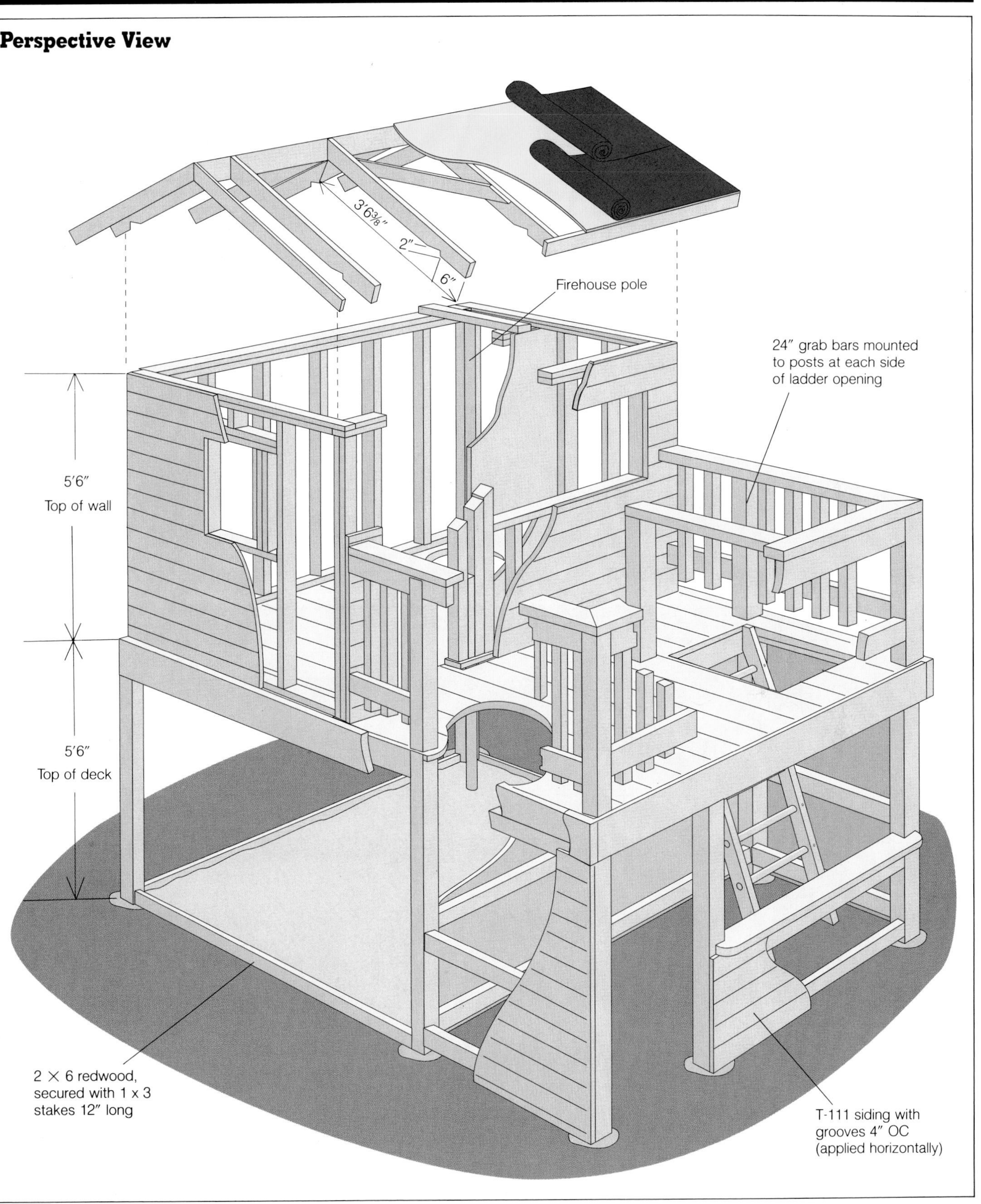

## Lower-Level Plan

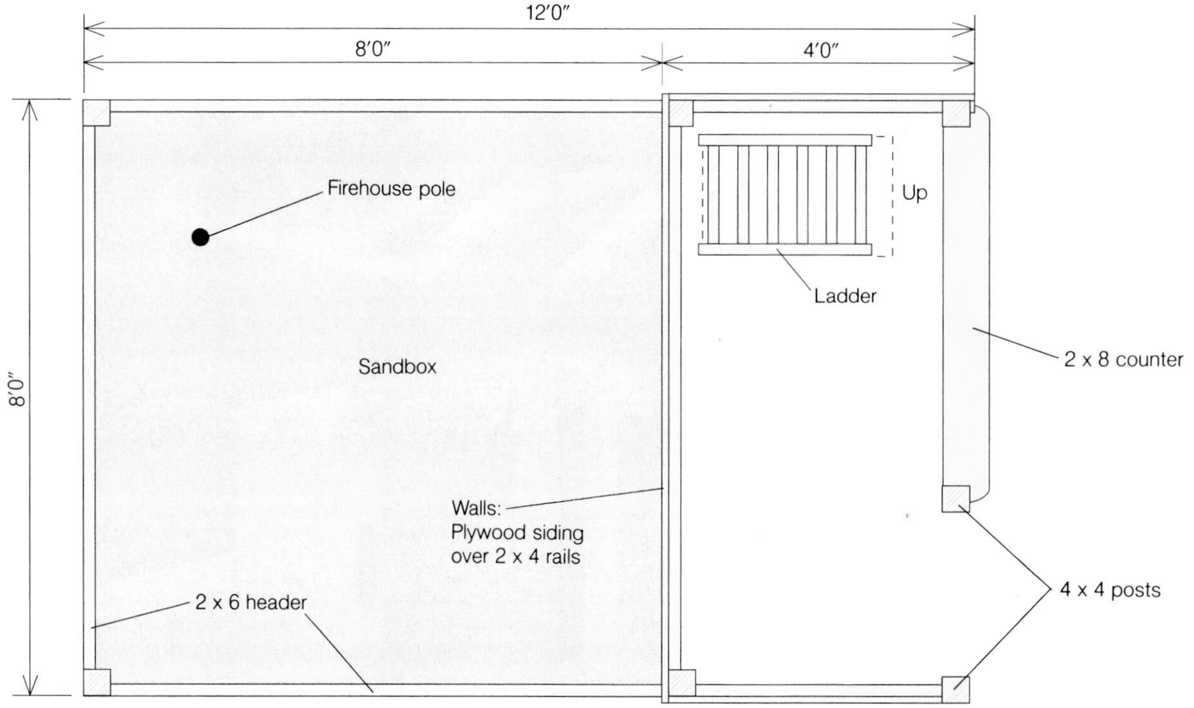

12'0"
8'0"
4'0"
8'0"
Firehouse pole
Sandbox
Up
Ladder
2 x 8 counter
Walls:
Plywood siding
over 2 x 4 rails
2 x 6 header
4 x 4 posts

## Floor Framing Plan

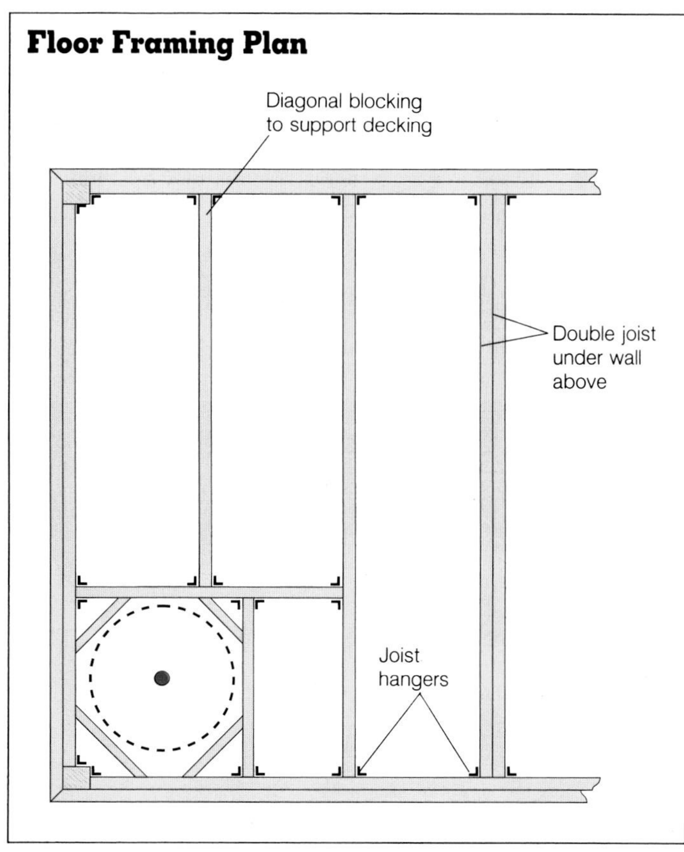


## Deck Framing Plan

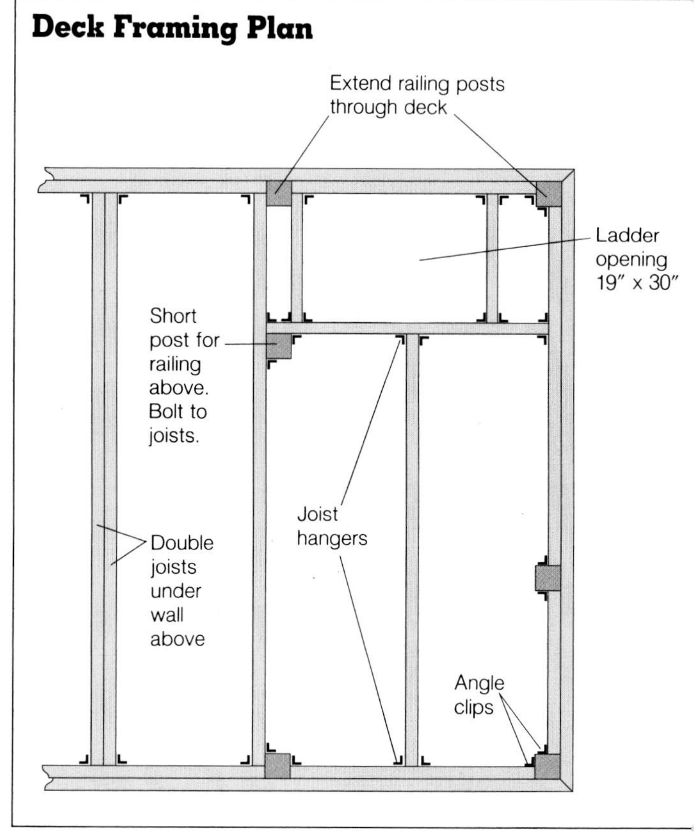

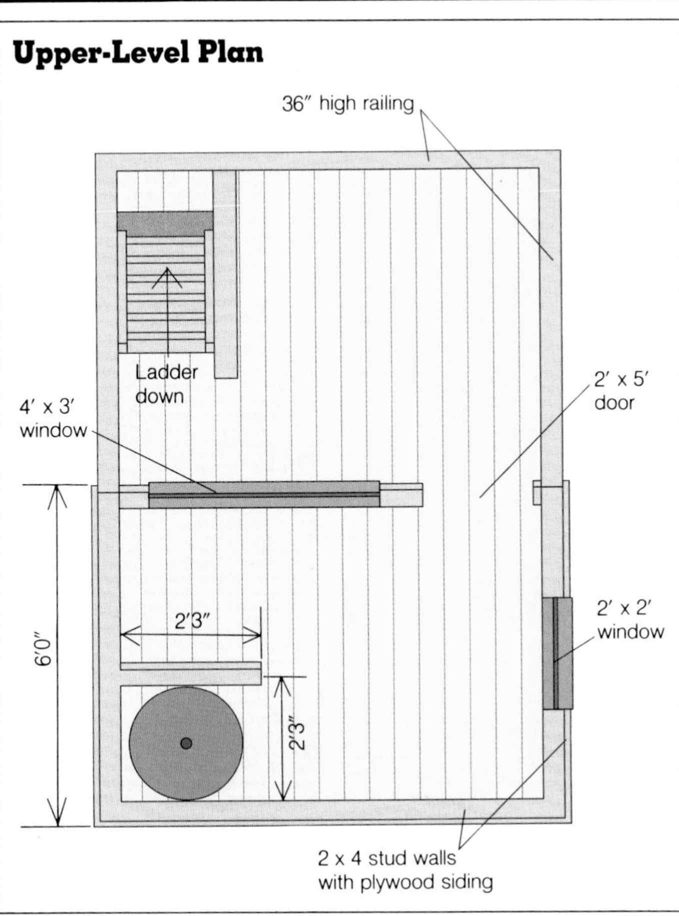


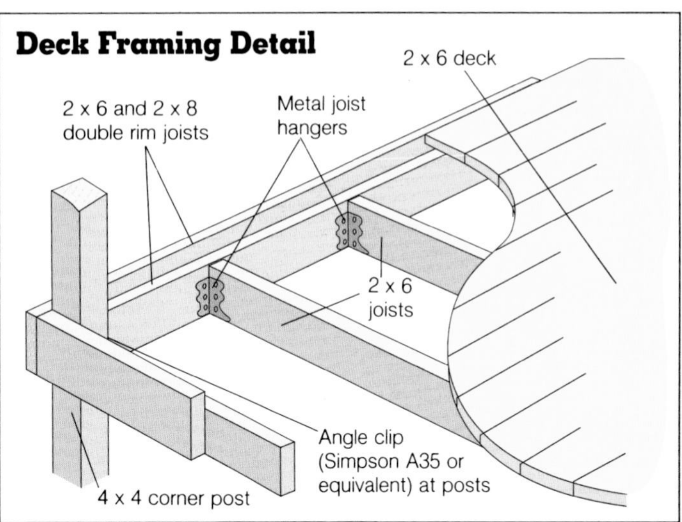


Before you run the 2 by 6 decking, install the short post that supports the guardrail next to the ladder opening. Bolt it to the joists with two ⅜-inch carriage bolts in each direction.

## Downstairs Walls

The walls for the lower floor are built much like a fence. Toenail 2 by 4 horizontal rails to the posts with four 8d nails in each end. Apply the plywood siding horizontally, with 6d HDG nails spaced 6 inches apart. Be sure to leave a gap of an inch or two between the bottom of the siding and the ground, otherwise surface moisture will eventually rot the siding.

The countertop for the front wall is cut from a section of 2 by 8. Notch it around the posts and cut the rounded corners with a saber saw; then fasten it in place with 16d finish nails.

## Upstairs Shed

Unlike the downstairs room, the shed on the upper level of the playhouse is constructed with conventional stud-wall framing. For a little building like this one, studs spaced 2 feet on center provide adequate support. (See page 52 for more on framing sheds.)

Remember to install the 2 by 6 block that will support the top end of the firehouse pole before you build the roof.

To frame the roof, cut five pairs of rafters as shown on page 77. Toenail them to the wall plates and ridge with three 8d nails at each end. Install a 1 by 4 collar tie across the center pair of rafters. Place it high enough that it won't be a hazard to the occasional adult visitor. Nail the 2 by 4 fascia to the rafter tails and ridge as shown, and cover the roof with ½-inch plywood. Roll roofing applied over the plywood provides quick, inexpensive, and effective protection from the weather, but you can use shingles (or any other type of roofing) if you prefer.

A note of caution: When you are working on the roof, you will be at least 12 feet off the ground. Protect yourself with roof safety brackets and a toe board.

Install plywood siding over the walls, again with the sheets applied horizontally. Start at the bottom of the wall and work up; orient the lap joint on each sheet so that it will shed rainwater to the outside. To make the best, most efficient use of the material, use the scrap from one wall as the first course for the next.

## Ladder, Firehouse Pole, and Railing

To construct the ladder that goes from the downstairs room to the deck, start with two 6-foot 2 by 4s. Lay out seven equal spaces on one piece; then clamp the 2 by 4s together and drill 1¼-inch-diameter holes through both pieces for the rungs. Cut 1¼-inch-diameter dowels to length for the rungs, about ¼ inch shorter than the width of the deck opening, and assemble the ladder. Use a mallet if you have to, but don't

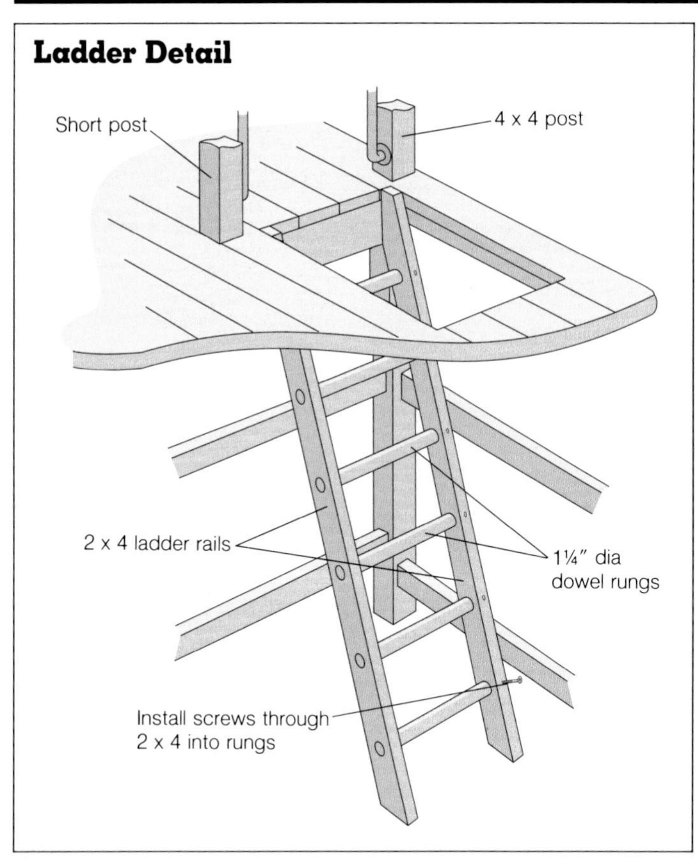


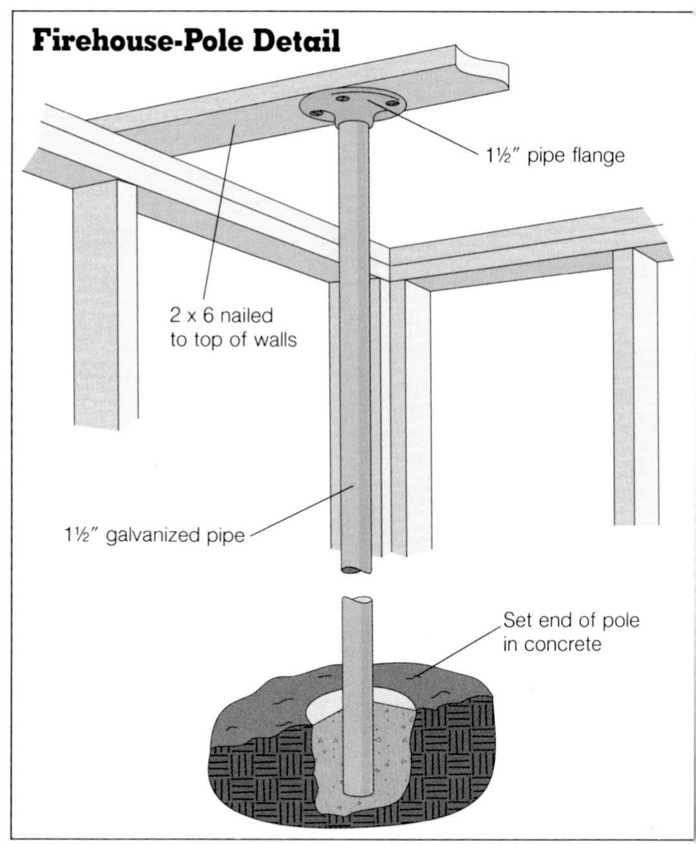


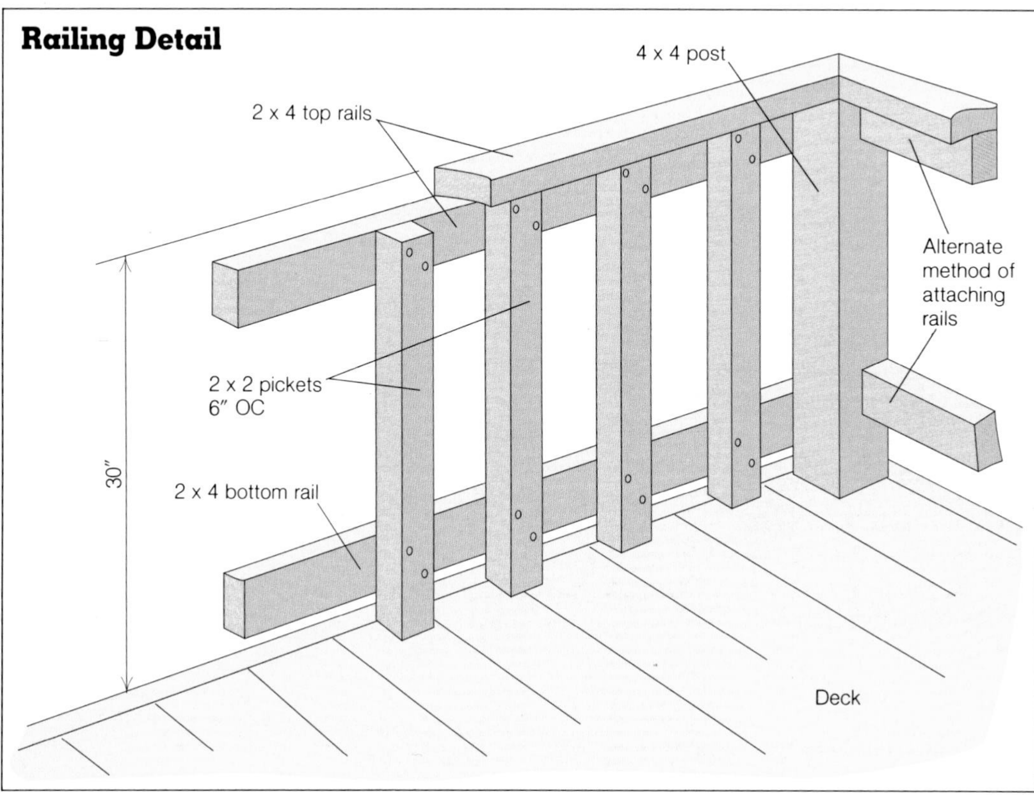


force it—you may split the 2 by 4 rails. Secure the rungs with 3-inch screws driven through the edges of the 2 by 4s. Countersink them to avoid sharp edges.

Make the angled cuts at the top and bottom of the ladder (the trial-and-error method is as easy as any) and secure the ladder in place with screws. Mount 24-inch-long grab bars to the railing posts on each side of the ladder opening.

The firehouse pole is simply a 12-foot length of 1½-inch-ID galvanized pipe, held in place at the top with a pipe flange and at the bottom with a small concrete footing, shown above. Attach the flange to the 2 × 6 first. Then screw the pipe to it and pour concrete around the base. The footing should be approximately 1 foot deep.

To build the sandbox, stake a 2 by 6 around the perimeter of the pole, with its top edge about 2 inches above the surface of the ground. Excavate the area inside to a depth of 6 or 8 inches and fill it with sand. Washed plaster sand (available from concrete- and masonry-supply businesses) is clean, relatively inexpensive, and ideal for making sand castles.

The figure at left shows one type of railing that is fairly easy to construct, but you can choose any style you like. With any design, however, be sure that the railing has no openings more than 6 inches wide, to prevent small children from getting their heads caught.

## Finishing Touches

As shown here, this playhouse is simple and unadorned, more like a stage set than a finished building. You can make it into a real dollhouse, though, with a few extra touches. Install a swinging gate in the door opening of the downstairs room, put in windows and a door upstairs, and install trim on the corners and around all the openings. When you're done, give everything a coat of latex paint or approved stain. You may even want to go all out and finish the interior, too, with wallboard walls, carpeting, and kid-sized furniture.

## Materials List

| Description | | Material/Size | Length | Quantity |
|---|---|---|---|---|
| Framing | Posts | 4×4 PT or heart rwd or cedar* | 8'<br>12' | 2 ea<br>5 ea |
| | Fascia joist | 2×8 | 10'<br>14' | 2 ea<br>2 ea |
| | Deck joists | 2×6 | 8' | 13 ea |
| | Decking | 2×6 | 12' | 17 ea |
| | Upper and lower walls | 2×4 | 12' | 25 ea |
| | Rafters and fascia | 2×4 | 10' | 9 ea |
| | Ridge | 2×6 | 10' | 1 ea |
| | Roof sheathing | ½" plywd | 4×8 sh | 3 ea |
| | Siding | T-111 plywd siding | 4×8 sh | 9 ea |
| Miscellaneous | Roofing | 90-lb roll roofing | — | 1 roll |
| | Firehouse pole | 1½" dia. galv pipe (threaded 1 end)<br>1½" pipe flange | 12'<br>— | 1 pc<br>1 ea |
| | Countertop | 2×8 | 6' | 1 ea |
| | Sandbox header | 2×6 | 8' | 4 ea |
| | Sand | washed plaster sand | — | 1½ cu yd |
| | Ladder rails | 2×4 | 6' | 2 ea |
| | Ladder rungs | 1¼" dowels | — | 9 l.f. |
| | Grab bars | 24" | — | 2 ea |
| Railing | Rails | 2×4 | 12' | 6 ea |
| | Pickets | 2×2 | RL | 160 l.f. |
| Hardware | Joist hangers | 2×6 joist hgr<br>double 2×6 hgr | —<br>— | 9 ea<br>2 ea |
| | Angle clips | std | — | 12 ea |
| | Screws (railing and ladder) | 3" coated deck screw | — | 2 lbs |
| | Bolts (short rail post) | ⅜" carriage bolt (n/w) | 6" | 4 ea |
| | Fascia joist screws | ⅜" lag screw (w) | 4½" | 22 ea |
| | Nails | 16d sinker<br>8d sinker<br>16d HDG<br>10d HDG<br>8d HDG<br>1½" joist hgr | —<br>—<br>—<br>—<br>—<br>— | 5 lb<br>2 lb<br>6 lb<br>2 lb<br>5 lb<br>1½ lb |
| | Assorted metal fasteners as per text | | | |

*or other naturally durable species
See page 105 for materials list abbreviations.

# THREE GAZEBO PLANS

*The gazebo is perhaps the most classic and renowned outdoor shelter there is. These stand-alone structures can add a striking dimension to a landscape, serve as a romantic garden retreat, and provide shelter from the elements throughout the year.*

*Although the elaborate Victorian gazebo is probably the most well known, there are a multitude of other designs that can make quite an impact on their surroundings. The photographs on the following pages show just a few of the many configurations and architectural styles of gazebos, and how each is successful in its particular location.*

*The three plans, beginning on page 86, start with the classic Victorian, followed by a screened, tiered-roof summerhouse, and a more modern model with skylights. Construction of these structures is usually more involved than that of a shed or overhead, so study the instructions, drawings, and materials lists carefully before you begin. "Planning Your Outdoor Shelter" (page 5) and "Materials, Tools, and Techniques" (page 104) provide additional information that is critical to the successful construction of these elegant outdoor rooms.*

*Built up from a platform deck set snugly against a garden slope, this graceful gazebo serves as a tranquil retreat and provides welcome shade along the poolside. A cedar shake roof and simple one-piece fascia between the posts give the structure a natural and uncluttered look.*

*Complementing its companion buildings in color and design, this gazebo is an inviting belvedere at the edge of the pond. The 1 by 4 horizontal slats on the hip roof provide substantial shelter from the sun. The grouped posts are notched into the beams, as are the rails and horizontal members, for an interlocking-style structure.*

*For those who feel uneasy about taking on the substantial project of building a gazebo from scratch, kits are available that can be assembled with a few simple tools in a short time. As an added benefit for some, many kit designs include prefabricated pieces that are more detailed and ornate than can be fashioned by hand. This painted kit model sports an upper raised roof, and plywood arches provide lateral stability. Lattice panels along the sides lend privacy to the finished product.*

*Top left: A cupola roof adds interest to the structure of this rectangular gazebo set at poolside for needed shade.*
*Top right: This little Victorian-style retreat at the end of a garden walkway is enhanced with scroll-sawn brackets in its corners and lattice-type railings.*
*Bottom left: A gazebo needn't be fancy to add interest to a landscape. Simple and straightforward in design, this model beckons as a cozy retreat.*
*Bottom right: A fence is incorporated into the structure of this Japanese-style pavilion; the fence gate even serves as its door.*

# VICTORIAN GAZEBO

*This is a classic gazebo in the Victorian tradition, built on an octagonal plan. Its arched bracing, pierced railings, and painted finish give it a comfortable, old-fashioned look with only a little extra detailing.*

## Construction

While no polygonal structure is easy to build, this one is less difficult than many. The posts are octagons shaped from 6 by 6s, which requires more work than when using square posts, but it simplifies installation of brackets and railings and adds elegance. The roof sheathing is 2 by 6 tongue-and-groove decking, which can span from corner to corner without sagging; this eliminates the intermediate rafter framing and a lot of the tricky angle cuts typical of many gazebos.

Fabrication of the arches, octagonal posts, and railing pieces is somewhat involved, but this work could be done indoors during the winter months in order to get a head start on spring construction.

Like the turn-of-the-century belvederes it is modeled after, this gazebo is meant to be painted, rather than stained or left unfinished. Many parts can be made of woods that might not otherwise be suitable for outdoor structures; pine and fir, for instance, will hold up to the weather quite well when properly protected by enamel paint (try to use kiln-dried wood for arches, railings, and other trim pieces). As an added bonus, if any of the joints don't fit perfectly, they can be caulked or puttied and then painted over.

## Footings

This gazebo can be built on a concrete slab or brick patio, or it can be incorporated into a raised wooden deck, but in either case it must be securely anchored to concrete footings. Keep in mind that a strong wind can uproot a poorly anchored gazebo and carry it away like an oversized umbrella. Prefabricated metal post bases, sized for 6 by 6 posts, provide protection against wind uplift. Try to find some with straps that are no more than 2¼ inches wide (the width of the flat faces on the octagonal posts).

To plot the octagonal outline of the gazebo, start with a square 12 feet on each side. Measure the diagonals from corner to corner—unless these dimensions are equal, the corners won't be square. Then measure in from the corners as shown on page 88 in order to establish the eight corners of the octagon.

The footings for the posts should be at least 18 inches square and 12 inches deep, but local conditions may require

## Perspective View

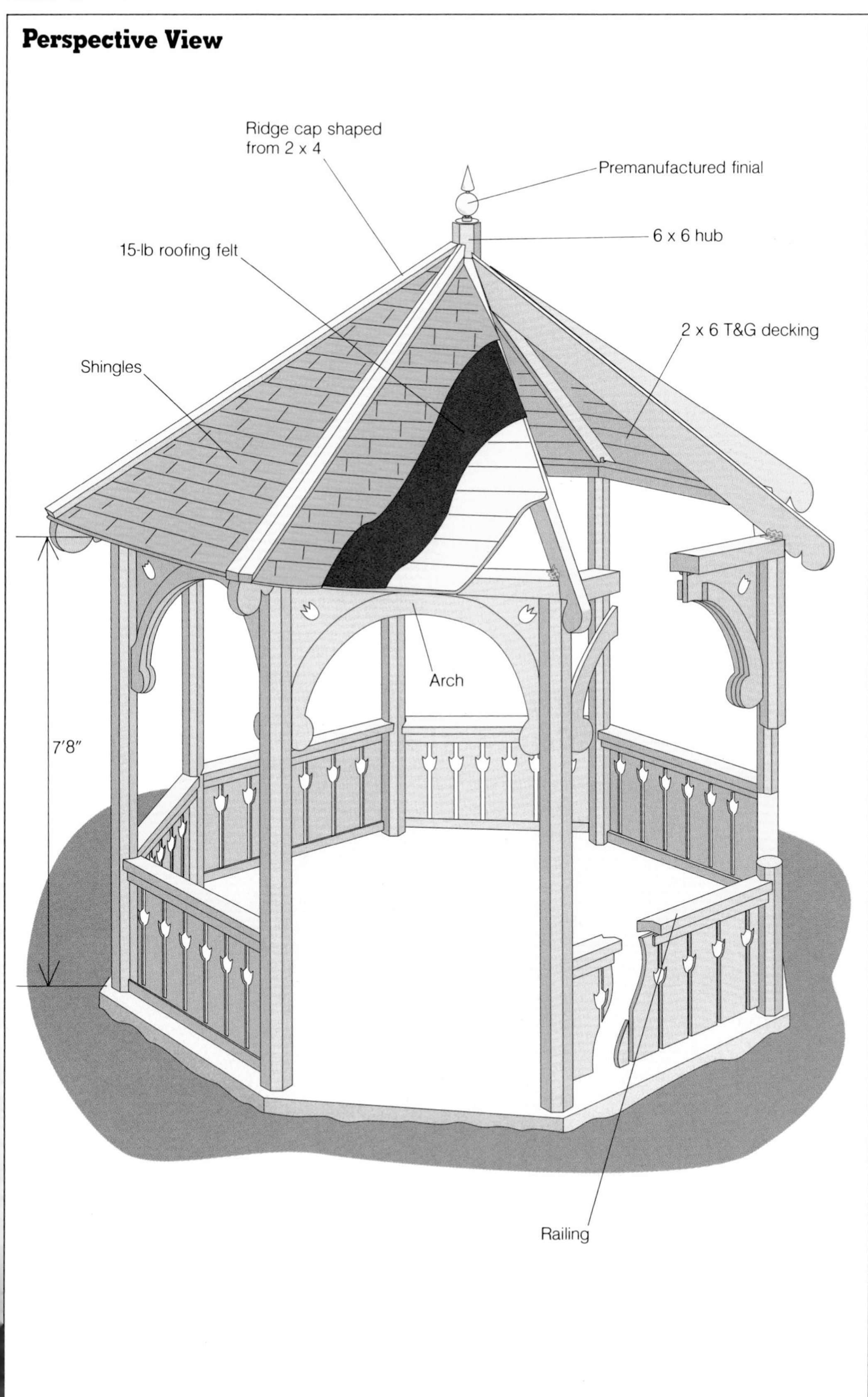


footings that are wider or deeper. Consult your building department for requirements in your area.

Fill the footing holes with concrete and set the post bases while the concrete is still wet. Locating the post bases accurately is crucial: A mislocated post will plague you through every phase of construction, right up to the peak of the roof. One way to help set the post bases properly is to make a cardboard template of the post shape and trace this outline onto each post base with a felt-tipped pen. This will show you where the corners of the posts will be when the gazebo is finished.

If the gazebo is to be built on a deck, the post bases can be concealed beneath the decking, but if you will be building on a patio or slab, be sure to orient the straps so they won't be in the way when you're ready to install the railings.

## Posts and Top Plates

To shape the octagonal posts, lay out the cut lines on all four sides of each post as shown on page 88. Lay out seven posts alike, plus one that is about 2 feet longer than the others. The excess length will be cut off later to form the hub for the center of the roof.

Set your circular saw to cut a 45-degree bevel, and rip-cut the corners of each post. A rip guide, sold as an accessory for most saws, will help keep the cut straight. A sharp blade is essential; with a standard 7¼-inch blade, you'll be cutting to the maximum capacity of the saw and taxing it to the limit. If the saw bogs down or the

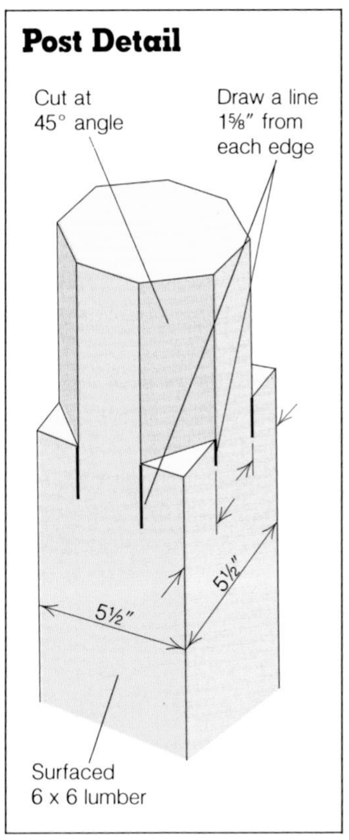


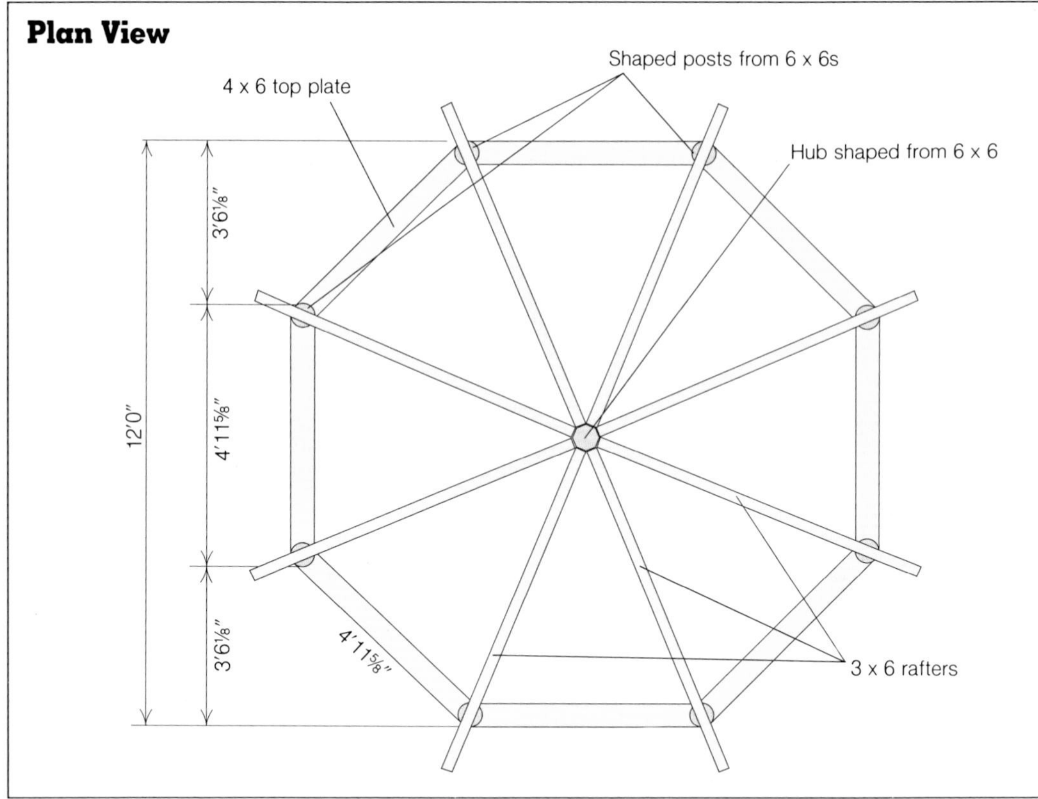


motor starts overheating, set the depth adjustment on the saw for a shallower cut and make two passes.

You can remove the saw marks on the posts with a hand plane or belt sander, but a portable power plane (available at most tool-rental yards) will make short work of what is an otherwise tedious job. Go easy, though; this tool can remove a lot of wood in a short time.

Cut the posts to 7 feet, 8 inches, but before you do, go back and check the post bases to see if they're all at the same elevation. If some are a bit too high or too low, you will be able to allow for the difference when you cut the posts. Use a circular saw to cut around all eight sides of each post; complete the cuts with a handsaw.

Cut the 4 by 6 top plates as shown. To lay out the 22½-degree angles at the ends of each piece, use a framing square with the 5-inch mark on the tongue and the 12-inch mark on the blade aligned with the edge of the 4 by 6 (mark on the 5-inch side).

If you will be using the plywood tongue-and-groove method of installing the arches (see page 89), you must cut the grooves in the posts and top plates before assembling them. Make the grooves with either a dado blade in a table saw or a fence-guided router, or by making repeated passes with a circular saw.

Set the posts in place and brace them temporarily with 2 by 4s. Toenail the top plates to the posts with 16-penny (16d) hot-dipped galvanized (HDG) finish nails. Add straps or L-brackets for a stronger connection. Tie the gazebo corners together with 12-inch-long plate straps on top of the 4 by 6s.

## Arched Bracket Construction

The eight arches that ring the walls of this gazebo are an elegant decorative touch, but they serve an important structural function as well: They brace the gazebo against wind and earthquake loads. It's imperative, therefore, that these arches be strongly built and rigidly connected to the posts and top plates.

Each bracket is composed of two ¾-inch-thick solid-wood arches glued and screwed to a plywood core. The edge of the plywood projects from the sides and top of the arch, forming a tongue that fits into grooves cut into posts and top plates. A simpler alternative to this tongue-and-groove method is shown on page 90; although not as strong, it is easier to construct.

Carefully lay out and cut one plywood half arch as shown on page 89, and use it as a pattern to lay out and cut 15 others. If you lay out the half arches on the plywood as shown, you can get all 16 pieces from two sheets. Save time by stacking the sheets together so you can cut two pieces at once.

If you wish, put decorative cutouts in the plywood before assembling the arches.

Lay out and cut the ¾-inch by 2¼-inch solid-wood arches. Use a plywood arch to trace them onto 1 by 8s. Make each half arch in two sections, with an extra inch or two at the ends for trimming and fitting.

Use waterproof, powdered urea-formaldehyde glue (commonly known as brown glue) to assemble the laminated arches. Dry-fit, then glue and clamp all the parts for one half arch. Drive 2-inch wallboard screws through the sandwich from both sides, 6 to 8 inches apart, and remove the clamps. Use a wet rag to clean up any excess glue before it hardens. Build up the rest of the arches the same way. After the glue dries, putty the screw heads and the exposed plywood edges and sand everything smooth.

When you install the arches, start at the back of the gazebo and work around toward the front. That way you can make your mistakes where they won't show; by the time you get to the front you'll have your technique perfected.

Test-fit each pair of half arches in its opening, trimming the joint in the middle as necessary to get a smooth fit. Fasten the arches to the framing with 8d toenails through the plywood into the grooves in the posts and beams, and with 4-inch wallboard screws through the solid-wood portion of the arches into the posts and top plates. Drill pilot holes before inserting the screws.

Install the ⅜-inch quarter-round moldings next. This trim will cover any gaps between the plywood and the framing and will give a finished appearance to the completed arch. You'll have to make a long, tapered cut where the molding meets the arch. Make the cut a little long and shave it down with a utility knife until it fits.

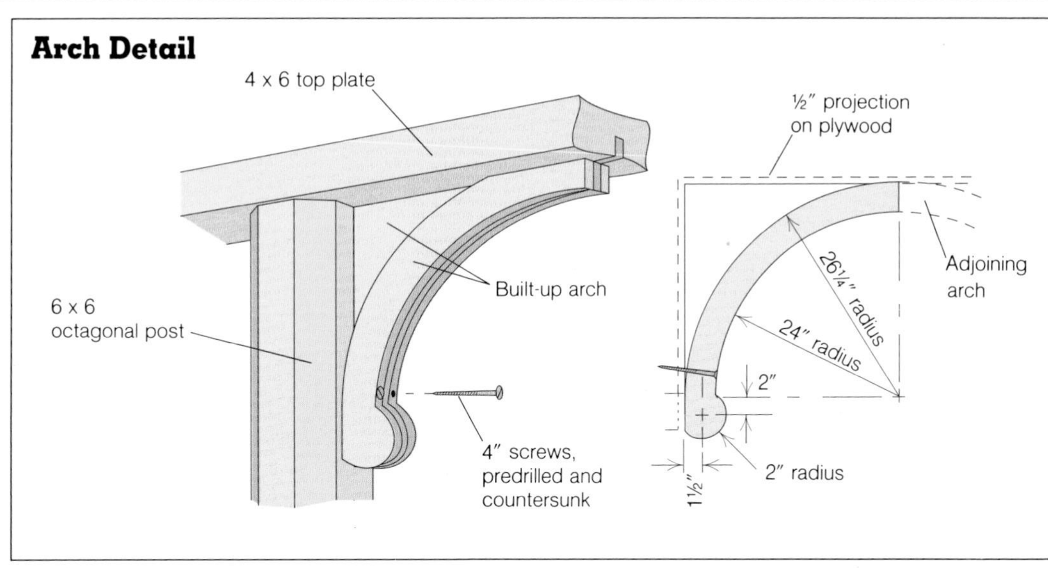


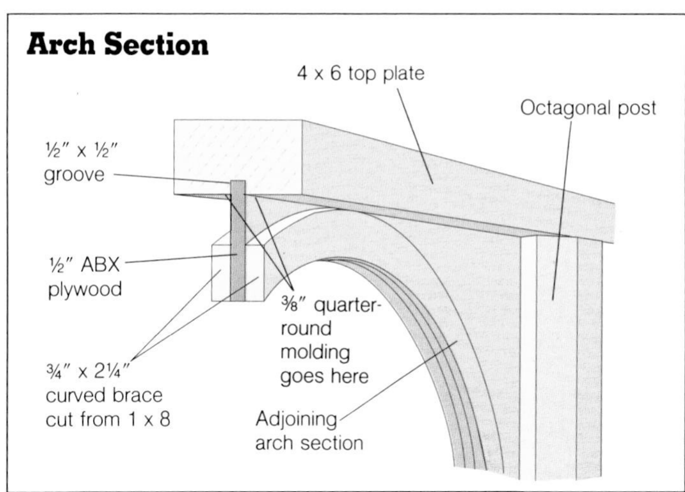


## Roof Framing

The rafters for this gazebo are made of 3 by 6s. The 2½-inch thickness of this material is heavy enough to hold the nails for the 2 by 6 decking, yet is just narrow enough for all the rafters to meet at the center hub. Not all lumberyards keep 3 by 6s in stock, but most will special-order them for you or mill them from heavier stock for a small fee.

Search out the scrap piece from the long post and cut it to length for the center hub of the roof. Make it 16 inches long, not counting the decorative finial on top. The finial can be lathe-turned as part of the hub, but it's easier to cut square the ends of the hub and apply the finial as a separate piece. Get one that's nearly the same diameter as the hub. It might seem too big at first, but once it's on top of the gazebo it will look just right.

Cut the first rafter according to the rafter diagram on page 90 and use it as a pattern to lay out and cut the other seven. You will have to bevel a little off the sides of the cut at the top of each rafter where it fits against the center hub so it won't crowd adjacent rafters—two passes with a block plane should do it.

Make the circular cuts at the ends of the rafter tails with a saber saw, using a blade designed for thick wood. Smooth and refine the shape with a rasp and coarse sandpaper.

In order to assemble the roof you'll need a couple of sturdy scaffold planks as well as an assistant. Place the planks on the 4 by 6 top plates to form a working platform. Fasten two rafters to opposite sides of the hub with 4-inch wallboard screws through the point of each rafter; then tip the whole assembly up, with the hub situated over the center of the gazebo and the bird's-mouth cuts of the rafters centered on opposite corners. Toenail the rafters to the top plates while your assistant supports the center hub, then install the rest of the rafters, one at a time, again with a 4-inch wallboard screw through each rafter into the hub (drill pilot holes for the screws and lubricate the threads with wax or soap). Finally, install the small metal framing clips on both sides of each rafter as shown on page 90. These will counteract the outward thrust of the rafters at the walls.

## Rafter Diagram

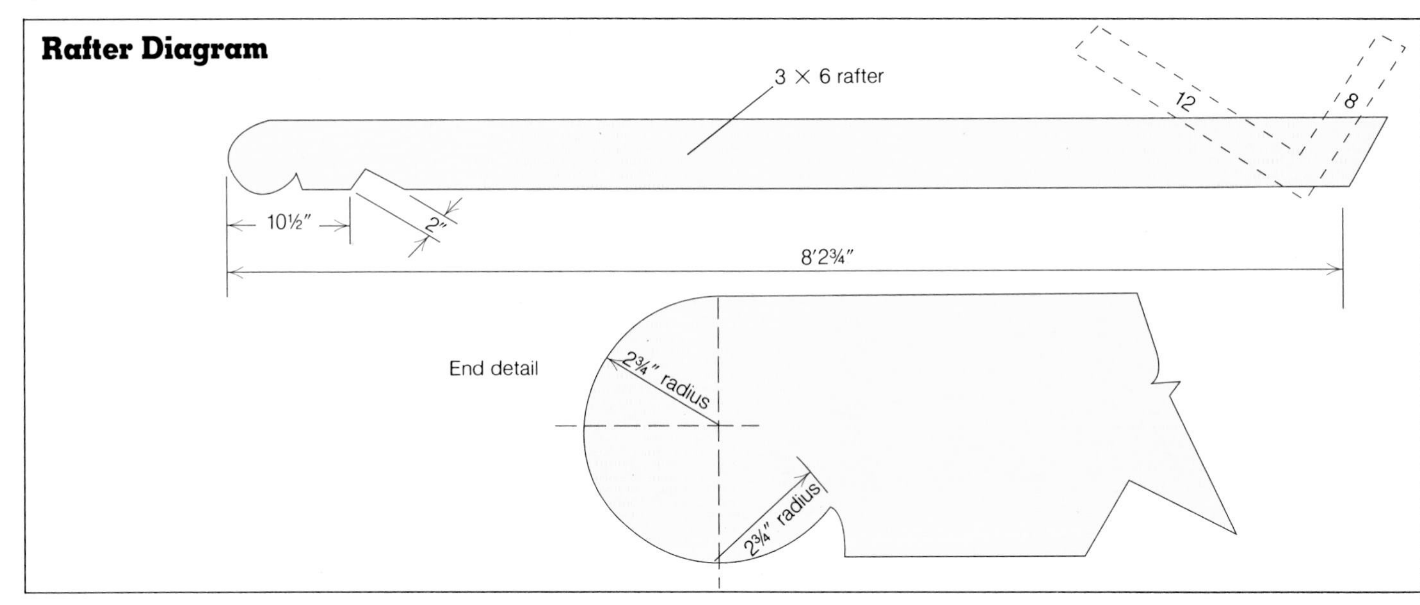


## Rafter Connection

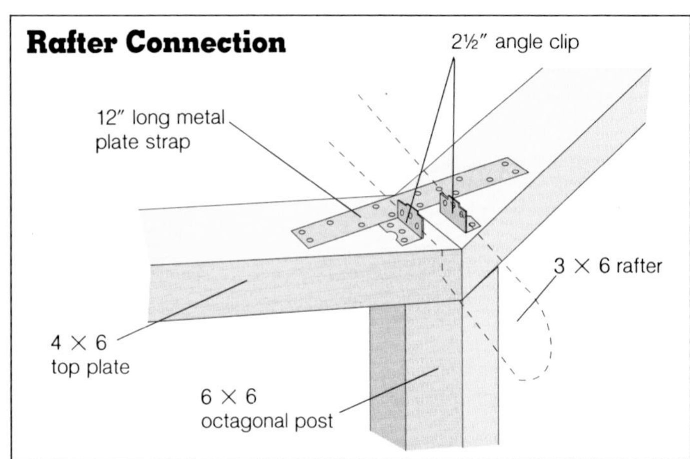


## Railing Detail

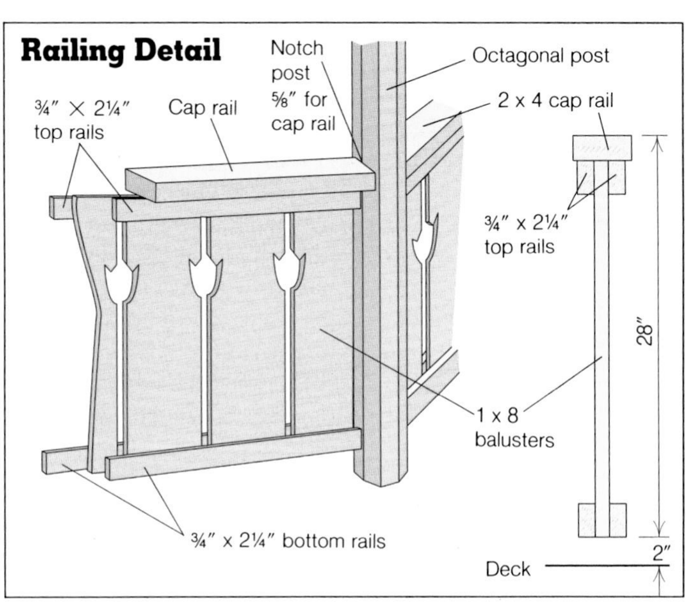


## Flush Method of Arch Construction

If you can't cut the grooves in the posts and beams, then assemble the arches in one piece, with the solid-wood portions overlapping the joint in the plywood. Test-fit each arch—if the opening is too wide, shave off the top corners of the plywood and flex the arch open enough to make it fit. To fit an arch into an opening that's too small, shave a little off both ends until it slides into place. Fasten the arches with 4-inch wallboard screws as shown on page 89.

### Alternate Arch Section (Flush)

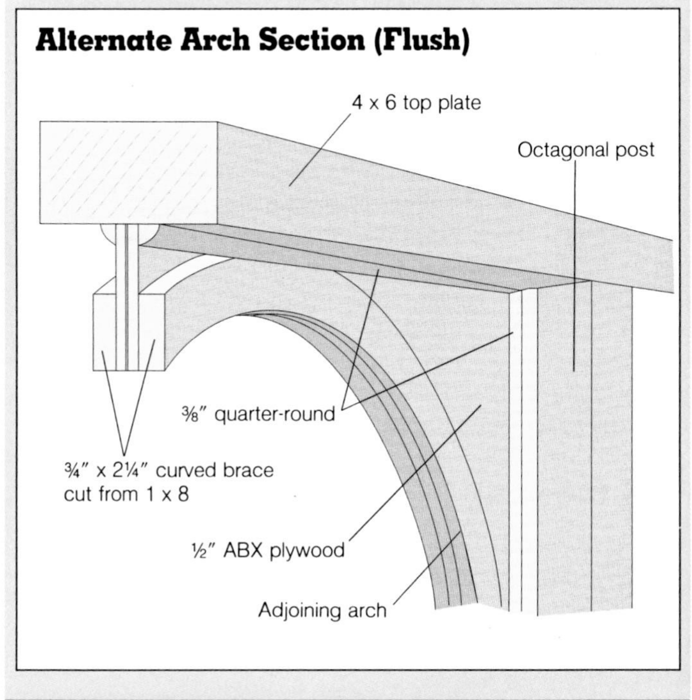

To install the 2 by 6 tongue-and-groove decking, first cut one end of each piece to the correct miter. The angle on the wide face of the board is 19 degrees (4⅛ and 12 on the framing square); the circular saw should be set to cut a 15-degree bevel. It's easiest to install three or four boards at a time, with two 10d nails in each end, then trim the uncut ends in place before proceeding. Be careful to place nails so that you won't cut through them when you trim the decking to length. When you get close to the top, drill pilot holes for the nails to avoid splitting the short pieces of decking.

Roof the gazebo with the shingles of your choice. Cover the hips with a wood cap shaped from a 2 by 4, or use special hip-and-ridge shingles.

## Railings

This gazebo has a simple board-and-rail type of railing, with a decorative pattern jigsawn into the edges of the boards. The tulip motif shown is only a sample of the many possibilities for this kind of railing. Copy other examples, or use your imagination if you'd like to try something different.

Build railings for seven sides of the gazebo as shown in the drawings on page 90. Assemble them with 6d HDG finish nails. Cut notches in the posts for the 2 by 4 cap rails, ⅝ inch deep, and slide the rails into place from the outside. Toenail them in with 16d finish nails.

## Finishing Touches

Except for painting, the gazebo is complete at this point. Caulk any open joints, sand any rough spots, and putty the nail and screw heads. Give the gazebo a coat of primer and two coats of enamel. Here's a tip: It's a lot easier to paint some parts before they're installed, especially the items you'd have to paint overhead, such as the rafters and roof decking.

## Materials List

| Description | | Material/Size | Length | Quantity |
|---|---|---|---|---|
| Foundation | Footings | concrete | — | 1 cu yd |
| | Post bases | 6×6 post or column base | — | 8 ea |
| Framing | Posts and hub (use longer pieces for gazebo on wood deck) | 6×6 | 8′<br>10′ | 7 ea<br>1 ea |
| | Top plates | 4×6 | 12′ | 4 ea |
| | Rafters | 3×6 | 10′ | 8 ea |
| | Roof sheathing | 2×6 T&G decking | RL | 380 l.f. |
| | Finial | 5″ dia | — | 1 ea |
| Arches | Plywood | ½″ ABX | 4×8 sh | 2 ea |
| | Solid-wood arches | 1×8 | RL | 120 l.f. |
| | Moldings | ⅜″ quarter-round | RL | 130 l.f. |
| Railings | Top and bottom rails | 1×3 | 10′ | 16 ea |
| | Board infill | 1×8 | 12′ | 10 ea |
| | Cap rails | 2×4 | 10′ | 4 ea |
| Roofing | Underlayment | 15-lb roofing felt | — | 1 roll |
| | Roofing | shingles, type as choosen | — | — |
| | Ridge caps | 2×4 rwd or cedar* | 10′ | 8 ea |
| Hardware, miscellaneous | Post-base bolts | as required by mfg | — | — |
| | Straps | 12″ plate strap | — | 8 ea |
| | Angle clips | 2½″ | — | 16 ea |
| | Glue | powdered brown glue | — | 1 lb |
| | Screws | 2″ drywall screw<br>4″ drywall screw | —<br>— | 2 lb<br>1½ lb |
| | Nails | 10d box or sinker<br>16d HDG finish<br>6d HDG finish | —<br>—<br>— | 10 lb<br>2 lb<br>2 lb |
| | Assorted metal fasteners as per text | | | |

*or other naturally durable species
See page 105 for materials list abbreviations.

# SCREENED SUMMERHOUSE

*The traditional screened summerhouse was initially developed to cope with the insect problem inherent in many areas of the world. This version, with its wide eaves and raised cupola roof, is a shady, airy, and bug-proof retreat. Its screen panels are removable for easy repairs and off-season storage.*

## Foundation

This summerhouse can be built on a concrete slab or a wood deck. (See page 57 for information on how to construct a concrete slab.) If you build on a wood deck, you may want to extend the deck surface beyond the walls of the summerhouse to provide more room for outdoor activities; if this is the case, make provisions to support the structure with footings, girders, and joists located under the summerhouse walls. Consult the building department to determine local requirements.

## Wall Framing

To frame the walls, first cut the pressure-treated (PT) sill plates to length. Drill for anchor bolts if you are building on a slab; if building on a deck, the walls can be screwed to the decking after they're erected. Cut the 4 by 4 posts to length (7 feet, 10½ inches) and notch their upper ends for the 2 by 4 beam that wraps around the top of the walls. Cut the 2 by 4 beams to length, and miter the ends. Tack together the sill plate and 2 by 4 beam for each wall and mark the locations of posts on both pieces.

Assemble the first wall flat on the floor. Nail the sill plate to each post with three 16d HDG nails, and nail the 2 by 4 beam to the notched ends of the posts with two 16d HDG nails. Then frame in the short sections of wall between posts. Raise the wall into position, and brace it temporarily. Lean out the top of the wall enough to allow the 2 by 4 beams of adjacent walls to clear when they are lifted into place. Frame the other three walls in the same way. Remove the temporary bracing, one wall at a time, and nail the corners together with 16d sinker nails.

Install temporary bracing to hold the summerhouse corners plumb, and apply the plywood siding to the lower portion of the walls. This plywood is the permanent bracing that keeps the building standing upright.

Install the 2 by 6 blocks between posts at the top of the walls, toenailed to the posts and facenailed to the 2 by 4 beams as shown on page 95. Besides reinforcing the 2 by 4s,

## Perspective View

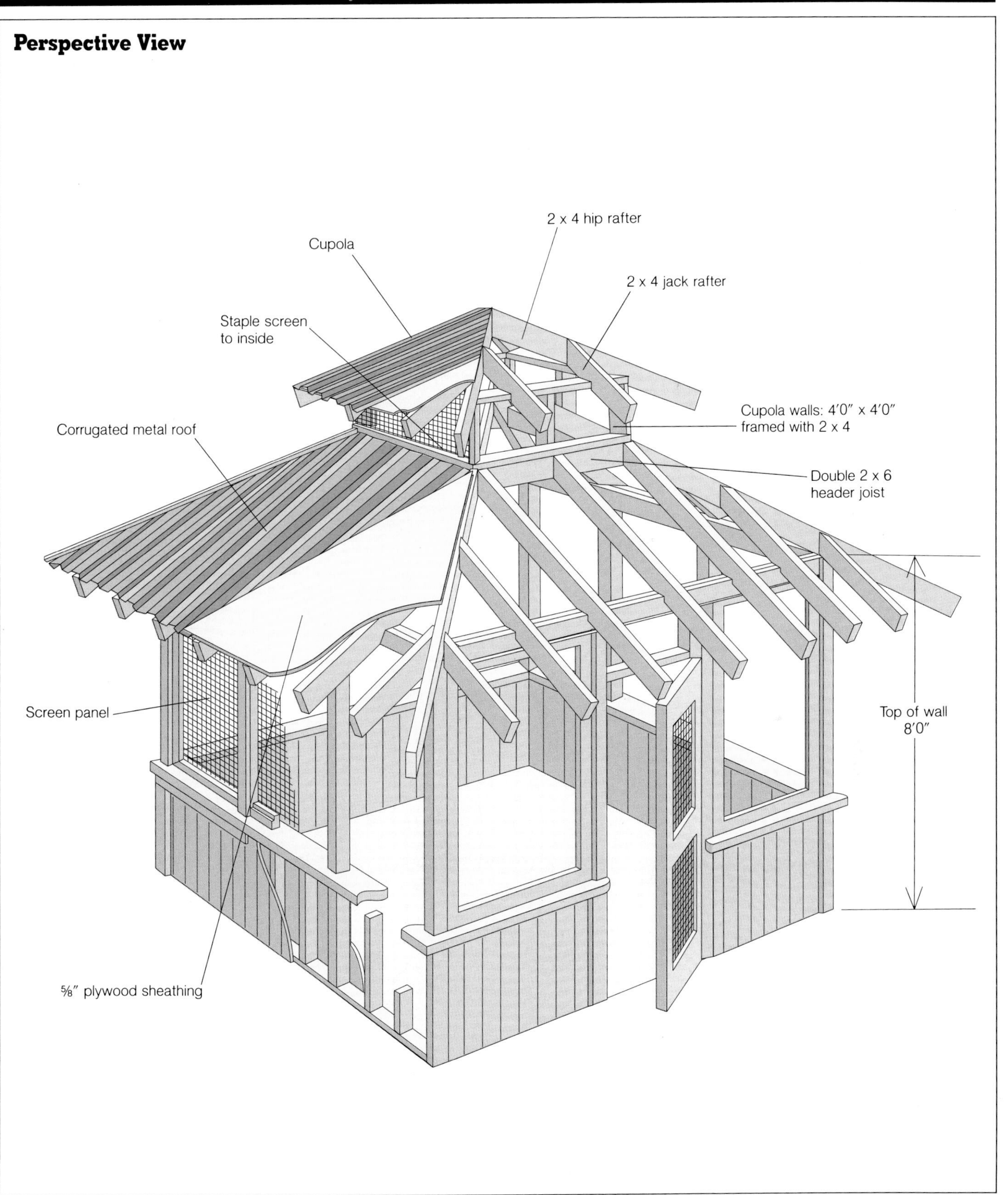

these blocks will support the upper edge of the screen panels.

## Roof Framing

There are actually two roofs on this summerhouse: the main roof, and a raised cupola that sits atop its peak. The main roof is somewhat unusual in that only the hip rafters run all the way to the peak; the common rafters are supported by doubleheader joists, which also support the cupola roof above (see page 95).

Begin by cutting all the rafters according to the rafter diagrams. Note that two of the four hip rafters for each roof are cut ¾ inch shorter than the others. This is so the longer rafters can be toenailed to each other, with the shorter pair nailed to the sides of the first two. For a more detailed discussion of hip-roof cutting, see page 62.

Install the four main hip rafters first; then use one of the common rafters to locate the position of the doubleheader joists. Next, cut and install the doubleheaders; when in place, they should form a square 4 feet across at the outside. Install the remaining rafters as shown, and nail on the roof sheathing.

It's easiest to build the cupola on the ground as a complete unit, including sheathing and screens. You can then lift it up onto the roof and fasten it to the framing (see page 96).

**Lower-Wall Detail**

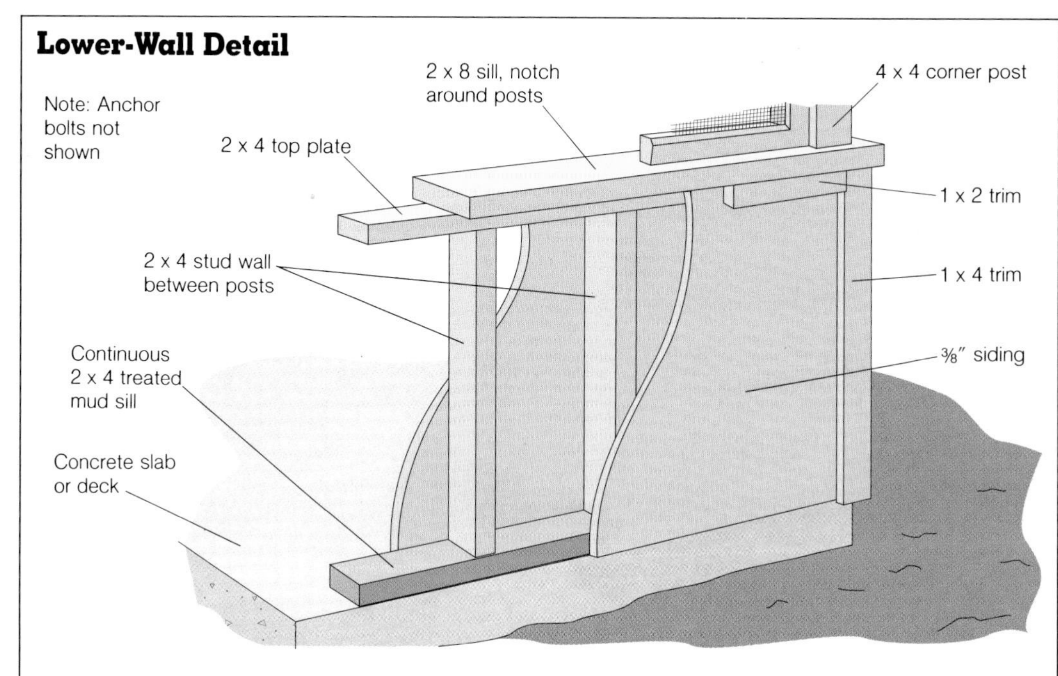


**Roof Framing**

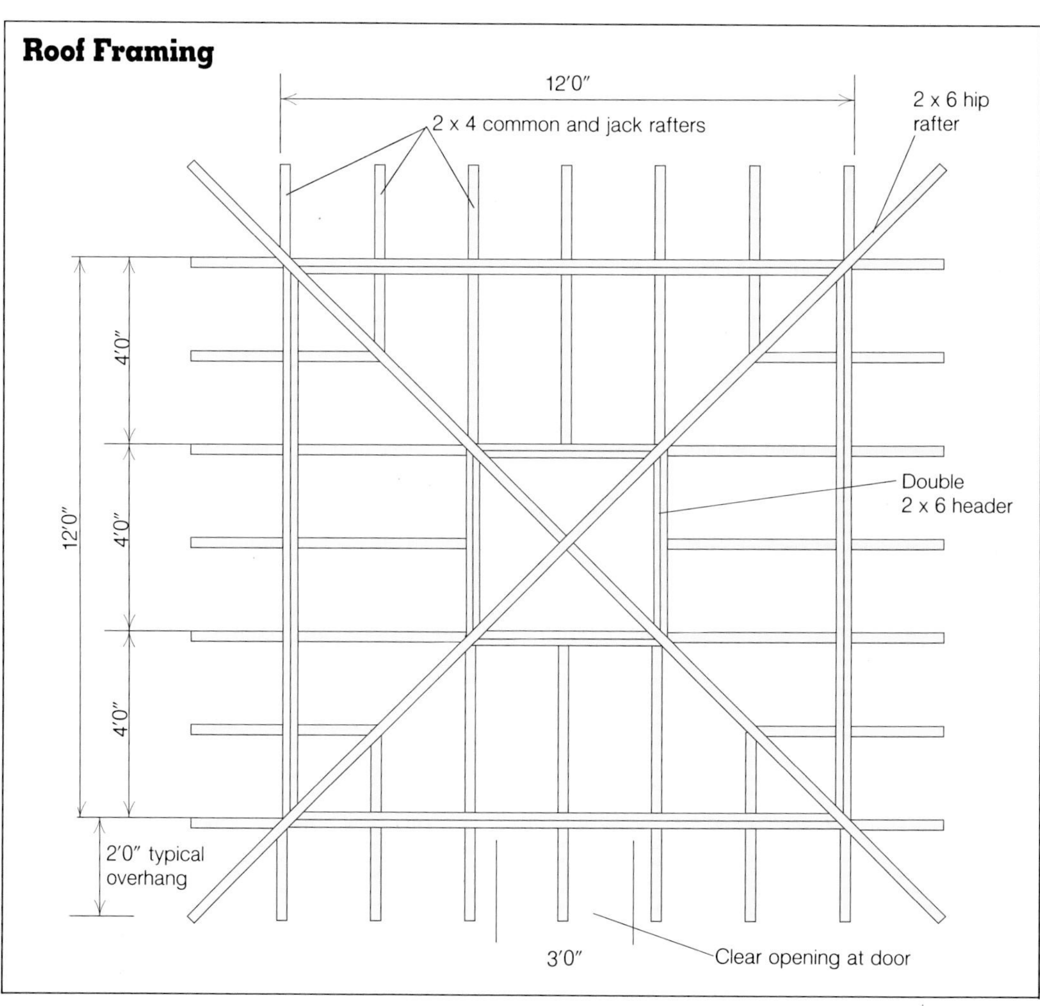

## Upper-Wall Detail

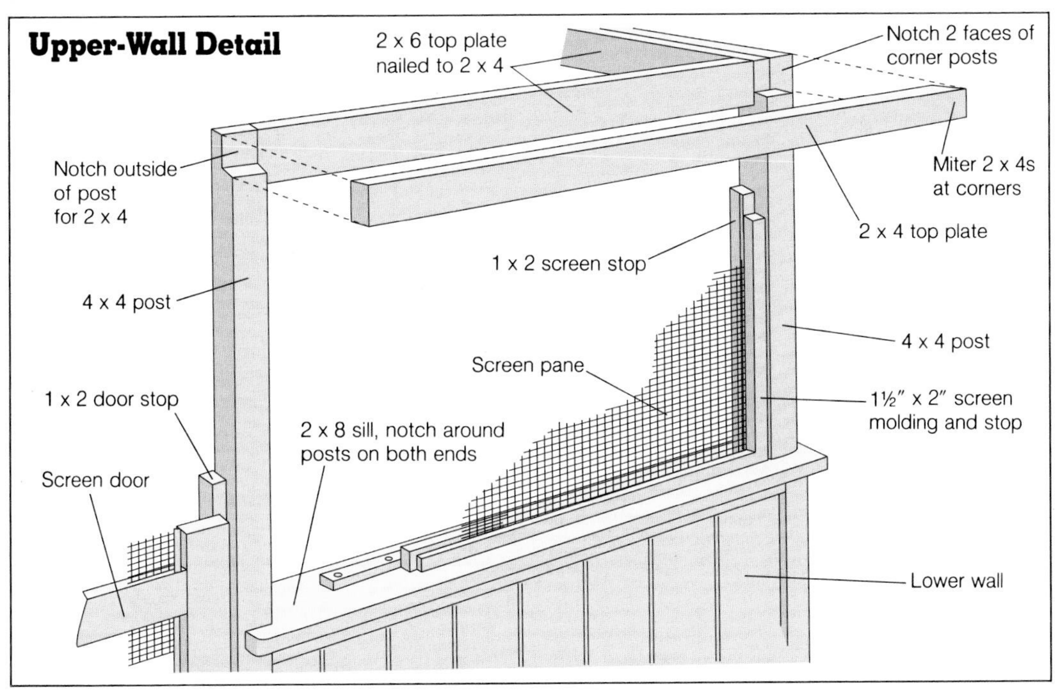

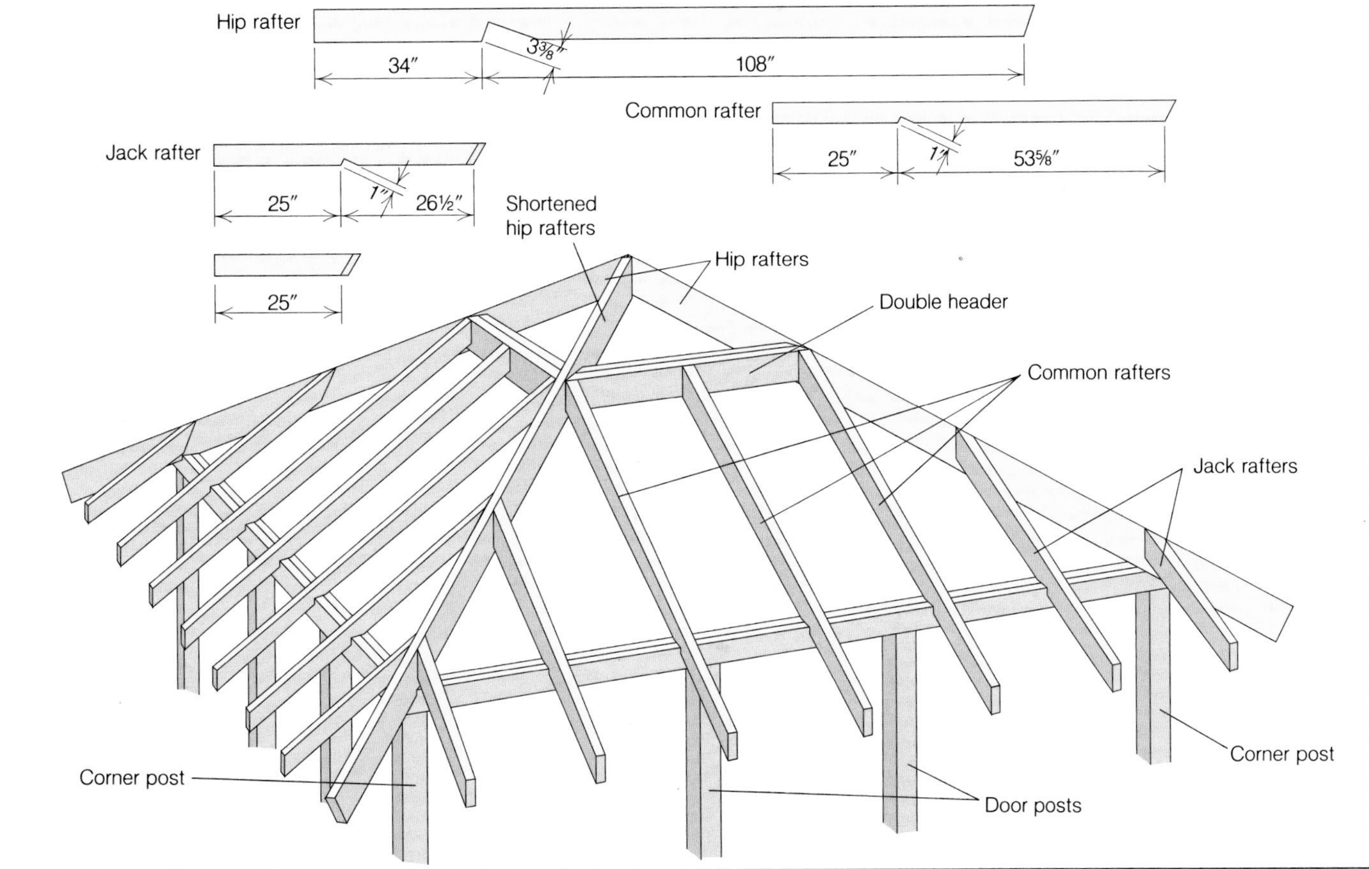

## Roofing

The summerhouse shown here has corrugated metal roofing to give it the feel of a rustic outbuilding, but any kind of roofing will do, so long as it is appropriate to the building and its surroundings. If you use metal roofing, the supplier should also be able to furnish the sheet-metal hip caps and any special fasteners that you might need.

## Windowsills and Trim

The low walls around this summerhouse are capped with 2 by 8 sills, which serve to cover the framing and plywood edges and

## Main Roof and Rafter Diagrams

Hip rafter
3⅜"
34"
108"
Common rafter
1"
25"
53⅝"
Jack rafter
1"
25"
26½"
Shortened
hip rafters
25"
Hip rafters
Double header
Common rafters
Jack rafters
Corner post
Corner post
Door posts

### Cupola Roof Detail

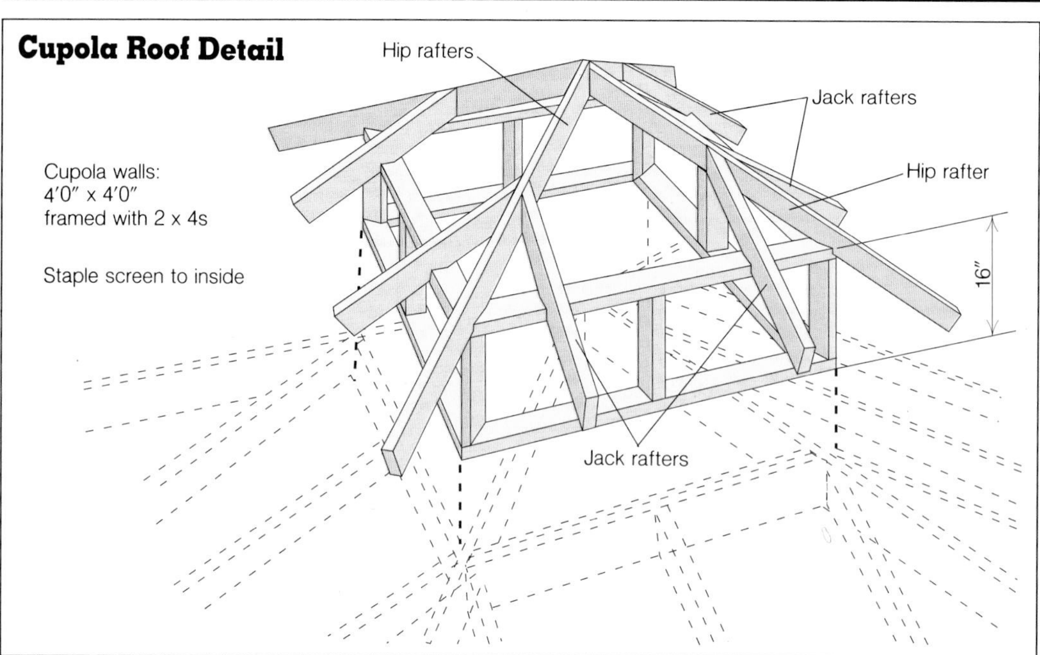


provide a convenient place to set a tall glass of something cool. Install the sills in sections, notched around the posts. Cut the notches with a saber saw. A bit of custom fitting may be necessary, especially if some of the posts have become twisted or out of square.

Install the 1 by 4 corner trim, the 1 by 2 trim strips under the windowsills, and the 1 by 2 screen stops on the posts. Nail a 2 by 4 between the posts that form the door opening, with its bottom edge 6 feet, 8½ inches above the floor; and install 1 by 2 stops for the door and the small screen panel in the opening above it.

### Cupola Roof Rafters

Cut rafters from 2 x 4s

Hip rafter (4)

17″ — 1″ — 36″

Jack rafter (8)

Shorten two by ¾″

Bevel at 45° angle

12½″ — 1″ — 13″

## Screen Panels

The screen panels are built like picture frames, with the screen held in place by a vinyl spline in a groove, as shown below. Begin by ripping the frame stock to width from 1½-inch-thick material. Cut a rabbet on one corner of all the frame pieces (save the scraps—they will be used later to cover the screen splines). Note that the

### Windowsill Detail

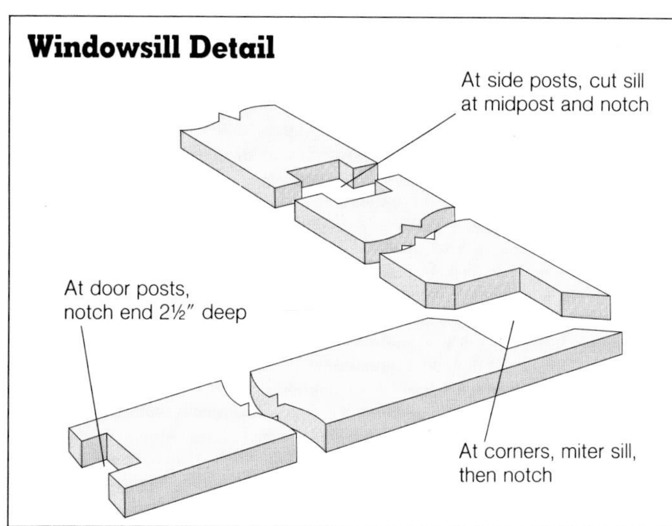


### Screen-Panel Detail

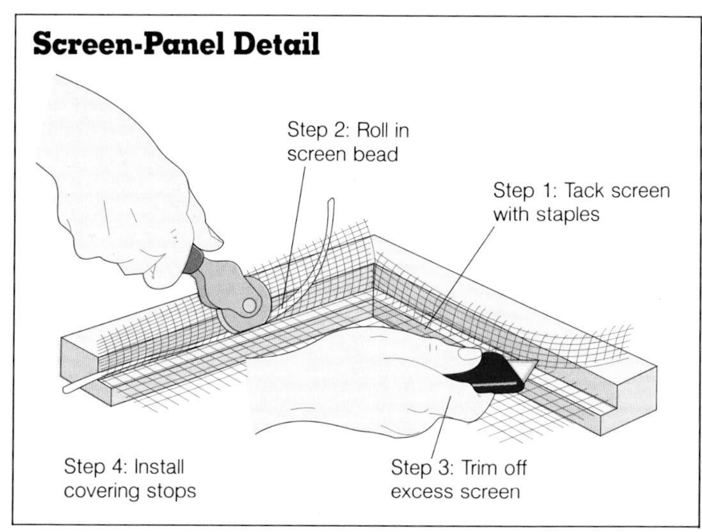

saw blade is set so that it leaves a ¼-inch-deep groove in the corner of the rabbet. Measure each opening in the summerhouse walls and cut the screen frames to fit. They will probably vary in size a little; number the parts so they won't get mixed up.

Although metal insect screen is stiffer and somewhat tougher than the fiberglass variety, fiberglass is easier to work with and its neutral color is less obtrusive than metal. The vinyl spline that holds the screen into the groove is available in several diameters. You may have to experiment to find the size that best fits the groove cut by your saw blade. For a saw with a ⅛-inch-thick blade, a ⁵⁄₃₂-inch spline is about right.

Cut the screen approximately 1 inch larger than the frame opening all around, and tack it into the frame rabbet with staples at the corners. Use a screen-splining tool (available at most hardware stores) to roll in the spline, working from opposite sides of the panel to stretch the screen evenly. Trim off excess screen with a sharp knife, and install the covering stops with ¾-inch brads.

Install the screen panels with 3-inch deck screws through the edge of the frames into the posts. If a screen gets damaged, it's a simple matter to remove the panel, pry off the covering stops, and replace the screen.

Unless you are feeling especially industrious, do not bother trying to build your own screen door. It's not easy to make one that won't sag, and factory-built doors are not expensive. This summerhouse is designed for a 3-foot-wide by 6-foot, 8-inch-high door. Install it with a door closer so you won't have to shut it manually.

## Materials List

| Description | | Material/Size | Length | Quantity |
|---|---|---|---|---|
| Framing | Sills | 2×4 PT | 12′ | 4 ea |
| | Posts | 4×4 | 8′ | 12 ea |
| | Beams & blocks | 2×4<br>2×6 | 12′<br>12′ | 4 ea<br>4 ea |
| | Hip rafters | 2×6 | 12′ | 4 ea |
| | Short walls; hip, common, jack rafters; blocking | 2×4 | RL | 420 l.f. |
| | Rafter headers | 2×6 | 8′ | 4 ea |
| | Roof sheathing | ⅝″ BCX plywd | 4×8 | 16 sh |
| Roofing | Corrugated metal roofing w/hip caps and fasteners | — | — | 250 s.f. |
| Sills, siding, and trim | Windowsills | 2×8 rwd or cedar* | 14′ | 4 ea |
| | Siding | ⅜″ plywd siding | 4×8 sh | 4 sh |
| | Corner trim | 1×4 | 8′ | 4 ea |
| | Sill trim, stops | 1×2 | RL | 280 l.f. |
| Screen panels | Frames | cut from 2×6 | 10′ | 12 ea |
| | Screen | fiberglass insect screen | 4′ width | 70 l.f. |
| | Spline | vinyl screen spline | — | 250 l.f. |
| | Screen door | 3′0″×6′8″ screen door w/hardware | — | 1 ea |
| Hardware | Nails | 16d sinker<br>8d sinker<br>16d HDG<br>10d HDG<br>6d HDG | —<br>—<br>—<br>—<br>— | 10 lb<br>5 lb<br>2 lb<br>2 lb<br>4 lb |
| | Mounting screws for screens | 3″ deck screw | — | 2 lb |
| | Assorted metal fasteners as per text | | | |

*or other naturally durable species

See page 105 for materials list abbreviations.

# SKYLIGHT GAZEBO

*This is a gazebo your plants will thrive in. It's roofed like a greenhouse, with clear acrylic glazing that provides shelter from the elements while letting in light and a view of trees and sky. A solid railing built around the gazebo walls serves as a backrest for a wraparound bench that seats people as well as potted plants.*

## Foundation

This gazebo can be built on a patio or wood deck. (See page 86 for techniques involved in laying out an octagon and setting up post bases.) This gazebo is 10 feet across, or 49⅝ inches on a side. Note that the posts are set in from the corners of the octagon 1½ inches (see page 100). This is so the framing constructed above will accommodate a standard-sized skylight in the center of the roof.

## Post-and-Beam Framing

Begin construction by cutting the posts to length, making sure they will all be the same height at the top (7 feet above the floor). Install the metal post caps and erect the posts with temporary bracing.

Cut the two main 4 by 8 beams to length (11 feet, 4 inches), and chamfer their ends. Set them into the post caps, with an equal overhang on each end, and nail them in place. Use string lines pulled across the remaining posts to lay out the intersections where the 4 by 8 beams mount to the main beams. Cut the four projecting beams to length (3 feet, 8¾ inches), chamfered on one end, and cut the two 4 by 8s that fit between the main beams. Toenail these beams in place temporarily; before fastening them permanently, check to make sure that everything is plumb, square, and parallel (adjust the temporary bracing if necessary). Install the metal plate straps across the tops of the short 4 by 8s and the metal framing clips where the beams meet (see page 100).

## Roof Framing

The roof is framed in three stages. First, a built-up plate is installed around the perimeter of the roof; then a 2 by 8 is wrapped around four short posts located over the intersections of the beams (this 2 by 8 acts both as a ledger to support the rafters and as a curb for the center skylight). Finally, rafters are installed from the plate to the 2 by 8 ledger as shown on page 101.

To install the built-up plate, start by cutting the double 2 by 4 plates; cut them so the pieces will overlap at the corners. When installed, they should

## Perspective View

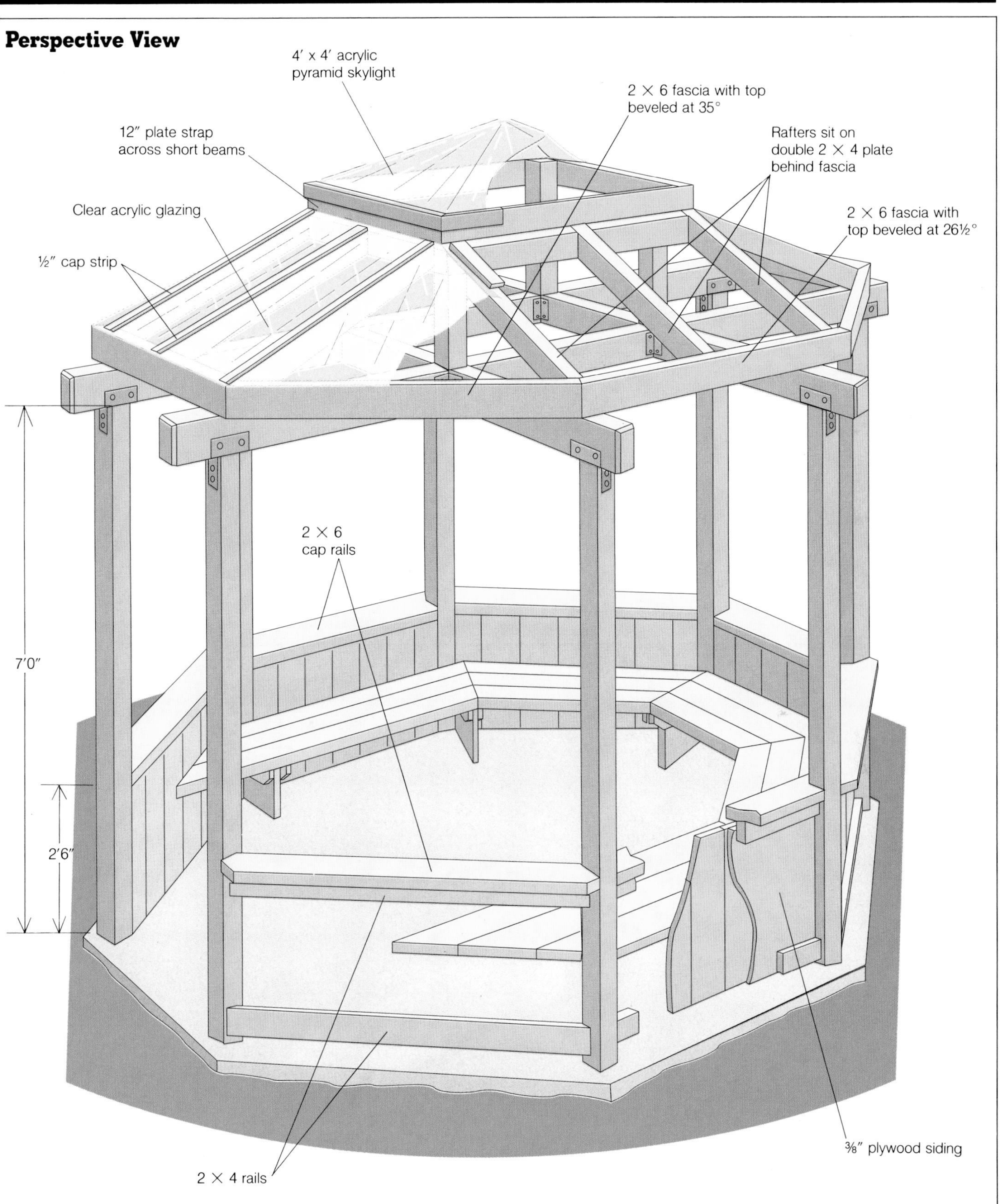

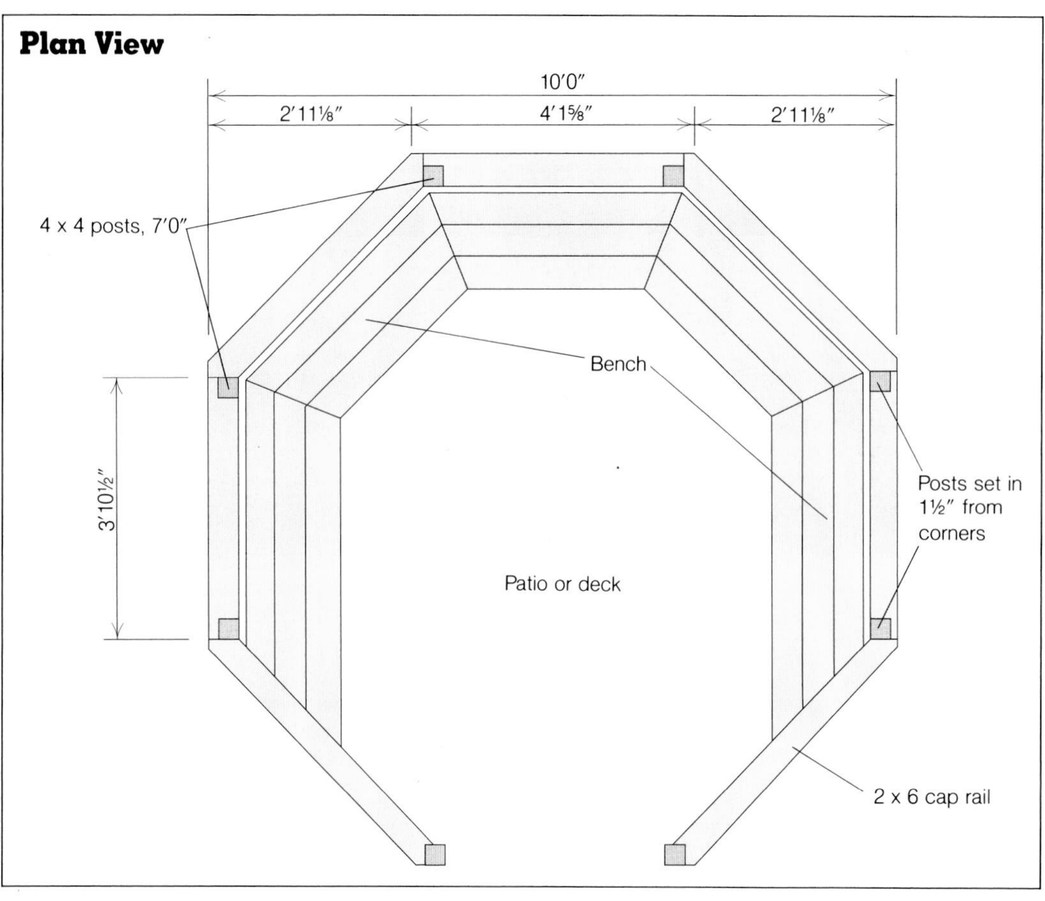


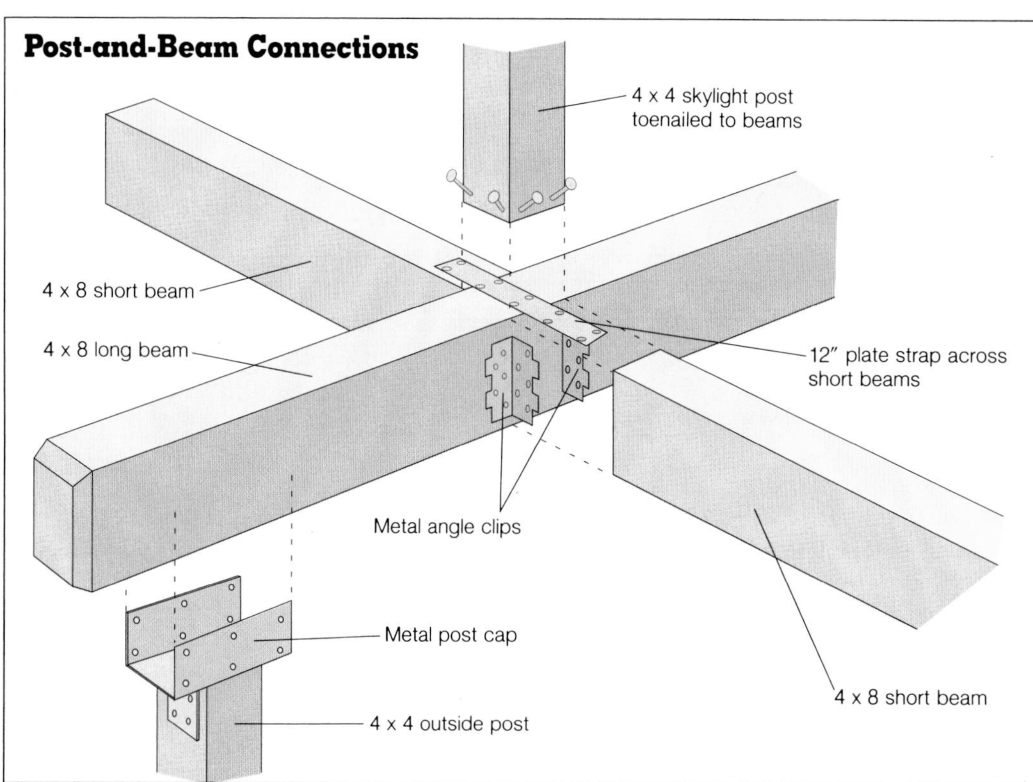


form an octagon that is 10 feet across and 49⅝ inches on a side. Keep the octagon centered on the beam layout when you fasten the plates to the beams. Then install the 2 by 6 fascia around the perimeter, mitering the corners. The sections of fascia that rest on the beams should be beveled 26½ degrees on top, and measure 4¾ inches wide on the outside face. The sections that span the corners are beveled at 35 degrees and measure 4¼ inches wide at the outside.

Next, install the four 4 by 4 posts over the beam intersections. These posts should be 26 inches long; toenail them to the 4 by 8s with two 8d nails on each side. Install the 2 by 8s around the posts, with their lower edges 18¾ inches above the beams. These 2 by 8s should form a square 49⅝ inches on a side (the skylight curb). Measure the diagonals in order to check for squareness.

Cut 12 rafters according to the rafter diagram on page 101. One edge of the rafters that face the triangular corners should be beveled 24 degrees to support the corner glazing. Nail the rafters in place and install beveled 2 by 4 blocking between them at the top.

## Roof Glazing

Acrylic glazing is available in a variety of sizes, thicknesses, and colors. For areas subject to intense sunlight, gray or bronze-tinted acrylic will reduce heat and glare; clear glazing is better for cool, shady

## Roof at Skylight Detail

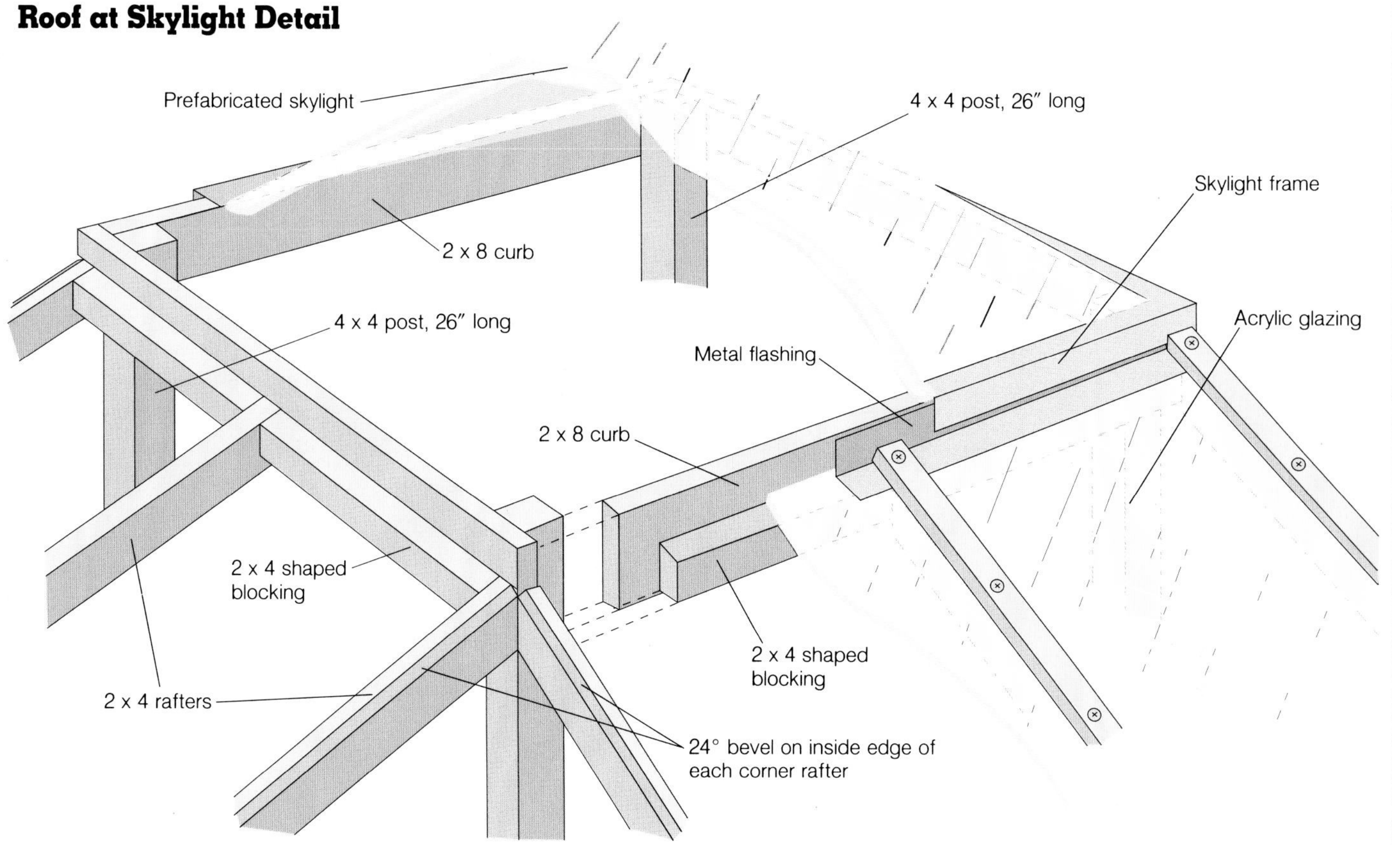

Prefabricated skylight
4 x 4 post, 26″ long
Skylight frame
2 x 8 curb
4 x 4 post, 26″ long
Acrylic glazing
Metal flashing
2 x 8 curb
2 x 4 shaped blocking
2 x 4 shaped blocking
2 x 4 rafters
24° bevel on inside edge of each corner rafter

## Rafter Diagram

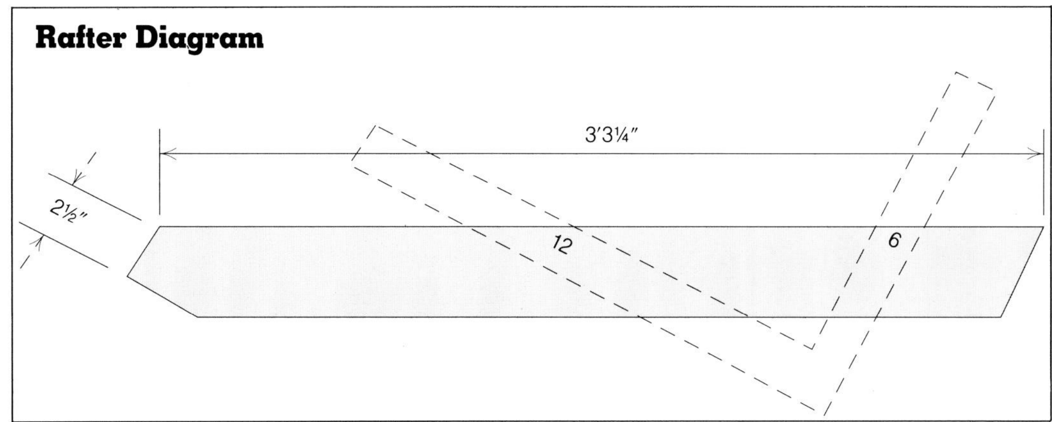


spots. The 3/16-inch thickness shown in the drawings is suitable for areas with a temperate climate, but if you anticipate snow on the roof you should use ¼-inch (or thicker) panels.

The plastic sheets come from the factory with a protective film of paper or plastic on both sides. This film should be left on to prevent scratching and scuffing while the sheets are cut and drilled; peel off the protective layer just before installing the individual panels.

Plastics expand and contract with temperature changes more than most building materials. For instance, a temperature variation of 80 degrees will cause a 4-foot-wide panel to move more than ⅛ inch. Therefore, provisions must be made to allow for normal movement. When installing the panels, fasten each one to the framing with two galvanized wallboard screws near the top edge, no more than a foot apart, and leave a gap of about ¼ inch between adjacent panels.

Joints in the roof are sealed with ½-inch-wide by ⅛-inch-thick glazing tape, available from glass suppliers. Glazing tape is a heavy, self-adhesive caulk with a peel-off paper

### Skylight Glazing Detail

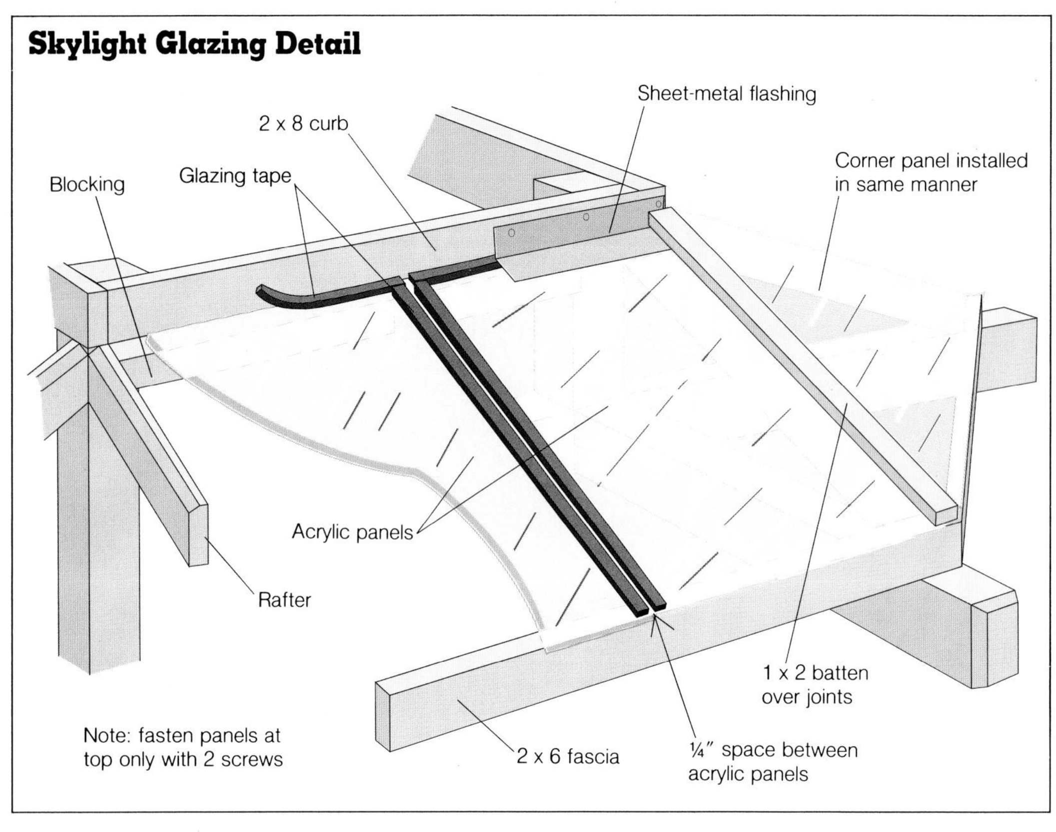


backing on one side; it's easier to use than caulk from a tube and is much less messy. Run a strip of the tape along the top and down both sides of each panel. Peel off the backing, and press the skylight curb flashing into the caulk. Overlap the flashing at the corners, and nail it to the curb with 8d HDG nails. Install the 1 by 2 battens over the rafters with screws that are driven into the space between glazing panels, as shown at left.

Install the center skylight last. Although these plans show one that is pyramid shaped, the bubble type will work just as well. The gazebo is designed so that most manufacturers' standard 4-foot by 4-foot units will fit the skylight curb. Verify the recommended curb size for the skylight you

### Railing and Bench Detail

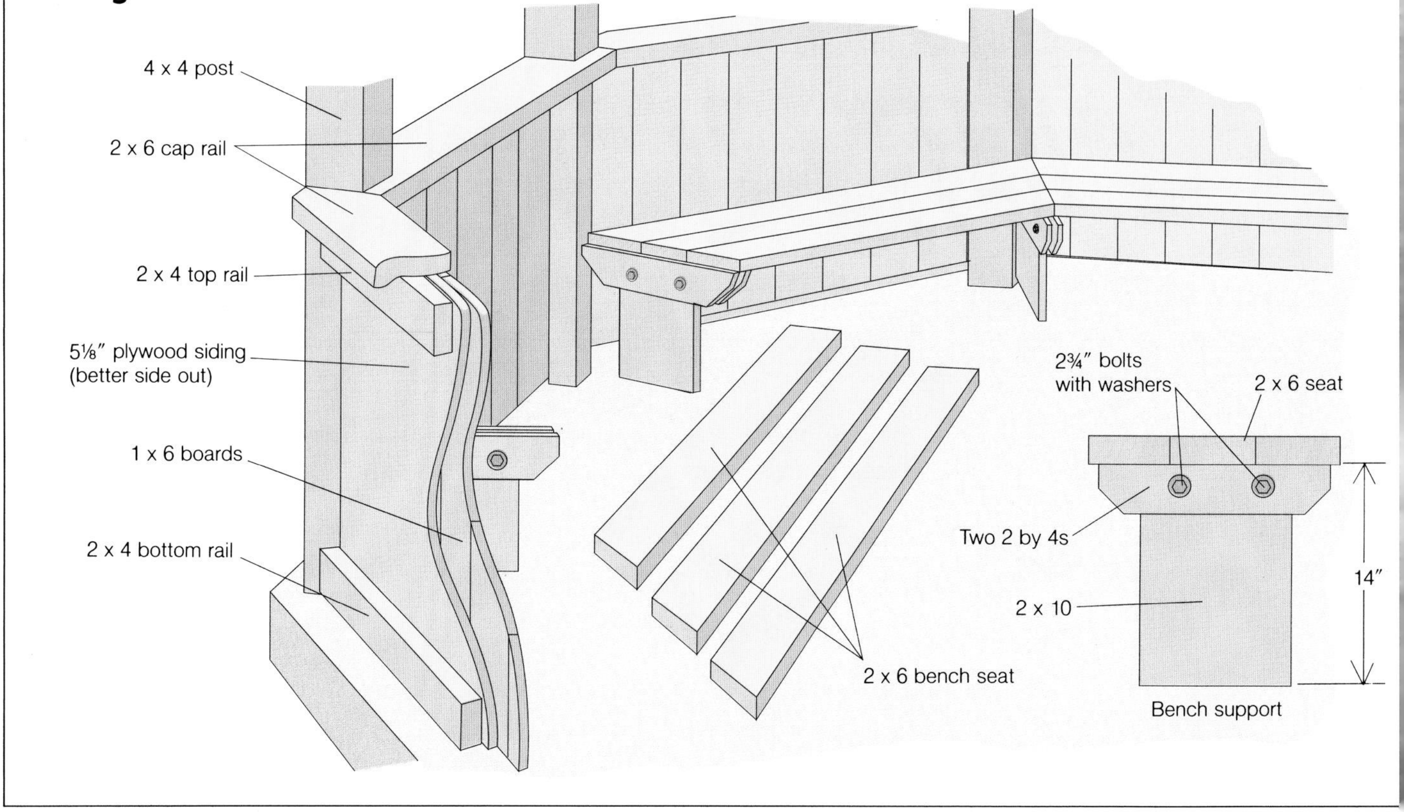

4 x 4 post
2 x 6 cap rail
2 x 4 top rail
5⅛″ plywood siding (better side out)
1 x 6 boards
2 x 4 bottom rail
2¾″ bolts with washers
2 x 6 seat
Two 2 by 4s
14″
2 x 10
2 x 6 bench seat
Bench support

purchase—you may have to adjust the framing layout to accommodate a special size.

## Railings and Benches

The railings for this gazebo consist of plywood siding panels over 2 by 4 horizontal rails, with vertical 1 by 6 boards nailed over the plywood on the inside of the railing. The plywood panels act as braces, strengthening the structure against wind loads. Install them with the better side facing out, fastened to the posts and rails with 1⅝-inch wallboard or deck screws every 6 inches. Install the cap rail and the 1 by 6 boards on the inside of the railing—these cover the top edge and the rough side of the plywood.

A low bench wraps around five sides of this gazebo. (See page 102 for construction details.) Install bench supports at each corner. On a deck, the 2 by 10 uprights can usually be bolted to the deck framing; if you're building on a slab, fasten the uprights to the concrete with metal brackets.

## Maintenance

Periodic cleaning will keep the skylight roof looking bright and clear. Wash acrylic surfaces with a sponge or soft cloth, using a mild soap or detergent solution and plenty of water. Although you can use naphtha or kerosene to clean up excess caulk and other smudges, avoid commercial window cleaners and other solvents—they may react chemically with the acrylic surface and cause clouding or discoloration.

## Materials List

| Description | | Material/Size | Length | Quantity |
|---|---|---|---|---|
| Framing | Posts | 4×4 | 8′<br>10′ | 8 ea<br>1 ea |
| | Beams | 4×8 | 12′ | 4 ea |
| | Plates/rafters | 2×4 | 10′ | 14 ea |
| | Ledgers or curbs | 2×8 | 10′ | 2 ea |
| | Fascia | 2×6 | 10′ | 4 ea |
| Roof | Prefabricated skylight | 4′×4′ pyramid or dome type of skylight | — | 1 ea |
| | Acrylic panels | 3/16″ acrylic sheet | 4′×8′<br>5′×5′ | 2 sh<br>1 sh |
| | Flashing | 2½″×2″ L-flashing | — | 20 l.f. |
| | Battens | 1×2 rwd or cedar* | 8′ | 6 ea |
| | Glazing tape | ⅛″×½″ tape | — | 100 l.f. |
| Railings, benches | Rails | 2×4 rwd or cedar*<br>2×6 rwd or cedar* | 10′<br>10′ | 9 ea<br>4 ea |
| | Siding | ⅜″ plywd siding | 4×8 sh | 3 sh |
| | Paneling (inside of railing) | 1×6 rwd or cedar | RL | 200 l.f. |
| | Bench supports | 2×10 | 10′ | 1 ea |
| | Bench tops | 2×6 decking | 10′ | 9 ea |
| Hardware | Post caps | 4×4 post or column cap | — | 8 ea |
| | Plate straps | 1¼″×15″ | — | 4 ea |
| | Angle brackets | 5″ long | — | 16 ea |
| | Bench support bolts | ⅜″×5½″ carriage bolt | — | 12 ea |
| | Nails | 16d HDG<br>8d HDG | —<br>— | 10 lb<br>3 lb |
| | Screws | 1⅝″ galv wallboard screw<br>2½″ deck screw | —<br>— | 2 lb<br>1 lb |

*or other naturally durable species
See page 105 for materials list abbreviations.

# ATERIALS, TOOLS, AND TECHNIQUES

*This section is designed to work in conjunction with the plan instructions in this book by providing more-detailed information on the subjects of construction materials, tools, building techniques, and basic tricks of the trade.*

## Materials

Wood and concrete are the primary materials used in the construction of nearly all outdoor shelters. Following are detailed descriptions of the various types of wood available and their suitability for these structures; and an explanation of the properties of concrete and how it should be handled.

### Wood

By virtue of its strength, versatility, and appearance, wood is the material of choice for most outdoor structures. Pound for pound, wood is nearly as strong as steel. It is easy to cut, shape, and join together with basic tools. And with proper maintenance, it can be long lasting, too—some wood structures in Europe and Japan are more than eight hundred years old and still going strong.

Lumber is available in a bewildering array of grades and species. The confusion is compounded by the different rules and markings for grading different types of wood. What follows is a field guide to lumberyard wood products.

#### Pressure-Treated Lumber

Wood that has been chemically treated to resist insects and decay is called pressure treated, or PT. A preservative is forced deep into the pores of the wood with pressure, where it binds chemically to the cell structure of the wood. The process is very effective—test stakes driven into the ground more than forty years ago still show no signs of decay.

Treated lumber is ideal for any location where wood comes in contact with the ground or with a concrete foundation. Depending on the amount of preservative used, pressure-treated wood is rated for ground contact (suitable for direct-burial uses, such as fence posts) or above-grade use (for bottom plates of walls, sills, framing members within 6 inches of the ground, and similar applications).

One drawback of pressure-treated lumber is the greenish tint imparted to the wood by the treatment process. If the wood will be exposed, it is usually stained or painted to conceal the factory color. Some manufacturers offer brown-tinted wood.

#### Decay-Resistant Species

Some types of trees have an inherent preservative (usually tannic acid) that protects them from decay. Only the darker heartwood from the center of the tree contains this natural preserving agent, though; the lighter-colored sapwood is not rot-resistant. Redwood, cypress, and some (but not all) species of cedar are the most common types of decay-resistant lumber.

Because of their beautiful coloration and excellent weathering properties, these woods are highly desirable for outdoor structures. They are also more expensive and are usually restricted to siding, railings, trim, and other uses where appearance and durability outweigh the higher cost.

#### Structural Lumber

This type of lumber can be made of nearly any species, usually a softwood. Douglas fir and southern yellow pine are the most common, but larch, spruce, hemlock, and other kinds of pine predominate in some regions.

Structural lumber is sold either surfaced or rough-sawn. Surfaced lumber is available in all grades and is used for posts, beams, studs, rafters, and other framing members. Rough-sawn lumber may not be available in every grade, but its coarse, natural texture and somewhat thicker dimensions make it a sensible choice for many outdoor structures.

Every piece of structural lumber is marked with a grade stamp. This stamp includes the name of the mill where the wood was processed, the initials of the grading agency, the wood species, an indication of whether the wood is unseasoned (S-grn) or kiln-dried (S-dry), and the structural grade of the lumber.

**Standard Lumber**

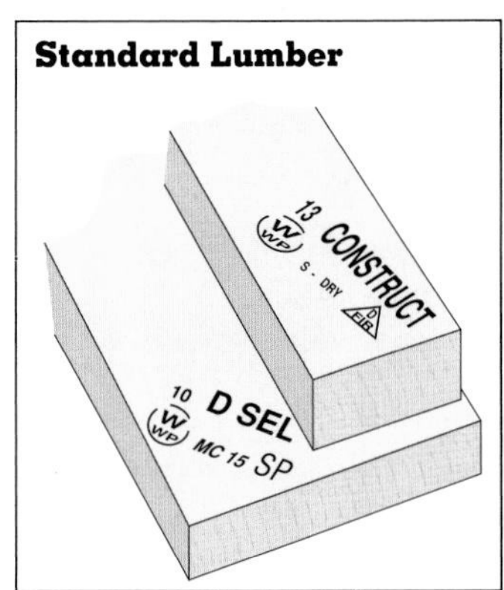


**Pressure-Treated Lumber**

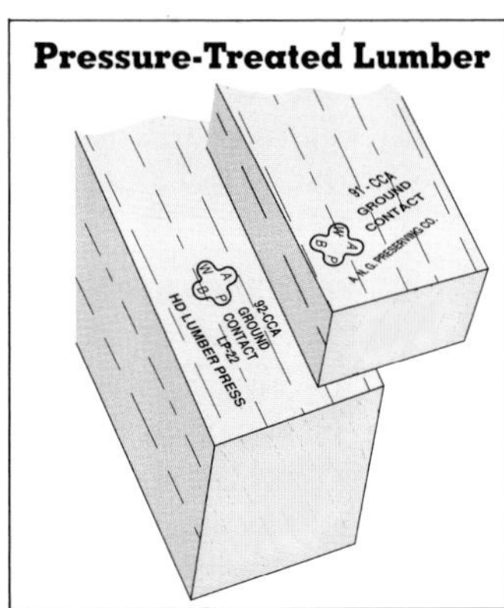


**Plywood**

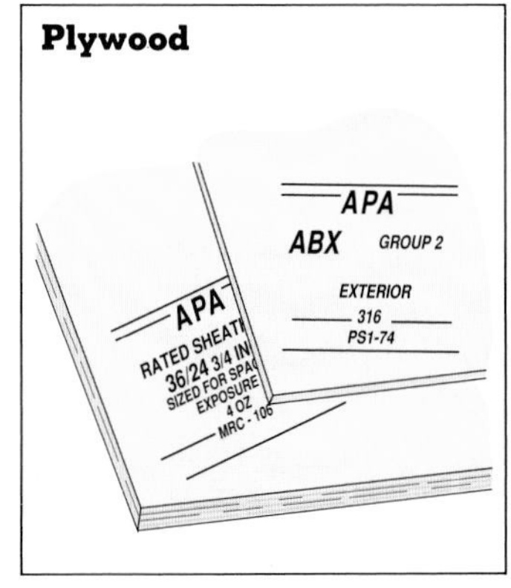


Grades for 2 by 4s and 4 by 4s range from utility (low grade), to standard (medium grade), to construction (better grade). There are as many as 10 possible grades for 2 by 6s and larger, but for practical purposes three will do. In ascending order, these are: grade 2

lumber, for general-purpose construction; grade 1, for situations where strength, appearance, and resistance to warping and twisting are considerations; and select structural, where extra strength is critical. As one might expect, the better grades are more expensive.

**Finish Lumber**

Used for outdoor construction, finish lumber is nearly always from softwood (evergreen) species. It is usually kiln-dried to control shrinkage and other seasoning defects, and is available only in thicknesses of 2 inches or less.

Where finish lumber will be exposed to the weather and simply stained or left unpainted, decay-resistant woods are the best choice; painted trim and interior finish wood can be of any species.

Different types of finish lumber are graded by different agencies, each with its own rules, so shop around to see what's available in your area.

**Plywood**

This multipurpose lumber is manufactured by laminating wood veneers into a sandwich, with the grain in alternating layers turned at 90 degrees. This results in a panel with great strength and dimensional stability, ideal for floor and roof sheathing, wall bracing, and siding. The large panel size makes it easy to cover large areas quickly.

Structural plywood is graded on a scale from A to D, with A being the highest grade. Each sheet has a two-letter grade mark; the first letter indicates the quality of the front side of the sheet and the second letter the back. C-D interior plywood is commonly used for subfloors and roof sheathing where appearance is not a factor. A-B and B-C plywood panels are better where one side will show, as for the underside of exposed roof decking. Try to buy structural plywood that is marked "interior-exterior glue"; this means it will withstand exposure to wet conditions without delaminating.

Plywood siding is rated for continuous outdoor use. It usually comes with a saw-textured face, sometimes with a grooved pattern cut into the surface. Because it's easy to apply and provides excellent lateral bracing, it's a natural for covering the walls of sheds and gazebos.

Some composite type of panels are also useful in outdoor structures. Oriented strand board, made by fusing large wood chips into a solid sheet, can be substituted for structural plywood of the same thickness. Hardboard siding provides a relatively inexpensive wall covering for painted outbuildings.

## Abbreviations Used in Materials Lists

| | |
|---|---|
| ABX | a grade of plywood for exterior use |
| BCX | a grade of plywood for exterior use |
| bds | boards |
| comp | composition |
| const | construction |
| cu ft | cubic feet |
| cu yd | cubic yards |
| dia | diameter |
| ea | each |
| elev | elevated |
| ft | feet (also abbreviated: ') |
| galv | galvanized |
| HDG | hot-dipped galvanized |
| hgr | hanger (as in "joist hanger") |
| in. | inch (also abbreviated: ") |
| lb | pound(s) |
| l.f. | lineal feet |
| MB | machine bolt |
| min | minimum |
| mfg | manufacturer |
| (n) | with nut |
| (n/w) | with nut and washer [(n/2w) is nut and 2 washers] |
| OSB | oriented strand board |
| pc(s) | piece(s) |
| plywd | plywood |
| PT | pressure treated |
| RL | random lengths (specific lengths not required) |
| rwd | redwood |
| s.c. | solid-core (door) |
| s.f. | square feet |
| sh | sheet(s) |
| SMS | sheet-metal screw |
| std | standard |
| T&G | tongue and groove |
| (w) | with washer |

## Concrete

Most outdoor structures are built on concrete foundations, usually a flat slab or a series of individual footings. Concrete is a strong, versatile, and permanent material, easily worked and relatively inexpensive.

Concrete is sold by the cubic yard (27 cubic feet). Strength is determined by the number of sacks of cement per cubic yard. A 5-sack mix is usually adequate for most conditions. Special additives are available to modify the working properties of the mix, accelerate or retard setting time, or reduce water content. Of special interest in cold climates are air-entraining agents, which form microscopic bubbles in the concrete that serve to reduce cracking and frost damage.

Small batches of concrete (up to ½ cubic yard) are usually easiest to mix on site. You can either purchase premixed concrete in sacks, or buy the ingredients and mix them yourself.

Purchase larger loads of concrete from a concrete company and have it delivered in a ready-mix truck. If the truck can't back up to the site, the concrete will have to be moved in wheelbarrow loads. If this sounds like too much hard work, hire a concrete pumper to pump the concrete directly into the forms; this is worth the added cost for all but the smallest jobs. Most concrete-pumping outfits will even order the concrete and arrange delivery for you.

## Tools

You do not need a lot of fancy equipment to build an outdoor structure. A set of basic hand tools and two or three power tools are all you need. Purchase a few high-quality tools to start with, and rent or buy the ones you don't have as the need for them arises.

### Hand Tools

The core of the carpenter's tool kit are the hand tools, which can be roughly divided into layout tools, cutting tools, and fastening tools.

#### Block Plane

This is a small, compact plane about 6 inches long and 2 inches wide. It's ideal for rounding over sharp edges and shaving joints for a tight fit. Like chisels, planes must be kept sharp at all times.

#### Chalk Line

Basically, this is a reel of string in a box filled with powdered chalk. The string is stretched taut between two points and then plucked to produce a long, straight line.

#### Chisel

A chisel is used for chopping out waste wood, trimming joints, and mortising for door hardware. A 1-inch-wide chisel is good for starters; other sizes can be added as needed. Do not use a chisel as a paint-can opener or pry bar.

Chisels must be kept razor sharp to work effectively, so buy a sharpening stone and learn how to use it. Remember to sharpen only the bevel side; the back of the blade should be kept absolutely flat.

#### Claw Hammer

This type of hammer is used for driving and pulling nails. Framing hammers are relatively heavy and have a corrugated face to bite into the nail head; their use is restricted to rough carpentry where neatness doesn't count. Use a smooth-face hammer with a 16- to 20-ounce head for exposed work.

#### Combination Square

This adjustable device is used to mark 90- and 45-degree angles on a board for cutting. It is also useful to mark a line parallel to the edge of a board.

#### Framing Square

This tool is indispensible for marking out rafters and stairs, laying out walls, and squaring across wide boards. In the hands of an expert, it can lay out octagons, figure lumber quantities, calculate the hypotenuse of a right triangle, and perform several other arcane tricks.

#### Handsaw

Even if you do most of your cutting with a power saw, a handsaw is useful for reaching into places the power saw can't go, cutting into corners, and completing cuts in very thick lumber. Handsaws are designed for either crosscutting or ripping, and have varying

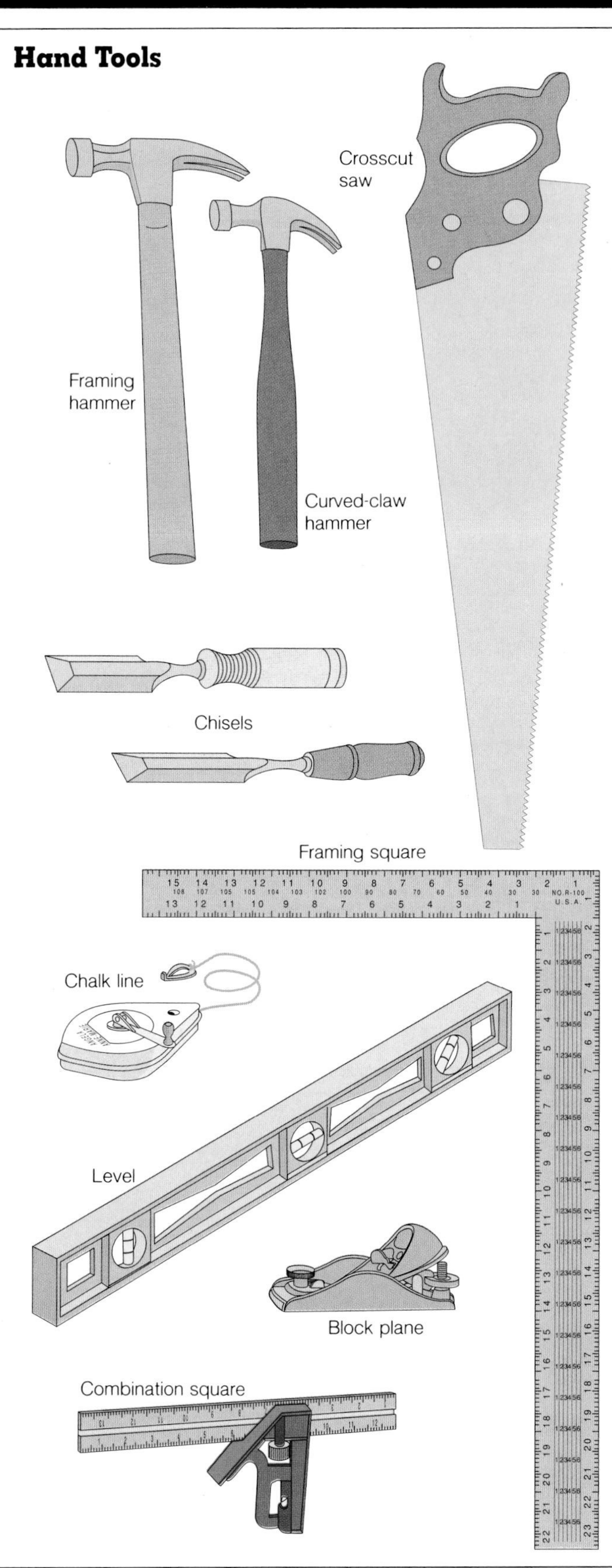

## Hand Tools

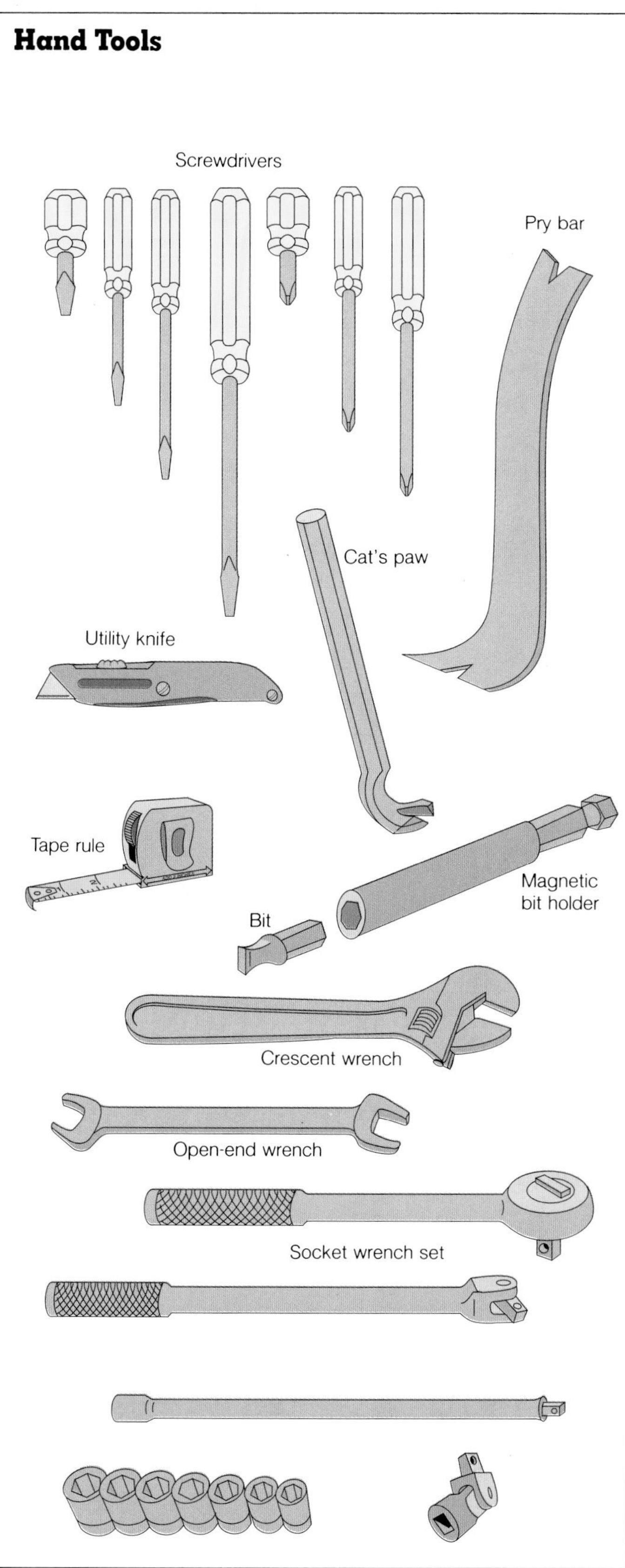


numbers of teeth, designated as points per inch. An 8- or 10-point crosscut saw is adequate for all-purpose work.

### Level

This tool is used to plumb and level foundations, walls, and the like by means of a bubble in a vial of liquid. A 4-foot level is suitable for general-purpose construction work.

Most levels have adjustable vials, which aren't always accurate, even on a new tool. To check accuracy, place the level against a door jamb or some other reasonably plumb surface; flip the level so the vial is turned end for end. If it reads differently, loosen the screws on the vial and adjust it until it reads the same in both positions.

### Pry Bar

This small crowbar is used for pulling nails, coaxing things into place, and disassembling mistakes. The best pry bars are made of spring steel, with slim ends for getting into tight spots. A cat's paw loosens nails and may be hit with a hammer.

### Screwdrivers

Everybody has a few of these lying around. If you have a lot of screws to drive, get a driver bit that can be used in a drill motor or cordless screwdriver.

### Tape Measure

For general construction, a self-rewinding tape 16 to 25 feet long is best, though tape measures are available in lengths from 8 to 100 feet. A tape with a wide blade (usually one inch) is easier to use when working alone because the stiffer blade gives you a longer reach.

### Utility Knife

This tool is useful for cutting string, sharpening pencils, and myriad other jobs. Some models have a retractable blade, which makes for less apprehension when reaching into a tool bag to pull it out.

### Wrenches

These are used for driving lag screws and tightening bolts. A 10-inch adjustable wrench is suitable for just about any construction project, but box-end or socket wrenches are less likely to cause knuckle injuries.

## Power Tools

It's difficult to deny the simple pleasures of working with hand tools. They are quiet, they put you in touch with the materials, and they lend a more relaxed pace to your work. There's a fine line, however, between the pleasures of hand craftsmanship and downright drudgery. Power tools can speed up the construction process tremendously and move you toward the real goal, which is to finish your project.

For most outdoor construction projects, just two power tools are sufficient: an electric drill and a portable circular saw. Some projects require more tools. If you think you will have a future use for them, go ahead and buy them; otherwise, just rent the tools you need and put the money you saved into the project at hand.

### Circular Saw

This is the carpenter's workhorse. It can make rip cuts, crosscuts, miters, and bevels quickly and efficiently. In general, a saw with a 2-horsepower rating is adequate for most work.

The quality of the blade is at least as significant as the quality of the saw or its horsepower. A saw blade should always be sharp. If the saw seems to be working too hard, it's probably time to change blades.

One common mistake made by beginners is to feed the saw too slowly into the cut. When this happens, the saw teeth stop cutting and instead start to rub against the end of the cut. This creates heat and friction, and dulls the saw teeth instantly. Try to maintain a smooth, even rate of feed at all times.

### Electric Drill

The electric drill is one tool that is almost universally well made. Even the inexpensive models seem to last forever. In addition to drilling holes, an electric drill is also handy for driving screws. For outdoor construction, you'll need one with at least a ⅜-inch capacity chuck.

Drill bits come in dozens of shapes and sizes for drilling in every kind of material. Start with a basic set and add more bits as you need them.

**Power Tools**

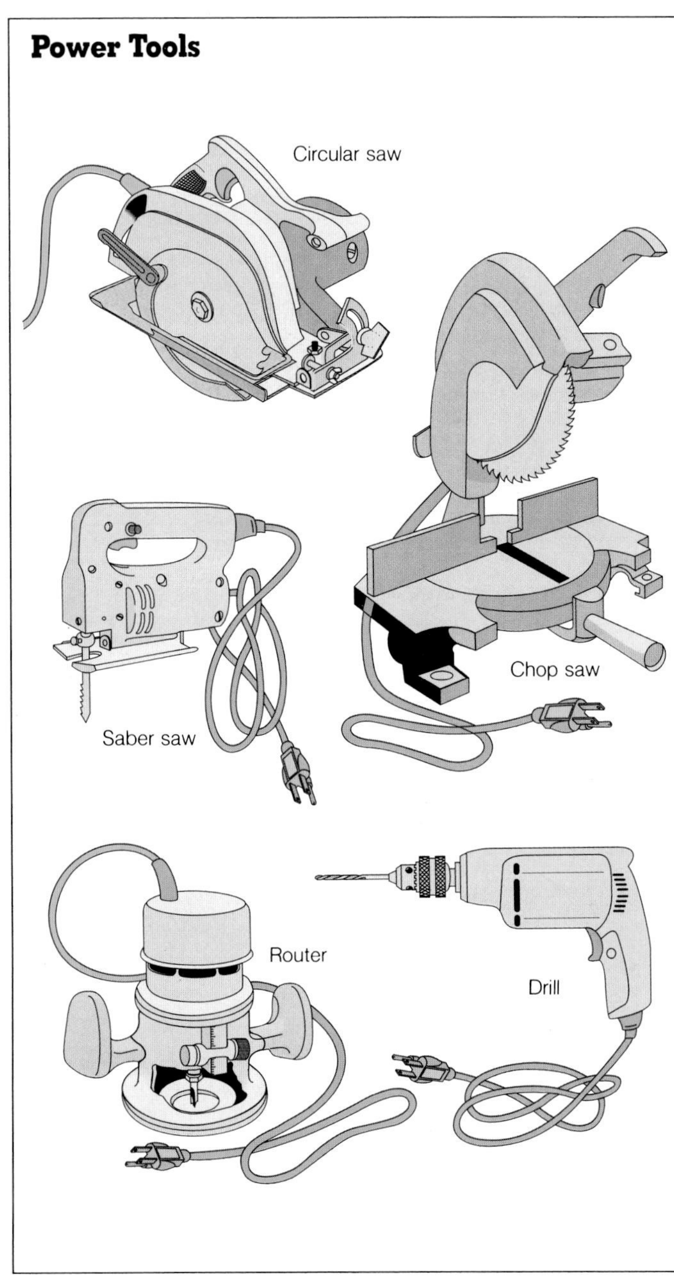


### Other Power Tools

Some of the projects in this book have parts that are cut on a curve. You can make curved cuts in material up to 2½ inches thick with an electric jigsaw (sometimes called a saber saw or bayonet saw). Orbital-action models cut fastest and are less likely to break blades.

A chop saw can be a real timesaver for making crosscuts, miters, and bevels. It will consistently make clean, accurate cuts, and is especially effective for trim work.

The electric router is another useful tool. It is used to cut decorative edges, grooves, dados, and cabinet joints.

There are many other power tools available for just about any job imaginable. If you are up against a task that seems to be taking forever, there is probably a power tool that will make the job go faster.

## Construction Techniques

A complete discussion of construction techniques is beyond the scope of this book. However, there are a few tricks of the trade you ought to know to successfully complete the projects outlined in the previous pages.

## Foundation Layout

Use string lines and batter boards to lay out the structure and establish the height of its foundation, as shown on page 109. Batter boards are placed 2 to 3 feet outside the foundation line; this allows you to locate the critical corners of the structure, remove the strings to dig the footings, and then put the strings back up again to set forms or install posts.

Start by marking with stakes the approximate locations of the corners of the structure. Then drive the batter-board stakes a few feet outside the building line. Use a water level, line level, or builder's transit to mark all the stakes at the same height. Nail crosspieces to the stakes, even with the marks. Brace the batter boards with more stakes so they won't move when you pull the strings across them.

Stretch string lines across the batter boards so they intersect over the temporary corner stakes. Adjust the strings back and forth until they are at the correct dimensions, parallel, and square. You can check for square with the 3-4-5 triangle method or by measuring diagonals. When everything is lined up just right, make shallow saw cuts in the batter-board crosspieces to mark the string locations; later you can use the saw cuts to reset the strings in exactly the same position.

## Mixing and Pouring Concrete

When mixing concrete by hand, it's easiest to use a large contractor's wheelbarrow. A typical concrete mix consists of one part portland cement, two parts washed sand, and three parts gravel, with just enough water to make a workable mix. Measure proportions by the shovelful.

Blend the dry ingredients together first; then push everything to one end of the wheelbarrow and add the water in the other end. With a shovel or hoe, pull a little of the dry mix into the water and stir it in; repeat until the whole batch is thoroughly mixed to the consistency of a thick milkshake. Take care not to add too much water—a mix that's too wet will be weak and crumbly when it hardens.

If you're mixing concrete in a rented cement mixer, put the gravel in first, then add the sand, cement, and water.

Slabs and foundations with continuous footings must usually be reinforced with steel bars. Rebars should be bent around corners and overlapped at splices by a minimum of 30 bar diameters. You can rent a cutter-bender for working with reinforcing steel, but in most cases this really isn't necessary. Cut rebar with a hacksaw or a circular saw fitted with a metal-cutting abrasive blade (wear safety goggles). To make a bend, stand on the bar where you want the bend to start. Slip a 2- or 3-foot length of pipe over the end of the bar, and use it as a lever to make the bend.

Concrete hardens because of the chemical reaction created when portland cement is mixed with water. This reaction takes from one to four hours to complete, depending on weather conditions. The clock starts ticking as soon as water is added to the concrete mix. Once you've started a pour, there's no turning back. Make sure everything is ready before you start, and have all your help lined up ahead of time.

Fill the forms to the top with concrete, and level it off by dragging a straight length of 2 by 4 over the forms with a sawing motion. Using a light touch, smooth the surface immediately with a wood float.

For concrete with a smooth finish, use a steel trowel. Knowing when to begin troweling is mainly a matter of feel. Use long, sweeping strokes, keeping the leading edge of the trowel slightly elevated so it won't dig in. As the concrete hardens, raise the edge of the trowel higher.

The smooth-troweled finish isn't the only way to treat a

### Finishing Concrete

### Foundation Layout

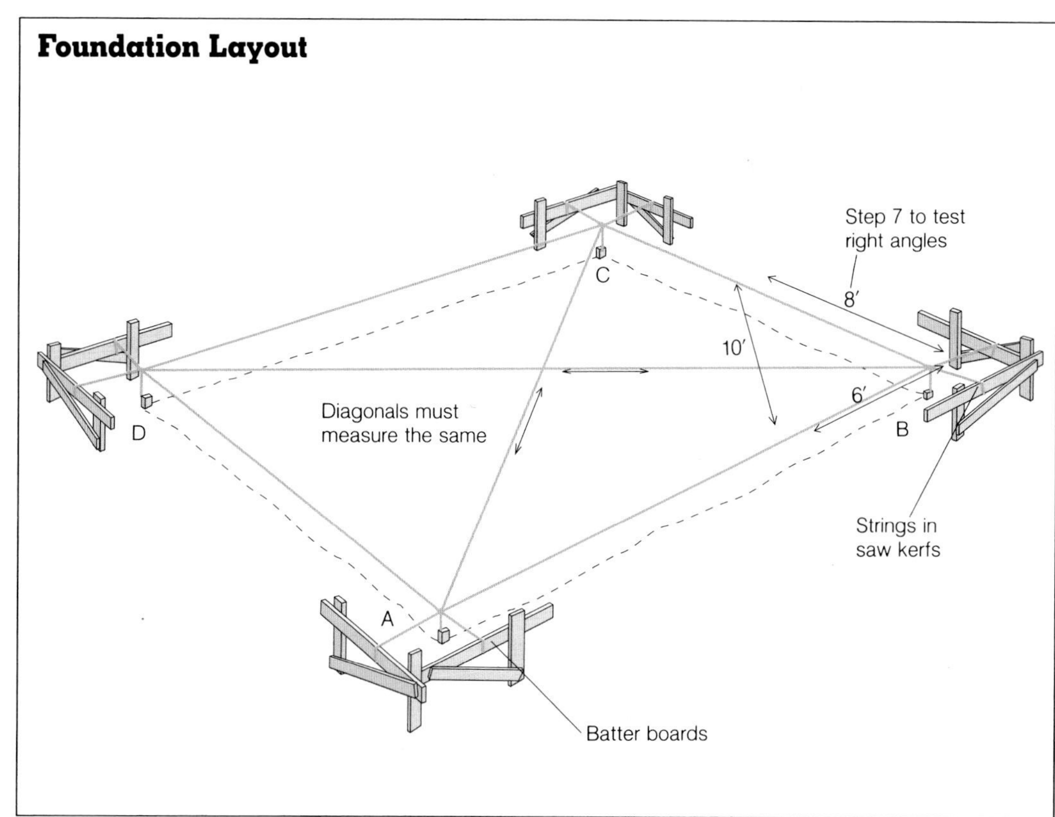

concrete surface. Concrete can be colored and textured in dozens of ways.

## Installing Fasteners

It is critical to use the right fastener for each and every connection on a construction project. Here are the various types of fasteners available and a rundown of the specific purposes they serve.

### Nails

Nails are the basic fasteners for wood construction. They're available in an astounding variety of shapes and sizes. Size is designated by penny, abbreviated *d* (from the Latin *denarius*).

For general framing work that won't be exposed to the weather, use box, sinker, or common nails. Sinkers, with a shank thicker than a box nail but thinner than a common nail, are the easiest to drive.

Use corrosion-resistant nails in all exposed locations. Galvanized box nails are the most common type. Be sure to specify hot-dipped galvanized nails (denoted HDG on the box). The electroplated (EG) kind aren't corrosion resistant for long. Aluminum, stainless steel, and bronze nails offer even better protection, although at a considerably higher price.

As a rule, use a nail that is at least three times longer than the thickness of the material being fastened. Drive nails with smooth, deliberate strokes of the hammer. When toenailing in places where your work will show, drive the nail most of the way down with a hammer, then finish off with a nail set.

Whenever you drive a nail close to the end of a board, especially on finish work, it's advisable to drill a pilot hole first to prevent splitting. Use a drill bit smaller than the diameter of the nail.

If, heaven forbid, you should lose your concentration for a second and put a hammer dent in your beautiful gazebo railing, don't despair. Place a wet rag over the mark and let it soak for an hour or two; then rewet the rag and iron over it with a household steam iron set on *high*. Repeat the process until the dent swells back up.

### Screws

These common fasteners come in nearly as many shapes and sizes as nails. For outdoor construction, coarse-thread wallboard screws (so called because they were originally developed for the wallboard industry), are the best choice. In exposed locations, they should be galvanized or coated to resist corrosion. The deck screw is a variation with a specially shaped tip that cuts its way through wood, eliminating the need for pilot holes. Wallboard screws have a Phillips-type head and are meant to be driven with power tools.

### Lag Screws

These are used to fasten ledgers to walls, beams to posts, and in certain situations where a connection can be made from only one side.

Always drill pilot holes for lag screws. If the head of the screw will be countersunk below the surface of the wood, drill the countersink hole first. Drill the pilot hole for the shank in two stages: first, drill as deep as the unthreaded portion of the shank with a bit the same diameter as the screw; then drill the rest of the way with a bit that's ⅛ inch smaller.

Lubricate the threads of a lag screw with wax or soap before installing.

### Machine Bolts

This type of bolt is used anywhere an extra strong connection is required. Drill the bolt hole with a bit ¹⁄₁₆ inch larger than the bolt diameter. If the pieces to be fastened aren't too thick, you can tack them together and drill through both at once; for very long holes, you may have to drill one piece first, use it to mark the second, and drill that piece separately.

For wood-to-wood connections, use washers under the bolt head and nut (washers aren't required when bolting metal hardware to wood).

### Carriage Bolts

Like machine bolts, carriage bolts are used for exceptionally strong connections, but with two differences: The bolt hole should be the same diameter as the bolt, and a washer isn't required under the bolt head (though one should still be used under the nut).

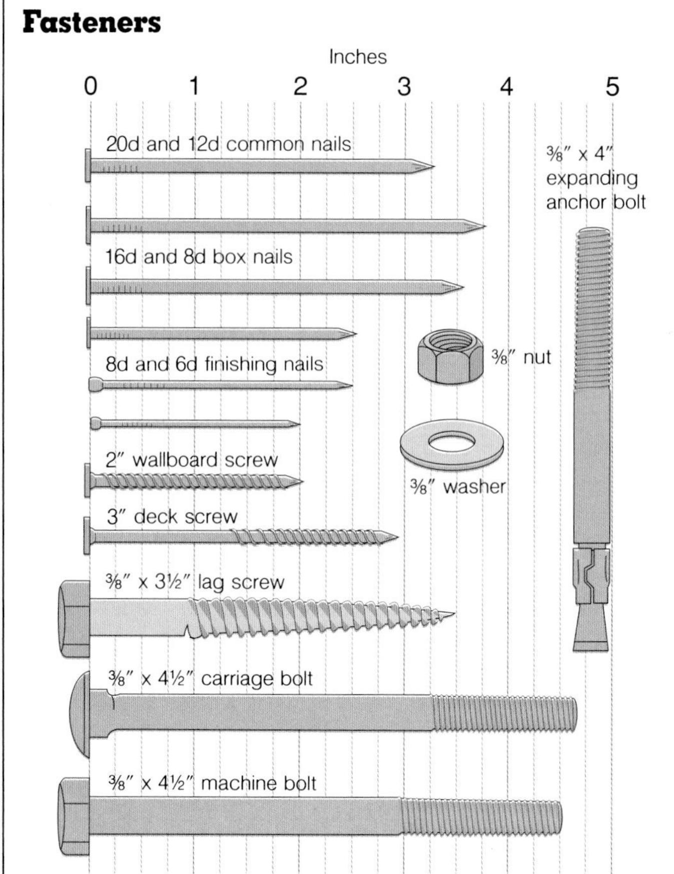

# INDEX

*Page numbers in boldface type indicate principle references. Page numbers in italic type indicate references to illustrations.*

## U.S./Metric Measure Conversion Chart

| | Symbol | When you know: | Multiply by: | To find: | Rounded Measures for Quick Reference | | |
|---|---|---|---|---|---|---|---|
| | | **Formulas for Exact Measures** | | | | | |
| **Mass (Weight)** | oz | ounces | 28.35 | grams | 1 oz | | = 30 g |
| | lb | pounds | 0.45 | kilograms | 4 oz | | = 115 g |
| | g | grams | 0.035 | ounces | 8 oz | | = 225 g |
| | kg | kilograms | 2.2 | pounds | 16 oz | = 1 lb | = 450 g |
| | | | | | 32 oz | = 2 lb | = 900 g |
| | | | | | 36 oz | = 2¼ lb | = 1000 g (1 kg) |
| **Volume** | tsp | teaspoons | 5.0 | milliliters | ¼ tsp | = 1/24 oz | = 1 ml |
| | tbsp | tablespoons | 15.0 | milliliters | ½ tsp | = 1/12 oz | = 2 ml |
| | fl oz | fluid ounces | 29.57 | milliliters | 1 tsp | = 1/6 oz | = 5 ml |
| | c | cups | 0.24 | liters | 1 tbsp | = ½ oz | = 15 ml |
| | pt | pints | 0.47 | liters | 1 c | = 8 oz | = 250 ml |
| | qt | quarts | 0.95 | liters | 2 c (1 pt) | = 16 oz | = 500 ml |
| | gal | gallons | 3.785 | liters | 4 c (1 qt) | = 32 oz | = 1 liter |
| | ml | milliliters | 0.034 | fluid ounces | 4 qt (1 gal) | = 128 oz | = 3¾ liter |
| **Length** | in. | inches | 2.54 | centimeters | ⅜ in. | = 1 cm | |
| | ft | feet | 30.48 | centimeters | 1 in. | = 2.5 cm | |
| | yd | yards | 0.9144 | meters | 2 in. | = 5 cm | |
| | mi | miles | 1.609 | kilometers | 2½ in. | = 6.5 cm | |
| | km | kilometers | 0.621 | miles | 12 in. (1 ft) | = 30 cm | |
| | m | meters | 1.094 | yards | 1 yd | = 90 cm | |
| | cm | centimeters | 0.39 | inches | 100 ft | = 30 m | |
| | | | | | 1 mi | = 1.6 km | |
| **Temperature** | ° F | Fahrenheit | 5/9 (after subtracting 32) | Celsius | 32° F | = 0° C | |
| | | | | | 68° F | = 20° C | |
| | ° C | Celsius | 9/5 (then add 32) | Fahrenheit | 212° F | = 100° C | |
| **Area** | in.$^2$ | square inches | 6.452 | square centimeters | 1 in.$^2$ | = 6.5 cm$^2$ | |
| | ft$^2$ | square feet | 929.0 | square centimeters | 1 ft$^2$ | = 930 cm$^2$ | |
| | yd$^2$ | square yards | 8361.0 | square centimeters | 1 yd$^2$ | = 8360 cm$^2$ | |
| | a. | acres | 0.4047 | hectares | 1 a. | = 4050 m$^2$ | |